Homemaking

Critical Perspectives on Theory, Culture and Politics

Critical Perspectives on Theory, Culture and Politics is an interdisciplinary series, developed in partnership with the Centre for Critical and Cultural Theory, which is based in the School of English, Communication and Philosophy at Cardiff University, UK. The series focuses on innovative research produced at the interface between critical theory and cultural studies. In recent years much work in cultural studies has increasingly moved away from directly critical-theoretical concerns. One of the aims of this series is to foster a renewed dialogue between cultural studies and critical and cultural theory in its rich, multiple dimensions.

Series editors:
Glenn Jordan, Visiting Research Fellow, Cardiff School of Journalism, Media and Cultural Studies, Cardiff University. Former Director of Butetown History & Arts Centre.
Laurent Milesi, Reader in English, Communication and Philosophy and Chair of the Centre for Critical and Cultural Theory, Cardiff University.
Radhika Mohanram, Professor of English and Critical and Cultural Theory, Cardiff University.
Chris Norris, Distinguished Research Professor, Cardiff University.
Chris Weedon, Professor Emerita and Honorary Chair, Centre for Critical and Cultural Theory, Cardiff University.

Titles in the Series

Culture Control Critique: Allegories of Reading the Present, Frida Beckman
Prometheanism: Technology, Digital Culture and Human Obsolescence, Günther Anders and Christopher John Müller, translated by Christopher John Müller
Creole in the Archive: Imagery, Presence and the Location of the Caribbean Figure, Roshini Kempadoo
The Attention Economy: Labour, Time, and Power in Cognitive Capitalism, Claudio Celis
Performative Contradiction and the Romanian Revolution, Jolan Bogdan
Chinese Subjectivities and the Beijing Olympics, Gladys Pak Lei Chong
The Extreme in Contemporary Culture: States of Vulnerability, Pramod K. Nayar
Superpositions: Laruelle and the Humanities, edited by Rocco Gangle and Julius Greve
Credo Credit Crisis: Speculations on Faith and Money, edited by Laurent Milesi, Christopher John Müller and Aidan Tynan
Materialities of Sex in a Time of HIV: The Promise of Vaginal Microbicides, Annette-Carina van der Zaag
From Shared Life to Co-Resistance in Historic Palestine, Marcelo Svirsky and Ronnen Ben-Arie
Affective Connections: Towards a New Materialist Politics of Sympathy, Dorota Golańska
Homemaking: Radical Nostalgia and the Construction of a South Asian Diaspora, Anindya Raychaudhuri
Partitions and Their Afterlives: Violence, Memories, Living, edited by Radhika Mohanram and Anindya Raychaudhuri (forthcoming)

Homemaking

Radical Nostalgia and the Construction of a South Asian Diaspora

Anindya Raychaudhuri

**ROWMAN &
LITTLEFIELD**
─────── INTERNATIONAL
London • New York

Published by Rowman & Littlefield International, Ltd.
6 Tinworth Street, London SE11 5AL, United Kingdom
www.rowmaninternational.com

Rowman & Littlefield International, Ltd., is an affiliate of
Rowman & Littlefield
4501 Forbes Boulevard, Suite 200, Lanham, Maryland 20706, USA
With additional offices in Boulder, New York, Toronto (Canada), and London (UK)
www.rowman.com

Copyright © 2018 by Anindya Raychaudhuri

All rights reserved. No part of this book may be reproduced in any form or by any electronic or mechanical means, including information storage and retrieval systems, without written permission from the publisher, except by a reviewer who may quote passages in a review.

British Library Cataloguing in Publication Information
A catalogue record for this book is available from the British Library

ISBN: HB 978-1-78348-262-7

Library of Congress Cataloging-in-Publication Data Is Available

978-1-78348-262-7 (cloth: alk. paper)
978-1-78348-263-4 (pbk. : alk. paper)
978-1-78348-264-1 (electronic)

∞ ™ The paper used in this publication meets the minimum requirements of American National Standard for Information Sciences Permanence of Paper for Printed Library Materials, ANSI/NISO Z39.48-1992.

Printed in the United States of America

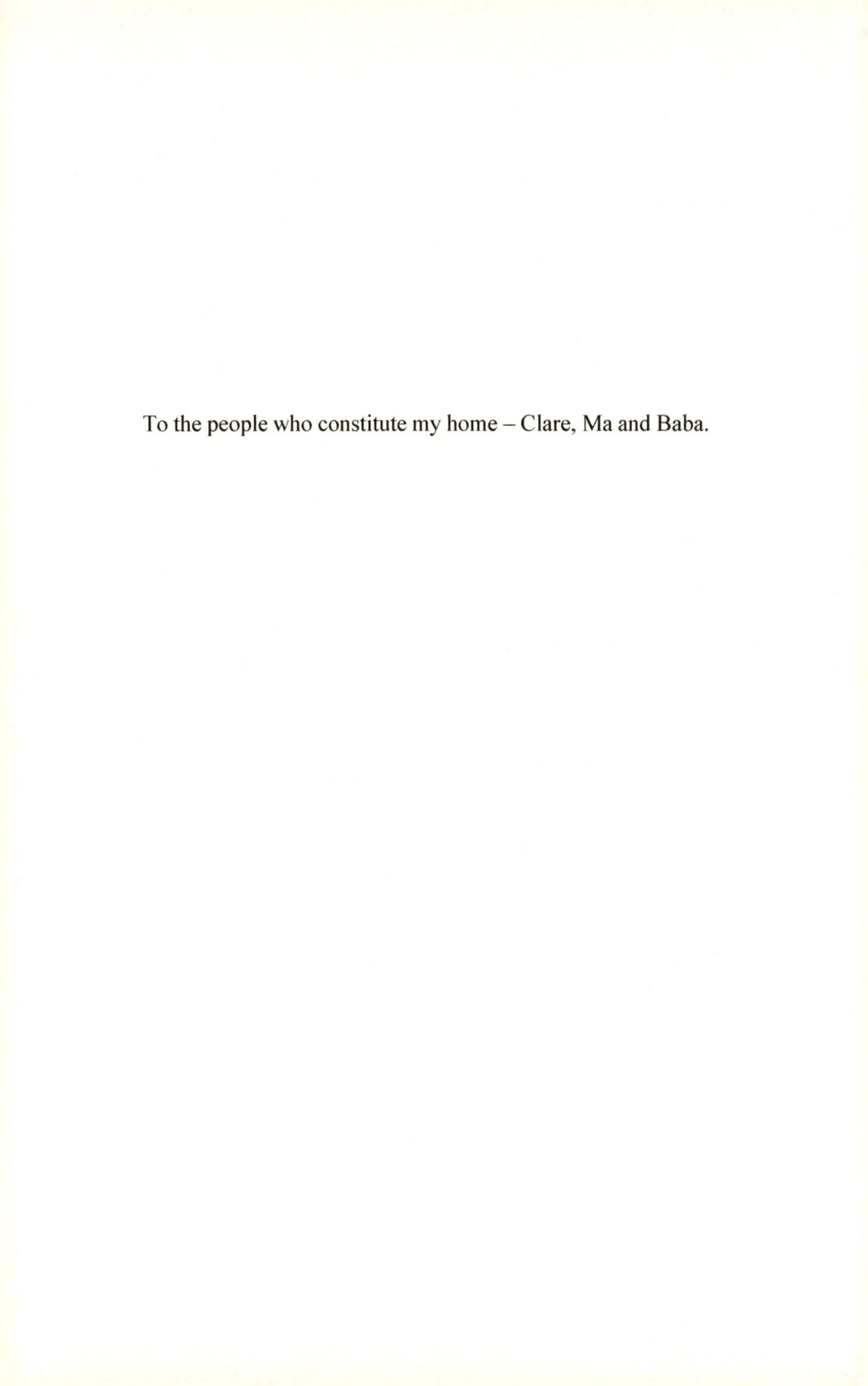

To the people who constitute my home – Clare, Ma and Baba.

Contents

Acknowledgements	ix
Preface	xi
Introduction: 'Ich Will Heim': Nostalgia and the Radical Possibilities of Homemaking	1
Johannes Hofer, Robert Hamilton and the Origins of a Nostalgia of the Marginalized	5
Contemporary Nostalgia and Its Discontented Scholarship	8
Homemaking, Domophilia and Diasporic Nostalgia	11
Chapter Outline	17
Notes	18
1 'Doubly Expatriated': Duleep Singh and the Politics of Nostalgia	21
Maharajah Duleep Singh: A Life of Nostalgia and Rebellion	22
Nostalgia and the Legacy of Duleep Singh's Life	35
Notes	44
2 A Teacher, a Factory Worker, and a 'Battered' Housewife: Rebellious Nostalgias, Nostalgias of Rebellion	47
'The Wrath of the Asian': Altab Ali, Asian Dub Foundation and Claiming Tower Hamlets	49
'A Village in Punjab': Blair Peach and the Rebels of Southall	56
'Better than No Cause at All': Kiranjit Ahluwalia and the Nostalgic Communities of Sisterhood	64
Notes	71
3 Aloo-gobi, Mangoes and a Small Aubergine: Food, Foodscapes and Nostalgia	75
Jhumpa Lahiri and the Piracy of Food	79

	Nostalgia and Its Discontents – The Gendered Nature of Food Production	86
	'The Old Secrets Your Mother's Mothers Knew': Nostalgia for Food and a Matrilineal Inheritance	89
	Memories of Food	94
	Notes	99
4	'Straight from the Village': Diasporic Public Spaces and the Heterotopias of Nostalgia	101
	Diasporic Heterotopias	102
	Home and the World: Inside/Outside	104
	'No Place like It': The South Asian Grocery Shop	109
	Space Invaders	115
	Food and Music – Examples of Critical Diasporic Heterotopias	118
	Notes	126
5	Salaam, London: Bollywood, Wish Fulfilment, and the Fictive Geographies of the Diaspora	129
	Bollywood and Nostalgia for the Future	132
	Nostalgia beyond Borders	134
	Bollywood, Nostalgia and Diasporic Dreaming	139
	Diasporic Nostalgia, India, Pakistan and the Male Muslim Body	140
	Diasporic Nostalgia and the Self-Referentiality of Bollywood	148
	Notes	150
6	Making Yourself at Home: Homemaking and Diasporic Asian Broadcasting	153
	Nostalgia and the History of BBC Asian Broadcasting	155
	Going 'Old Skool': Nostalgia and the BBC Asian Network	165
	Nostalgia and Diasporic Asian Broadcasting: *Psychoraag* and *Salaam Namaste*	170
	Notes	175

Conclusion: Going Back Home: Looking Backwards, Looking Forwards	179
'The Return of the Prodigal': Nostalgic Returnings in *Anil's Ghost* and *The Hungry Tide*	183
A Radical Hermeneutics of Nostalgia	187
Notes	191
Bibliography	193
Index	199

Acknowledgements

I first started working on the material that would end up in this book in 2011. Any project that has been this long in its preparation has inevitably benefitted from the advice and assistance of numerous people along the way.

I am very grateful to the staff of the libraries at Cardiff University, University of Edinburgh, University of St Andrews, and University College London for all their help over the years. Thanks are also due to the staff at the British Library, the BBC Written Archives Centre, the National Library of Scotland, the National Archives at Kew, and the Harry Ransom Center for Humanities, Austin, Texas.

BBC copyright content reproduced courtesy of the British Broadcasting Corporation.

'Chutney', Collected Poems, 2013. Sujata Bhatt. Copyrighted by Sujata Bhatt. Printed with permission from Carcanet Press, Manchester, UK.

Lyrics from 'Rebel Warrior' (Words and Music by Steve Chandra Savale, Aniruddha Das and John Ashok Pandit), 'TH9' (Words and Music by Lisa Thorpe, John Ashok Pandit, Saidullah Zaman, Aniruddha Das and Steve Chandra Savale) and 'PKNB' (Words and Music by Aniruddha Das and Steve Chandra Savale) reproduced with kind permission from Warner/Chappell Music Ltd.

Where applicable, all reasonable attempts to obtain permission from rightsholders have been made. If you have any information regarding outstanding permissions, please let the publisher know.

I am very grateful to Chris Weedon, Radhika Mohanram and the other series editors for their support, advice and insightful comments on the manuscript. Thanks are also due to the three reviewers who read and commented on the initial proposal and the final manuscript. They all made helpful comments and suggestions – their generosity and collegiality has made a huge difference.

Gurdeep Mattu, Natalie Linh Bolderston, Lisa Whittington and the entire team at Rowman & Littlefield have been very kind and patient throughout the writing and production process.

The bulk of this book was written while at the University of St Andrews, and I am so very grateful to everyone in the School of English and the University for advice and support. These are really too numerous to name, but they include: Matthew Augustine, Lorna Burns, Katie Garner, Clare Gill, Sam Haddow, Ben Hewitt, Tom Jones, Peter Mackay, Andrew Murphy, Katie Muth, Gill Plain, Neil Rhodes, Susan Sellers, Jane Stabler and all the other wonderful people in the School of English. A special mention is due to Akhila Yechury for her encyclopaedic knowledge of Bollywood cinema, to Alex Davis for allowing me to read an unpublished version of his article on nostalgia, and to Hannah Fitzpatrick for conversation and podcasts.

I have presented aspects of this work in conferences at Linköping University, Bangor University, the University of Tübingen, and the University of Stirling. I have benefitted from the useful feedback I have received from my fellow conference delegates.

Finally, and most importantly, thank you to my parents (Ma and Baba), and to Clare, for creating and preserving my sense of home while I was exploring the process of homemaking. None of this would have been possible without your love and support, and I owe you more than I can say. This book is dedicated to the three of you.

Preface

On 12 October 2008, BBC Radio 4's long-running programme *Desert Island Discs* featured comedian, actor and broadcaster Sanjeev Bhaskar. When the interviewer Kirsty Young asks him to describe his childhood home, he says that 'it was a little bit of India that was existing in west London'. This little bit of India was maintained within and without the interior of the home. Later on in the programme, for example, Bhaskar remembers their family weekend outings to Southall, where there were three cinemas that would only show Bollywood films:

> Thinking back on it now, the capacity of the cinemas – they may have been five or six hundred, may be seven hundred but about four and a half thousand people would turn up to each of these cinemas to watch . . . it was just fantastic, it was like a fair, it was like a festival.

This celebration of the south Asian in Southall is juxtaposed, in Bhaskar's narration, with the rise of the far-right in British politics as he remembers National Front signs being painted on their front door, and 'a major National Front march through Southall in 1979–80'. Southall becomes, in Bhaskar's narration, a place that is at once familiar and hostile, a place that is a home for British Asians, but a home that is constantly under threat.

Two years after appearing on *Desert Island Discs*, on 29 December 2010, Bhaskar would feature on the Channel 4 programme *The House That Made Me*, where he returned to his childhood home, above a launderette, in Heston. The format of this programme consists of taking a celebrity back to the house that they grew up in, which has been meticulously reconstructed to exactly how it was back when they lived there. This particular episode opens with a shot of Bhaskar driving the streets of West London, as the narrator intones: 'As the child of Indian immigrants, he walked the tightrope between English and Asian cultures'. The door that had the hated letters 'NF' painted on it makes an appearance in this show as well. When Bhaskar first arrives in front of the flat that was his childhood home, he describes the door and 'the thickness there' as representing the gap between the inside and the outside, the public and the private. The outside represents 'England, Government and Empire' while on the other side of the door, there was 'a whole different world in there', characterized by the distinctive 'smells of the home and the cooking and the language'. The door is not the only thing that these two programmes share, however. *The House That Made Me* includes a trip to the recently closed Liberty cinema, where Bhaskar describes the 'carnival atmosphere' in a manner similar to his interview on *Desert Island Discs*. Watching Bollywood films, he says, helped him connect to his roots. The Bollywood cinemas of Southall become, in the narrative of the programme, part of the house that has made Sanjeev Bhaskar who he is.

At one point in the programme, the narrator asks Bhaskar, as he is sitting in the front room, whether any of his school friends would have visited when they lived there. Rarely, Bhaskar replied, imagining that if any of his friends had, the difference of their home, hidden behind the front door, would be experienced by them as 'something akin to a slap on the face'.

On one level, this book can be described as examining the literal and metaphorical versions of the front door that create and delineate a particular version of home in a world that is perceived to be hostile and alienating. What are some of the strategies used to create such doors, and why is it so important that doors like these are preserved? What role does the home, outlined and defined by material and symbolic doors, play in sustaining lives that are marked as different and foreign? What connects the smells and sounds that existed behind the closed doors of flats like Bhaskar's, for example, and the sense of the carnival that characterized the experience of going to watch Bollywood films in a cinema hall in Southall?

This book focuses on this process that leads to the creation of these little bits of south Asia within the context of twentieth- and twenty-first-century Britain, America and Australia. What is at stake for recognizing and valuing the presence of south Asia that exists within public and private life in the Occident? In the pages that follow, I identify and explore a number of these effects – through visual art, cinema, computer games, music, literature, food, broadcasting, and public and private spaces – in the process constructing an alternative history of the "West" within which the material and cultural presence of south Asian immigrants occupies a central position. I connect and arrange these diverse examples of south Asian traces under the framework of nostalgia, conceived as the varied collection of affects, strategies and processes through which a sense of home is first constructed, and then preserved and maintained in defiance of an ethnocentric hostility.

It is my contention that this provides us both a different and perhaps more productive way of understanding the ways in which memory has been mobilized by and for diasporic south Asians, as well as a different framework for understanding the complexities of nostalgia. In other words, if these cultural traces can be thought of as an effect of nostalgia, then how might this nostalgia itself be conceptualized as a tool of resistance against the normalizing tendencies of a neo-colonial nation-state that continually demands assimilation?

What I try to do in the pages of this book is to resurrect examples of diasporic Asian life and its material and cultural traces, through which nostalgia can be mobilized into something that is shocking, that can be said to represent a 'slap on the face' for the ethnocentric and neo-colonial mainstream. I want to resurrect nostalgia as a complex and complicated set of forces that can be potentially progressive. Using the south Asian diaspora as my case study, I study these various strategies of homemaking, and explore how, in its sheer persistence, in its refusal to assimilate or compromise, in its continual effort to maintain the visible presence of the south Asian in Britain, it can force us to re-examine nostalgia and recognize it for the complex and powerful thing it really is.

Introduction

'Ich Will Heim': Nostalgia and the Radical Possibilities of Homemaking

The year 2016 had been a big one for nostalgia. On 23 June of that year, the UK voted in a nationwide referendum to leave the European Union. In the debates that preceded and followed the referendum, liberal and progressive commentators, academics and politicians were clear about the role that nostalgia played in this decision. Writing in *The Sunday Times*, A.A. Gill argued that the pro-Brexit slogan 'getting our country back' is inextricably connected to a nostalgic view of the past:

> It's snorting a line of the most pernicious and debilitating Little English drug, nostalgia. The warm, crumbly, honeycoloured, collective 'yesterday' with its fond belief that everything was better back then, that Britain (England, really) is a worse place now than it was at some foggy point in the past where we achieved peak Blighty . . . it's a desire to shuffle back to a regret-curdled inward-looking yesterday. In the Brexit fantasy, the best we can hope for is to kick out all the work-all-hours foreigners and become caretakers to our own past in this self-congratulatory island of moaning and pomposity.[1]

Gill was writing before the referendum, though commentators were making similar connections between its result and a conservative nostalgia for months afterwards. Chris Haskins, writing in *The Guardian*, observed that:

> nostalgia for the past and resentment about the world in general were the deciding factors in the Brexit vote and were ruthlessly exploited by the Europhobic, often xenophobic outpourings of some Brexit politicians.[2]

Nadine El-Enany, writing for the LSE Blog, makes a similar case:

> The terms on which the EU referendum debate took place are symptomatic of a Britain struggling to conceive of its place in the world post-Empire. Present in the discourse of some of those arguing for a Leave vote was a tendency to romanticise the days of the British Empire, a time when Britannia ruled the waves and was defined by her racial and cultural superiority. Brexit is not only an expression of nostalgia for empire, it is also the fruit of empire.[3]

A few months later, the leader of the Liberal Democrats, Vince Cable, made a similar point, in an opinion piece in the *Daily Mail*:

> The old have comprehensively shafted the young. And the old have had the last word about Brexit, imposing a world view coloured by nostalgia for an imperial past on a younger generation much more comfortable with modern Europe.[4]

In the intervening months between the referendum and most of these pieces, the United States saw the election on 8 November 2016 of Donald Trump as the forty-fifth President. Like the Brexit result, this too was largely attributed to a similar brand of conservative, white-supremacist and neo-colonial nostalgia. In June of that year, Ronald Brownstein described Trump's appeal as the 'rhetoric of white nostalgia'[5] while, writing after the elections, Sarah Pulliam Bailey of the *Washington Post* sought to examine 'how nostalgia for white Christian America drove so many Americans to vote for Trump'.[6] Gregory Rodriguez and Dawn Nakagawa examine the commonalities of conservative nostalgia on both sides of the Atlantic:

> These emotions are being exploited by politicians peddling mournful nostalgia and narratives of a lost identity. As globalization marches forward, along with seismic demographic shifts in the developed world, the seductive pull to look backward and inward will intensify, with unfortunate consequences for our politics and social order. Indeed, we are already seeing this play out in the United States and Britain.[7]

With slogans like 'Getting our country back' and 'Making America Great Again', it is easy to see the nostalgic underpinnings that helped fuel these particularly reactionary political movements. In analysing the social effects of this brand of nostalgia, commentators have connected it to everything from restaurants and burger bars[8] to a desire for retro electronic devices,[9] in the process, helping to define nostalgia itself as white, neo-colonial, and xenophobic:

> The politics of nostalgia generally amount to more than just missing the old neighborhood or one's late grandmother. Many are longing for a past when the

country was less diverse, communities were more homogenous and self-contained and your immediate surroundings largely defined your experience of the world. . . . Nostalgia-driven movements are assertions of whom its followers stand against. . . . The fact that 81 percent of surveyed Leave voters said they saw multiculturalism as a 'force for ill' highlights the strong link between nostalgia and identity.[10]

Gurminder K. Bhambra has described how both the movements for Brexit and Trump could be characterized as attempts to define the United Kingdom and the United States respectively as 'nations that were represented as "white" into which racialized others had insinuated themselves and gained disproportionate advantage'.[11]

Of course, it would be foolish to assume that this type of white nostalgia arose with Brexit or Trump. At the start of 2016, before either of these phenomena, Owen Hatherley published a book called *The Ministry of Nostalgia*, in which he connects what he sees as 'austerity nostalgia' with a desire for the good old days of Empire that would resonate all the more in a few months, in a post-Brexit world where Trump was President. Hatherley identifies the emotional attachment on the part of both the British Right and the British Left to particular moments in its national history – the Blitz and the Second World War, and the creation of the Welfare State, respectively, as 'morbid fetishes, clung to as a means of not thinking about other aspects of recent British history – most obviously, its Empire.'[12] Hatherley's principal target, what he identifies as 'the emblem of austerity nostalgia',[13] is the phenomenon of the 'Keep Calm and Carry On' poster. Initially designed for the wartime Ministry of Information in 1939, it was never actually used as a propaganda poster during the war, but was rediscovered by Barter Books in Alnwick, and has subsequently become a design icon – generating reproduction posters, bags, t-shirts, and a whole range of other visual and linguistic echoes. Visible in shops across most of the world, this poster has since become a clichéd aspect of the way Britain sells itself at home and abroad. Hatherley argues:

> The power of 'Keep Calm and Carry On' comes from a yearning for an actual or imaginary English patrician attitude of stiff upper lips and muddling through. . . . The poster isn't just a case of the return of the repressed, it is rather the return of repression itself. It is *a nostalgia for the state of being repressed*. . . . At the same time as it evokes a sense of loss over the decline of an idea of Britain and the British, it is both reassuring and flattering, implying a virtuous (if highly self-aware) consumer stoicism.[14]

Hatherley does a great job of charting the ways in which this poster has taken on multiple different lives since being rediscovered and the experience of encountering it on journeys around London, as well as department stores in Warsaw. At the time of writing, the craze for this 'truly global design icon' may well have diminished, though its popularity can still create 'the horror film-like feeling' that one is being followed wherever one goes.[15] Certainly when I was reading the book in mid-2016, Hatherley's observations felt very familiar as I made journeys of my own across London.

On one of these journeys, however, I encountered a version of the poster in Watney Street Market, Tower Hamlets, East London, that does not feature in Hatherley's analysis. Emblazoned above a shop selling south Asian clothes was the poster 'Keep Calm and Say Mashallah', referring not just to the ubiquitous poster, but also to the common Islamic expression meaning 'God has willed it', used to express praise and gratitude for the munificence of the Almighty. Does this use of the poster help to complicate Hatherley's thesis identifying nostalgia as inherently pro-imperial, as necessarily harking back to a pre-immigration, white Britain? Given the complicated and painful history of marginalization of Muslims in Britain, surely the rewriting of this most prominent emblem of British imperial nostalgia deserves more attention? In the barrage of books, articles and opinion pieces that connect the success of the Leave campaign in Britain, and the Trump campaign in America to a particularly conservative, insular, and xenophobic majoritarian white nostalgia, there is little room for a nostalgia that might be experienced by minority groups. Is it then possible to also think of a counter-hegemonic, progressive nostalgia that celebrates and helps sustain the marginalized? And if it is, what progressive political significance might this alternative nostalgia have in a world that, in 2016, seems to have made such a decisive and transnational shift to the Right?

These are some of the questions this book seeks to answer. Using a series of examples from literature, cinema, visual art, music, computer games, mainstream media, physical and virtual spaces and many other cultural objects, I will make the case that cultural life in twentieth-century Britain, and to a lesser extent in Europe, North America and Australia, needs to be read as always already imbued with south Asian diasporic nostalgia. I will make the further case that this form of nostalgia is not only distinct from white and imperial nostalgia that is so clearly connected to Brexit and Trump, but can also be read as an important progressive antidote to the hegemonic conceptions of nostalgia as intrinsically conservative. Reading this counter-colonial nostalgia in contemporary culture amounts to a recognition of a presence, and valuing an other that has been 'here' for a long time, and whose presence necessarily complicates the here-there dynamic that is still far too often seen as structuring the world. It amounts to an affirmation of the importance of dreams, of celebrations, and the critical potential of the same.

JOHANNES HOFER, ROBERT HAMILTON AND THE ORIGINS OF A NOSTALGIA OF THE MARGINALIZED

This near-universal insistence on the nostalgia of the majority is even odder, considering the origins of nostalgia as a diagnosable medical condition, first identified in 1688 by Swiss physician Johannes Hofer. In his *Medical Dissertation on Nostalgia*, Hofer seeks to identify and name the condition caused 'by the grief for the lost charm of the Native Land ... those stricken with this disease grieve, either because they are abandoned by the pleasant breeze of their Native Land or because at some time they picture themselves enjoying this more.'[16] Looking around for a suitable name, Hofer coins the word *Nostalgias*:

> Greek in origin and indeed composed of two sounds, the one of which is *Nosos*,[17] return to the native land; the other, *Algos*, signifies suffering or grief; so that thus far it is possible from the force of the sound Nostalgia to define the sad mood originating from the desire for the return to one's native land.[18]

While Hofer's more famous cases involve the homesickness of Helvetian soldiers, Swiss mercenaries fighting in wars across Europe, the case that speaks to me most powerfully is the anonymous country girl who developed nostalgia after an enforced stay in a hospital following an injury:

> When she saw that she was being handled about among the wrangling and querulous old women, immediately homesickness took hold of her; she spat back the foods and medicaments, of which she stood in need against the great loss of her strength. Especially she wailed frequently, groaning nothing else than '*Ich will heim; Ich will heim*', nor responding to anything else to questions than this same 'Ich will heim'.[19]

Alex Davis has astutely pointed out the significance of Hofer's decision to render the girl's speech in German as opposed to Latin:

> In this episode, the vernacular might be construed as subordinate on a variety of fronts: female, rural, ignorant, irrational. ... Yet 'Ich will heim' breaks through Hofer's Latin with great simplicity and force, and Hofer's point is that this appeal cannot and must not be denied.[20]

Davis is perfectly correct when he identifies in Hofer a sympathy for the disempowered, a sympathy that can seem to be at odds with his insistence on the importance of the 'Fatherland' in the health of his patients, an insistence that might begin to explain the hegemonic connection in subsequent scholarship between nostalgia and nationalism. In Hofer's own thought, however, this connection is at best tenuous, and always made more complicated by his equal stress on the importance of the commonplace and the quotidian:

> Nostalgia ... is originated by arousing especially the uncommon and ever-present idea of the recalled native land in the mind. ... It is easily clear ... that the imagination is affected because men thus oppressed are moved by small external objects and nothing creates a stronger impression than the desire recalling the homeland.[21]

Hofer's analysis straddles the macro-world of the 'fatherland' with all the self-aggrandizement that that involves, on the one hand, and the micro-world of the subaltern country girl and her insistence on breaking through with her vernacular into the pages of a learned Latin medical dissertation, on the other. This dichotomy in Hofer's thought, I argue, is more productive in terms of approaching a better, fuller understanding of the concept of nostalgia than the conventional insistence on its hegemonic nature. The importance of these 'small external objects' in the construction of an image of what Hofer calls the 'Native Land' cannot be overstated, and it is these small objects which prove to be much more powerful in generating nostalgia than any ideological sense of nationalism.

Hofer is certainly not alone among seventeenth-century physicians to have spotted a subaltern potential in this disease that they had just diagnosed. In 1781, the regimental surgeon of the 10th Foot regiment, Robert Hamilton, was stationed in barracks in Tinmouth. While there, he was asked to examine a soldier called Edwards who had, according to Hamilton, undergone a drastic transformation recently:

> but a melancholy hung over his countenance, and a wanness preyed on his cheeks. He complained of universal weakness, but no fixed pain; a noise in his ears, and giddiness of his head. Pulse rather slow than frequent; but small, and easily compressible. His appetite was much impaired. His tongue was sufficiently moist, and his belly regular; yet he slept ill, and started suddenly out of it, with uneasy dreams. He had little or no thirst.[22]

After a period of uncertainty, during which he admits he 'looked on him as lost', Hamilton learns from a nurse that the only topic on which 'he was able to speak ... constantly' was:

> the strong notions he had got in his head ... of home, and of his friends ... the alacrity with which he ... mentioned his never more being able to see his friends.[23]

Hamilton reported this case as part of the *Medical Commentaries* for the year of 1786. His diagnosis, though he only ever uses the word in the title of his contribution, was that Edwards was suffering from nostalgia. Like Hofer, Hamilton recognizes in Edwards a similar attachment to the apparently unimportant, the minor, the equivalent of Hofer's 'small external objects':

> I went immediately up to him, and introduced the subject; and, from the alacrity with which he resumed it (yet with a deep sigh, when he mentioned his never more being able to see his friends), I found it a theme which much affected him. He asked me, with earnestness, if I would let him go home.[24]

As Philip Shaw has argued, Hamilton's diagnosis was perfectly in line with medical thinking at the time, and, indeed, Hamilton displays an uncharacteristic sympathy to Edwards's sensitivity.[25] He promises Edwards that he will arrange for him to go home, though he admits in his account that he had no authority to do this. After Edwards recovers, Hamilton notes how he managed to persuade the authorities to allow him leave to return home.

While the work of Hofer and Hamilton, along with other contemporary physicians such as William Cullen and Joseph Leopold Auenbrugger, has been examined in very great detail by contemporary scholars in humanities and social sciences working on nostalgia, there is one, to my mind, quite key aspect that has so far been overlooked. I have mentioned above that Hamilton only uses the word 'nostalgia' in the title of his chapter. The full title of Hamilton's contribution is: '*History of a remarkable Case of Nostalgia affecting a native of Wales, and occurring in Britain*. By Dr Robert Hamilton physician at Ipswich.'

It seems surprising to me that no one, as far as I know, has commented on the careful distinction, both spatial and national, that Hamilton makes between the country where Edwards is from (Wales) and where he finds himself (Britain). Given that Hamilton himself was born in Coleraine in what is today Northern Ireland, and qualified in medicine in Edinburgh, and given the fact that events being described are happening a mere seventy years since the Act of Union, it is perhaps not unforgivably anachronistic to read a colonial dynamic to the relationship between Edwards and his regiment, and therefore, to the physical and psychological symptoms of nostalgia that he was exhibiting.

Nicholas Dames is one of a few scholars to recognize the ontological complexity of the home that Edwards misses and Hamilton writes about – Dames points out in his outline of the 'plot' of nostalgia, that it usually began with 'an initial displacement from home, whether that home be defined nationally, regionally, or even more locally'.[26] Thinking through the significance of Edwards's position as a Welsh soldier in the British army, or the position of that anonymous girl among the old women of the hospital, it is perhaps possible to begin to explore the different lines of power that delineate the national, regional and local homes that appear in Dames's argument. Going back to Hofer's analysis then, it is particularly noticeable that in his belief that the Helvetian is most prone to nostalgia, he implicitly recognizes relationships that might, in a future time, be deemed to be colonial:

> If nevertheless the Helvetian race are seized most frequently of all by this symptom, I do not know whether it is because the Helvetian has to search about for the morning broth, or by scarcity of the milk of this tribe, or because he is suddenly deprived of his own manner of feasting, or because rather the use of native liberty is prohibited him.[27]

Alex Davis has argued that Hofer's use of the vernacular 'Heimweh', like the country girl's refrain, 'embodies nostalgia at the level of sound rather than signification, since its patterns of articulation sound familiar (or, perhaps, do not sound unfamiliar) to native speakers',[28] i.e., the Helvetians who may be alienated both by Hofer's Greek neologism and his use of Latin to describe their condition.

It is interesting to note as well how both Hofer and Hamilton conceptualise nostalgia as an affect – whether it is through Hofer's use of the creative imagination or through his allusion to the importance of 'morning broth' and the 'mother's milk'.[29] I will go on to argue in a later chapter the vital role that food plays in evoking, maintaining and reinforcing nostalgias, but it is enough to point out for the moment, once again, that neither Hofer nor Hamilton, nor indeed their patients, are at all concerned with the nation as an ideological or political entity, nor with nationalism as a way of looking at their world. The lines of power are not the domineering ones of the nation-state, but the marginalized ones of valuing the apparently valueless and insignificant – the 'small external objects'.

If these lines of power can then be borne in mind while conceptualizing contemporary nostalgia as well, it may be possible to rethink the way nostalgia continues to function not just as a way of resurrecting and maintaining a particular version of the past, but also as a way of using it to challenge given assumptions in the present.

CONTEMPORARY NOSTALGIA AND ITS DISCONTENTED SCHOLARSHIP

In the transition that the concept of nostalgia made from seventeenth- and eighteenth-century medicine to twentieth- and twenty-first-century literary and cultural studies, nostalgia seems to have largely lost this alternative, subaltern and counter-hegemonic potential. With a few important exceptions, scholars have mostly accepted the Brexit-Trump version of nostalgia – the idea that nostalgia is only ever reactionary, that it is another opportunity for the majority to luxuriate in self-indulgent fantasies of a safe, uncomplicated past, that it does not recognize the ways in which said past was experienced as violent and brutal by groups not allowed into this nostalgically re-inscribed world. One of the first, pioneering accounts in this vein is Renato Rosaldo's landmark essay "Imperialist Nostalgias", in which he takes to task cinematic representations that evoke nostalgia for the empire: 'Evidently, a mood of nostalgia makes racial domination appear innocent and pure.'[30] As he goes on to argue:

> Imperialist nostalgia thus revolves around a paradox: a person kills somebody and then mourns his or her victim. In more attenuated form, someone deliberately alters a form of life and then regrets that things have not remained as they were prior to his or her intervention. At one more remove, people destroy their environment and then worship nature. In any of its versions, imperialist nostalgia uses a pose of 'innocent yearning' both to capture people's imaginations and to conceal its complicity with often brutal domination.[31]

In what seems to me a particularly egregious piece of misreading, he associates Hofer's Helvetian Swiss mercenaries 'with processes of domination',[32] rather than recognizing the much more ambiguous and alienated relationship the Swiss mercenaries had with the power centres of Europe.[33] It should be said, however, that I have no particular disagreement with Rosaldo's conception of neo-colonial nostalgia; I just disagree that this is the only possible role nostalgia might have in the afterlives of colonialism.

It is true that Rosaldo's line of argument has proved to be hugely influential among literary, cultural, historical and anthropological scholars. In 1989, David Lowenthal had described nostalgia as 'the search for a simple and stable past as a refuge from a turbulent and chaotic present.'[34] When he revisited his work in 2015, he identified the post-Thatcher generation as one marked by a 'nostophobia':

> Besides nostalgia's starry-eyed view of wretched times, falsified history, kitschy commerce, and regressive elitism, it is faulted for foolish faith that issues were faced, action taken, crises averted, and problems solved better and faster in the past ... a neoconservative plea for bygone virtues.[35]

Similarly, Susan Bennett has forcefully argued that the nostalgic 'representation of a seamless past has ... been an important strategy in the politically regressive governments of the New Right.'[36] She goes on to argue:

> In all its manifestations, nostalgia is, in its praxis, conservative (in at least two senses – its political alignment and its motive to keep things intact and unchanged): it leans on an imagined and imaginary past which is more and better than the present and for which the carrier of the nostalgia, in a defective and diminished present, in some way or other longs.[37]

Ryan Lizardi has pointed out the ways in which popular media encourage a nostalgic and therefore uncritical view of history:

> Our convergent media present[s] us . . . with our own mirror of narcissistic nostalgic desire. Where we could use the past as an adaptive functional mirror with which we could compare and contrast to our contemporary situation, possibly learning something along the way, the past instead . . . construct[s] us as uncritical citizens of our own culture.[38]

Susan Stewart has attacked nostalgia for its perceived reactionary insistence on authenticity: 'Nostalgia is the repetition that mourns the inauthenticity of all repetition and denies the repetition's capacity to form identity'[39] while, in the same vein, Raphael Samuel has argued that nostalgia is 'a contemporary equivalent of what Marxists used to call "false consciousness" and existentialists "bad faith"'.[40]

Even when nostalgia has been connected to immigration, this view of it as essentially conservative has largely persisted. Anita Mannur has argued that nostalgia leads immigrant communities to become invested in an image of the homeland as an 'unchanging and enduring cultural essence'.[41] There seems to be an all-pervasive agreement on the part of theorists that, in Carrie Hamilton's words, 'nostalgia must be an idealizing, and therefore conservative, form of memory'.[42]

Two major scholars who have attempted to produce more nuanced views of nostalgia still feel unable to fully endorse any critical potential it might have. Svetlana Boym's landmark *The Future of Nostalgia* is one example. Boym distinguishes between restorative nostalgia and reflective nostalgia – the former places the accent on the need 'to rebuild the lost home', while the latter 'dwells in . . . longing and loss'.[43] The former is conservative in that it aspires to a homogeneous whole, while the latter 'is ironic, inconclusive and fragmentary'[44] and therefore potentially creative and productive. While Boym's notion of reflective nostalgia does not really match my model of critical nostalgia anyway, there does seem to be signs in her own work that she herself is deeply unsure of the counter-hegemonic possibilities within nostalgia. In one of her more critical moments, she describes nostalgia as 'an abdication of personal responsibility, a guilt-free homecoming, an ethical and aesthetic failure'.[45] Similarly, Alistair Bonnett is equally critical of both nostalgia's attackers and defenders, arguing that in the former case, 'nostalgia is still routinely reviled as a lie, as the essence of reaction'[46] while, for the latter, the temptation 'to tip into a perverse celebration of this politically mobile emotion' is strong. Bonnett's central claim, that 'nostalgia is too ubiquitous and too diverse to need' defending may well be accurate enough, but in his understandable desire not to provide 'a prescriptive guide to nostalgia',[47] he arguably misses an opportunity to explore the ways in which it may have genuine political currency as a progressive, liberatory force, especially in the specific instance of the construction of diasporic communities that is the focus of this book.

What Bonnett does begin to develop, however, is a role for nostalgia that is not, as it is in Rosaldo, neo-colonial, but *anti-colonial*. Anti-colonial nostalgia can, for Bonnett, provide 'a transgression of, and a challenge to, monolithic visions of modernity' because it marks a break 'with the repression of themes of loss and attachments to the past.'[48] What is ironic, however, is that what, for Bonnett, constitutes anti-colonial nostalgia is also hugely Eurocentric – in his arguments, the anti-industrialism of Gandhi, and the return to the pastoral advocated by Tagore, is presented as almost derivative of William Morris and John Ruskin.[49] As a result, Bonnett is arguably unable to distinguish between the significantly different positions of Gandhi and Tagore, as well as not being able to explore the truly diverse forms that postcolonial nostalgia can take. His insight that nostalgia can be wielded to construct a counter-hegemonic anti-colonial politics is crucial, however, and has been very influential in my own work here.

Another attempt to conceptualize postcolonial nostalgia can be seen in the work of Dennis Walder. Walder is also limited to some extent by the hegemonic definitions of nostalgia, arguing for example that 'nostalgia and national identity are inextricably linked',[50] but he has simultaneously moved the argument forward significantly, in the process making a strong case for a counter-hegemonic, postcolonial nostalgia:

> The imaginative reconstruction of the past may be a conservative and parochial activity, reflecting a 'restorative' desire for belonging that overrides distance; equally, it may be a radical and disturbing activity, reflecting a challenging sense of the inadequacy of recalled or (to use Rushdie's language) reclaimed images of earlier times and places; or it may in complex ways address both possibilities.[51]

In the rest of this introduction, I will take this as my jumping-off point, in order to think through what a progressive, diasporic, postcolonial nostalgia might look like.

HOMEMAKING, DOMOPHILIA AND DIASPORIC NOSTALGIA

In this book, I attempt to move beyond Svetlana Boym's influential conception of nostalgia as a spectrum – with 'restorative' and 'reflective' as its two extremes. Instead of her contention that the attempt to restore the lost home is necessarily manifested through conservative politics, I wish to think through the consequences of placing the accent on the rather more fluid, and therefore more productive notion of homemaking. As a result, I can (loosely) define my use of nostalgia as the mourning of a home that has been lost in time and space, and the various social, creative and discursive processes that can be deployed in order to attempt to remake the home, in the here and now.

Nostalgia, then, is a diverse set of processes and discourse that represent a particular use of the past in order to re-create an imaginary, imaginative version of it in the present. Nostalgia is of course connected to cultural memory, but is a particular inflection of it. All remembering can be nostalgic, but it certainly does not have to be so. When cultural memory leads to particular narratives of home and homeliness, when these narratives can be said to be attempting a reimagining and reconstruction, then these acts of memory can be described as nostalgic. In the pages that follow, I look at a wide variety of textual and cultural examples from many different genres and representing many different discourses. Using the global south Asian diaspora as my case study, then, I examine some of the examples of nostalgia and try to evaluate the extent to which they may or may not aid the cause of progressive politics.

What makes the hegemonic connection between nostalgia and conservatism so puzzling is that, even at its most reactionary, it is, by definition, critical of the present. When Susan Bennett argues that nostalgia characterizes the present as 'defective and diminished', she is, of course, completely correct. What she fails to see, however, is its critical potential in recognizing the present as unsatisfactory. Nostalgia then, is fundamentally counter-hegemonic because it is always attempting to change the contemporary status quo. It represents a particular use of the past in order to change the present, and therefore the future. This counter-hegemonic change can be reactionary, absolutely, but it certainly does not have to be.

It is my contention throughout this book that, faced with the neo-colonial, racist reality of diasporic life, the self-indulgence that leads to the insistence on the right to belong can be seen as a powerful example of a progressive and liberatory nostalgia. In a sense, then, I would like to take nostalgia back to its roots, and explore the political significance of homes and homemaking.

I am calling this deeply personal, intensely powerful attachment to one's home *domophilia*. As Will Fellows has written in a different context, domophilia can be defined as 'this exceptional love of houses and things homey, this deep domesticity'.[52] Unlike Irfan Ahmad, who equates domophilia and nationalism by suggesting that the 'nation has been mainly conceived as home and vice versa',[53] I would argue that domophilia, and the nostalgia that helps to fuel it, is often cross-border, and pan-state in nature, and is therefore very different from patriotism or nationalism. In fact, and as I argue throughout the book, this form of nostalgia can be seen to represent a significant challenge to the apparent fixity of the nation-state. This is a crucially important point because it is this conflation between nostalgia and nationalism that accounts for much of the critical suspicion that it has received over the years. Jonathan Steinwand, for example, has argued:

Nations make use of nostalgia in the construction of national identity. The myths of any nation appeal to the national nostalgia and encourage identification with such nostalgic images as the nation's 'founding fathers' or some 'golden age', or decisive events in its history and the culture of the people. Nostalgia is a particularly useful tool for nations at times of crisis, despair, urgency and transition.[54]

Written almost two decades before Brexit or Trump, the parallels with the contemporary world are almost uncanny. Writing more specifically of the Indian diaspora, Arvind Rajagopal makes a similar case for the twinning of the nostalgic attachment to home, and a conservative project of nation building:

The liminal status of first generation Indians as immigrants inflects their expatriate nostalgia with a peculiar poignancy; 'home' gains in brilliance as a constellation of memories drawing closer emotionally even as it recedes in time. 'India' becomes a touchstone of their identity, assuring them of a place where they truly belong, or once belonged.[55]

The conflation of nostalgia and nationalism is matched with a similar conflation between the nation and the home. In *The Freedom of the Migrant: Objections to Nationalism*, Czech-born philosopher Vilém Flusser turns the physical space and architecture of the home into a thinly veiled symbol of the nation-state:

We can actually count on ever higher levels of homelessness, for we are everywhere tearing down walls, either because they impede traffic or because they get in the way of the free flow of people, goods, or information. Roofs supported by solid walls don't have much of a future.[56]

Flusser's objections to nationalism are at the root of his suspicions of home and people's attachments to their home:

The famous desire for home much celebrated in prose and poetry, this secret rootedness in infantile, fetal, and transindividual regions of the psyche, cannot stand up to the kind of cool analysis that the man without home is bound to and is capable of.[57]

What all of these theories share, I argue, is that they similarly underestimate the importance of the home as a fictional construction. It is indeed possible that the fictionalized home can easily map onto the ideological contours of the nation, but it is equally possible, and perhaps much more common, that the home represents an imaginary and imaginative rewriting of time and space. This imaginary rewriting can also be seen to help create a space where the ontological certainty, and therefore the ideological significance of the nation, can be challenged and undermined. If nostalgia can be used not just to mourn the loss of a fixed, stable home of the past, but to imagine a new home of the future, there is no reason why this new future must reflect the same oppressive forces that have structured the past.

In the context of imagining a future home, it is useful to remind oneself of the poetry that Gaston Bachelard finds in the domesticity of the home. He has famously argued that 'the house shelters day-dreaming, the house protects the dreamer, the house allows one to dream in peace'[58] – it is possible for my purposes here to think of the dreaming that the house allows as an example of the progressive nostalgia that I am trying to disentangle. Nostalgia is domophilic because it needs a home in order to protect itself, and therefore homemaking is absolutely central to the way in which nostalgia allows certain narratives of the past to be used in the present. Created through language and culture, nostalgia recognizes the literary, imaginative nature of this home, as Bachelard makes clear in his own work:

> All really inhabited space bears the essence of the notion of home . . . the imagination functions in this direction whenever the human being has found the slightest shelter: we shall see the imagination builds 'walls' of impalpable shadows, comfort itself with the illusion of protection – or, just the contrary, tremble behind thick walls, mistrust the staunchest ramparts.[59]

The home, for Bachelard, needs to be studied 'both in its unity and its complexity',[60] which implies the recognition that it is constructed 'in its reality and its virtuality, by means of thoughts and dreams'.[61] The home is thus a culmination of a number of contradictory narratives and as a result, a space of belonging and identity, memories and experiences that cannot be simplified under any kind of a simplistic symbol for nationhood. In other words, I would like to reinforce the distinction between home and nation that Rosemary Marangoly George sets up in her work:

> In fact, fictionality is an intrinsic attribute of home. The homes that are constructed . . . are multifarious experiences and desires which are at best vigorously interrogated, frequently challenged, and never quite rejected. I will examine the overlapping constructions of home and nation to suggest that while the nation is the object and subject of nationalist narratives, literary narratives are more centrally concerned with the idea of home.[62]

Even Flusser, whose view of the concept of home is diametrically opposite to that of Marangoly George, recognizes the intrinsic literariness of home, as the quote above demonstrates. Flusser might have failed to recognize the importance of the home, but he is completely correct when he points out that it is an object not just celebrated but created and maintained through literary and cultural production.

It is interesting that for both Johannes Hofer and Robert Hamilton, nostalgia is also and absolutely a literary construction, just as Marangoly George's vision of the home is. Philip Shaw has pointed out how Hamilton alludes to *Tristram Shandy*, 'a novel pointedly concerned with the effects of physical trauma on the soldier's mind and body'[63] in order to justify his claim that a well-read physician, using his developed literary sensitivities, would be better able to both 'focus on the emotional life of the patient'[64] as well as to serve their physical needs. Alex Davis has noted that Hofer's argument 'subtly foreground[s] the centrality of language to belonging',[65] and perfectly appropriately, his dissertation ends with two poetic tributes to Hofer, in one of which the poet P. Ancillon Metens declares: 'Hofer gave this, whose pages already reveal (that) by which the Helvetian corrects his own ill.'[66] Davis's account of the role played by the imagination in Hofer's conception of nostalgia is intriguingly reminiscent of what one might today call a creative, if not a distinctively literary imagination:

> This 'deepest part of the brain is afflicted constantly from infinite nerve fibres in which the spirits constantly move about in waves'. It is within this inner zone of incessant motion that that 'Wasting Disease' of nostalgia takes root, and it is this space that is incised and refashioned by the repeated thought of home, carving out familiar pathways from its fluid complexity. In the inmost precincts of the self, at the very seat of the creative imagination: a sea of waste.[67]

Helmut Illbruck has pointed out that the transition of nostalgia from a medical concept to a cultural one is connected to a change in the forms of scientific discourse itself:

> Nostalgia's exodus from the domain of medicine may be seen in conjunction also with medicine's increasing dissociation from literary styles ... as medical science struggled to adopt a ... persona ... [that was] rigorously objectivist and masculinist.[68]

It is this fictive nature of nostalgia and the home that it creates that helps to defend it from the attack of critics like Susan Stewart who argue that nostalgia is an inauthentic account of history 'because it does not take part in lived experience'[69] while indulging in the fantasy of authenticity. On the contrary, and as I hope this book will show, it is possible to read the various examples of diasporic nostalgia as self-consciously, almost joyously fictional. The home that is being created does not have to be a static, unchanging, essentialist version of the home that was left behind, but an imaginary, imaginative, discordant and vibrant entity that is able to transcend past, present and future, that is able to rewrite space and time, in order to produce a new sense of belonging that may well be utopian, but it is certainly not uncritical.

What follows in these pages, then, is an attempt, following Hofer, Hamilton and Marangoly George, to explore the ways in which the global south Asian diaspora is able to produce and consume literary and cultural texts in order to generate and reinforce the distinctively postcolonial, often counter-hegemonic, and always deeply political project of homemaking. In the pages that follow then, I examine various facets of diasporic life, looking at historical figures and memories of past rebellion, as well as more quotidian experiences such as food and music, to think about how each helps towards this homemaking. The home that is constructed using this nostalgia is fictional, often bears little resemblance to any kind of discernible geographical or historical reality, but also often contains within it enormous progressive and liberatory potential – potential that can be used to further active political resistance against hegemonic forces of neo-colonialism, racism and sexism, to name a few. Nostalgia does not have to be the preserve of the dominant majority, but in the hands of a counter-hegemonic minority can become a powerful tool with which to fight back.

It will be quickly obvious to the reader that I am very present in the arguments that follow. Perhaps inevitably, my reading of diasporic nostalgia is inflected in particular ways based on my own identity as a south Asian male living in the United Kingdom – my gendered, class, caste, occupational, regional, racial, political and religious identity all necessarily play a part in the ways in which I conceptualize diasporic nostalgia as progressive and counter-hegemonic. There is a temptation to apologize for this, but I will resist it – it would be foolish and perhaps intellectually dishonest to try to hide my own presence from the world that I am interested in exploring in these pages. My experience of a scholar of diasporic cultures is obviously inseparable from my own non-scholarly experiences of going shopping in an Indian grocery store, or turning on the BBC Asian Network while driving to work. I like to think that I have paid attention to the ways in which diasporic nostalgia might work for people who do not share my identity, and I certainly believe that the conceptions of nostalgia I provide could be applied to other, different case studies, but in the end my call for the scholarly necessity of recognizing a progressive nostalgia is connected to my own affective autobiography, my own nostalgic sensibility, as it were.

I should say that I am hardly the first person to identify the possibilities inherent in progressive nostalgia. Peter Glazer's account of the commemoration of the Spanish Civil War in America, *Radical Nostalgia: Spanish Civil War Commemoration in America*, and Gilad Padva's study *Queer Nostalgia in Cinema and Pop Culture*, which explores nostalgia as a means of empowerment, re-evaluating and re-creating lost gay youth, are two important books that have influenced my own thinking to a large degree. In later chapters, I will return to these books again, making clearer the connection between Glazer's and Padva's arguments and my own.

CHAPTER OUTLINE

In the first two chapters, I look at a few moments of resistance in British Asian history, from the failed rebellions instigated by the last Sikh Maharajah and the first British Sikh, Duleep Singh, to the anti-racist demonstrations caused by the deaths of Altab Ali and Blair Peach, and the campaign for the release of Kiranjit Ahluwalia, who was convicted for murdering her violent, alcoholic and abusive husband. I will examine how nostalgia can help to fuel acts of rebellion against the centre of power, and then the ways in which nostalgic memories of such resistance in the past can in turn help to generate further resistance in the present. These four figures – Duleep, Altab Ali, Blair Peach, and Ahluwalia are so different in every possible way, but cumulatively, they can help one chart a particular trajectory of British Asian history – one that recognizes the fights that had to be fought in order to be able to create a British Asian community, to create spaces where people could belong as British Asians.

The next two chapters together look at the importance of nostalgia in domesticity and everyday life, firstly through the role played by the production and consumption of food, and then by the construction of what Michel Foucault has called 'heterotopias'.[70] Using the theories of Michel Foucault and Walter Benjamin, I explore the importance of identifying this kind of everyday, domestic, quotidian nostalgia as also possessing important, progressive political potential. Nostalgia plays an important role in the various ways in which human beings occupy and imagine domestic space, and the material and discursive ways in which these spaces can be constructed and maintained. Moreover, when the human bodies doing the imagination and creation are hegemonically considered to be out of place, this nostalgia assumes great critical potential. I look at particular diasporic Asian spaces – places of worship, grocery stores, restaurants, and so forth, and the various literary and cultural texts through which they are imagined and created, in order to chart the ways in which, for example, the existence of an Asian grocery shop in one's life can aid the nostalgic process of homemaking that I am centrally concerned with in this book.

In Chapters 5 and 6, I turn my focus to the way in which popular media can help to create this sense of home and belonging, through looking at Bollywood representations of a global south Asian diaspora, and the development of British Asian radio and television broadcasting respectively. I try to make the case that the Bollywood representations of diasporic success needs to be separated from the neo-liberal, Islamophobic model of the stereotypical successful expatriate Hindu, and needs to be recognized for the deliberately fictional, self-referential world that it helps to create. This fictional world conjured on the screen can then be imaginatively used to provide solace against the alienation of diaspora, and support for the homemaking process that helps to overcome it. In Chapter 6, I read the examples and effects of nostalgia in the history of British Asian broadcasting. Using a combination of cultural texts and archival sources, I explore the nostalgia that underpinned the demand to be recognized as a legitimate part of British life, and therefore the right to have tailored broadcasting to suit one's interests. Approaching the BBC archives through the lens of progressive nostalgia helps to illuminate not just the translation of the affect of nostalgia into actual concrete activism, but also how both the affect and the activism it leads to become a threat to the status quo. This struggle between British Asian nostalgia on the one hand, and the pro-establishment BBC's ideology of assimilation on the other, provides an intriguing case study of the progressive role that nostalgic homemaking can have in the development of a marginalized minority community.

In the final, concluding chapter, I turn from homemaking and going back home as a metaphorical act, to an actual, material act, and examine examples of diasporic subjects returning home. Charting the ways in which their movement back to the place that had been the object of nostalgia both helps to reinforce the imaginative process of homemaking while exposing the home that is thus made as fictional. The home that is being imagined into existence is no more an accurate representation of the place that was left behind than it was of the diaspora in which one finds oneself. Homemaking leads, then, to the construction of a place that is tenuous, always out of reach. Utopian, but always critical of reality, and therefore perhaps able to challenge and undermine the unequal power structures that define it. It represents the persistent search for somewhere to belong, on one's own terms, for who one wishes to be. Constructed through word, image and music, preserved through dreams and imagination, the home emerges as a space of comfort and solidarity, a space where one can store up memories of one's past, something to draw sustenance from in the continuing struggle to change the present and the future for the better.

NOTES

1. A.A. Gill, "Brexit: AA Gill Argues for 'In'", *The Sunday Times*, 12 June 2016
2. Chris Haskins, "Ireland Is Looking Forward. Britain after the Brexit Vote Is Looking Back", *The Guardian*, 18 October 2016. Accessed on 11 August 2017, available at: https://www.theguardian.com/commentisfree/2016/oct/18/ireland-looking-forward-britain-brexit-vote-looking-back
3. Nadine El-Enany, "Brexit Is Not Only an Expression of Nostalgia for Empire, It Is Also the Fruit of Empire", 11 May 2017. Accessed on 11 August 2017, available at: http://blogs.lse.ac.uk/brexit/2017/05/11/brexit-is-not-only-an-expression-of-nostalgia-for-empire-it-is-also-the-fruit-of-empire/
4. Vince Cable, "Not Martyrs, Masochists", *Daily Mail*, 6 August 2017. Accessed on 12 August 2017, available at: http://www.dailymail.co.uk/debate/article-4764742/Lib-Dem-leader-SIR-VINCE-CABLE-attacks-Brexit-fanatics.html#ixzz4pRTclxIi

5. Ronald Brownstein, "Trump's Rhetoric of White Nostalgia", *The Atlantic*, 2 June 2016. Accessed on 12 August 2017, available at: https://www.theatlantic.com/politics/archive/2016/06/trumps-rhetoric-of-white-nostalgia/485192/

6. Sarah Puliam Bailey, "How Nostalgia for White Christian America Drove So Many Americans to Vote for Trump", *The Washington Post*, 5 January 2017. Accessed on 12 August 2017, available at: https://www.washingtonpost.com/local/social-issues/how-nostalgia-for-white-christian-america-drove-so-many-americans-to-vote-for-trump/2017/01/04/4ef6d686-b033-11e6-be1c-8cec35b1ad25_story.html?utm_term=.2d9420165789

7. Gregory Rodriguez and Dawn Nakagawa, "Looking Backward and Inward: The Politics of Nostalgia and Identity", *Berggruen [Insights]*, Issue 4, 22 July 2016. Accessed on 12 August 2017, available at: http://insights.berggruen.org/issues/issue-4/institute_posts/106

8. Kehinde Andrews, "Colonial Nostalgia Is Back in Fashion, Blinding Us to the Horrors of Empire", *The Guardian*, 24 August 2016. Accessed on 12 August 2017, available at: https://www.theguardian.com/commentisfree/2016/aug/24/colonial-nostalgia-horrors-of-empire-britain-olympic

9. Adam Scott, "Why Brexit and Trump Are to Blame for a Rise in Retro Gadgets – and How Brands Take Advantage", *Wired.com*, 24 May 2017. Accessed on 12 August 2017, available at: http://www.wired.co.uk/article/psychology-nostalgia-price

10. Gregory Rodriguez and Dawn Nakagawa, "Looking Backward and Inward"

11. Gurminder K. Bhambra, "Brexit, Trump, and 'Methodological Whiteness': On the Misrecognition of Race and Class", *British Journal of Sociology*, 68.S1, 2017, 214

12. Owen Hatherley, *The Ministry of Nostalgia* (London and New York: Verso, 2016), 16

13. Hatherley, *The Ministry of Nostalgia*, 14

14. Hatherley, *The Ministry of Nostalgia*, 21

15. Hatherley, *The Ministry of Nostalgia*, 14

16. Johannes Hofer, "*Medical Dissertation on Nostalgia* by Johannes Hofer (1688)" translated by Carolyn Kiser Anspach, *Bulletin of the Institute of the History of Medicine*, 1 January 1934, 380

17. Alex Davis has pointed out that this is a mistake in Anspach's translation, as she misreads a printer's contraction. It should read '*nostos*'. See Alex Davis, "Coming Home Again: Johannes Hofer, Edmund Spenser, and Premodern Nostalgia", *Parergon*, 33.2, 2016, 20, footnote 10

18. Johannes Hofer, *Medical Dissertation on Nostalgia*, 381

19. Johannes Hofer, *Medical Dissertation on Nostalgia*, 383

20. Alex Davis, "Coming Home Again", 19

21. Johannes Hofer, *Medical Dissertation on Nostalgia*, 381

22. Robert Hamilton, "History of a remarkable Case of Nostalgia affecting a native of Wales, and occurring in Britain" in Andrew Duncan (ed.) *Medical Commentaries for the Year 1786* (Edinburgh and London: C. Elliot & Co, 1787), 343

23. Robert Hamilton, "History of a remarkable Case of Nostalgia", 345

24. Robert Hamilton, "History of a remarkable Case of Nostalgia", 345–46

25. Philip Shaw, "Longing for Home: Robert Hamilton, Nostalgia and the Emotional Life of the Eighteenth-Century Soldier", *Journal for Eighteenth-Century Studies*, 39.1, 2016, 36

26. Nicholas Dames, *Amnesiac Selves: Nostalgia, Forgetting and British Fiction, 1810 – 1870* (New York and Oxford: Oxford University Press, 2001), 34

27. Johannes Hofer, *Medical Dissertation on Nostalgia*, 384

28. Alex Davis, "Coming Home Again", 20

29. Johannes Hofer, *Medical Dissertation on Nostalgia*, 383

30. Renato Rosaldo, "Imperialist Nostalgias", *Representations* 26, Spring 1989, 107

31. Renato Rosaldo, "Imperialist Nostalgias", 108

32. Renato Rosaldo, "Imperialist Nostalgias", 109

33. For more information about the relationship between nostalgia and the military history of Europe, see Helmut Illbruck, *Nostalgia: Origins and Ends of an Unenlightened Disease* (Evanston, IL: Northwestern University Press, 2012)

34. David Lowenthal, "Nostalgia Tells It Like It Wasn't" in Malcolm Chase and Christopher Shaw (eds) *The Imagined Past: History, and Nostalgia* (Manchester: Manchester University Press, 1989), 21

35. David Lowenthal, *The Past Is a Foreign Country Revisited* (Cambridge: Cambridge University Press, 2015), 52–54

36. Susan Bennett, *Performing Nostalgia: Shifting Shakespeare and the Contemporary Past* (London: Routledge, 1996), 4

37. Susan Bennett, *Performing Nostalgia*, 5

38. Ryan Lizardi, *Mediated Nostalgia: Individual Memory and Contemporary Mass Media* (Lanham, MD: Lexington Books, 2015), 1

39. Susan Stewart, *On Longing: Narratives of the Miniature, the Gigantic, the Souvenir, the Collection* (Durham, NC, and London: Duke University Press, 1993), 23

40. Raphael Samuel, *Theatres of Memory: Past and Present in Contemporary Culture* (London and New York: Verso, 2012), 17

41. Anita Mannur, *Culinary Fictions: Food in South Asian Diasporic Culture* (Philadelphia: Temple University Press, 2010), 31

42. Carrie Hamilton, "Happy Memories", *New Formations*, No. 63, Winter 2007, 70

43. Svetlana Boym, *The Future of Nostalgia* (New York: Basic Books, 2001), 41

44. Svetlana Boym, *The Future of Nostalgia*, 50

45. Svetlana Boym, *The Future of Nostalgia*, xiv

46. Alastair Bonnett, *Left in the Past: Radicalism and the Politics of Nostalgia* (New York and London: Continuum, 2010), 2

47. Alastair Bonnett, *Left in the Past*, 3

48. Alastair Bonnett, *Left in the Past*, 88

49. Alastair Bonnett, *Left in the Past*, 88

50. Dennis Walder, *Postcolonial Nostalgias: Writing, Representation, and Memory* (Abingdon: Routledge, 2011), 5

51. Dennis Walder, *Postcolonial Nostalgias*, 12

52. Will Fellows, *A Passion to Preserve: Gay Men as Keepers of Culture* (Madison: University of Wisconsin Press, 2004), 26–27.

53. Irfan Ahmad, "In Defense of Ho(s)tels: Islamophobia, Domophilia, Liberalism", *Politics, Religion & Ideology*, 14.2, 2013, 241

54. Jonathan Steinwand, "The Future of Nostalgia in Friedrich Schlegel's Gender Theory: Casting German Aesthetics Beyond Ancient Greece and Modern Europe" in Jean Pickering and Suzanne Kehde (eds) *Narratives of Nostalgia, Gender, and Nationalism* (New York: New York University Press, 1997), 10

55. Arvind Rajagopal, *Politics after Television: Hindu Nationalism and the Reshaping of the Public in India* (Cambridge: Cambridge University Press, 2001), 246

56. Vilém Flusser, *The Freedom of the Migrant: Objections to Nationalism* (Urbana, Chicago and Springfield: University of Illinois Press, 2003), 59

57. Vilém Flusser, *Writings* (Minneapolis: University of Minnesota Press, 2002), 93

58. Gaston Bachelard, *The Poetics of Space* (Boston: Beacon Press, 1994), 6

59. Gaston Bachelard, *The Poetics of Space*, 5

60. Gaston Bachelard, *The Poetics of Space*, 3

61. Gaston Bachelard, *The Poetics of Space*, 5

62. Rosemary Marangoly George, *The Politics of Home: Postcolonial Relocations and Twentieth-Century Fiction* (Berkeley and London: University of California Press, 1999), 11–12

63. Philip Shaw, "Longing for Home", 28

64. Philip Shaw, "Longing for Home", 29

65. Alex Davis, "Coming Home Again", 19

66. Cited in Johannes Hofer, *Medical Dissertation on Nostalgia*, 390

67. Alex Davis, "Coming Home Again", 38

68. Helmut Illbruck, *Nostalgia*, 143

69. Susan Stewart, *On Longing*, 23

70. Michel Foucault, *Aesthetics, Method and Epistemology Vol. 2* (New York: New Press, 1998), 178

Chapter One

'Doubly Expatriated'

Duleep Singh and the Politics of Nostalgia

Hauptbanhof station in the Stuttgart S-Bahn network is not a place where one would normally expect to find traces of south Asian diasporic nostalgia, so when I passed through it in June 2015, I was surprised to encounter a familiar face. I was in Germany to present a conference paper on postcolonial nostalgia and Bollywood representations of the south Asian diaspora, so nostalgia was, as it were, on my mind.

Out of the corner of my eye, I thought I saw a face I recognized, staring impassively out at me as I went down the escalator. At first, I thought I must be mistaken. A few extra trips on the escalator, and some consequent strange looks from Stuttgart's commuters, however, proved that I had been right. Dressed in exotic, royal finery, leaning nonchalantly on a ceremonial sword, he seemed to me to be incongruously out of place – called upon merely to attest to the excellence of the Prince of India chain of restaurants to be found, as the poster promised me, in Frankfurt, Mannheim and Stuttgart. The figure used to advertise this restaurant had been so summoned to corroborate the owner's claim, also emblazoned on the poster, that their restaurant provided 'Original Indian Ambience'.

It is impossible to know how many of the commuters and tourists who went through Hauptbanhof that day recognized the image as they glided by on the escalators, but the 'girlishly beautiful face smudged with adolescent masculinity . . . clad for the portrait in the splendour of an Eastern chieftain'[1] has a long and complex history, involving a much more critical, ambiguous and deeply counter-normative use of nostalgia than the arguably more simplistic orientalist use in this particular advertisement.

The image is from a painting, dating from 1855, and is by Franz Xaver Winterhalter, the nineteenth-century court painter from Frankfurt. The subject is not an imaginary, archetypal Oriental monarch, but a youthful Maharajah Duleep Singh, son of the Lion of Punjab, Maharajah Ranjit Singh, and the last emperor of the Sikh nation. Born in 1838, Duleep succeeded to his father's throne in 1843, following the series of coups and assassinations that were triggered by his father's death. Aged just five, Duleep was declared ruler under the care of the regent, his mother, Maharani Jindan Kaur. The next five years would see the two Anglo-Sikh Wars, culminating in 1849, with the defeat of the Sikh armies, and the signing of the Treaty of Bhyrowal, which effectively became the instrument of annexation, as Punjab became part of the British Empire. Duleep lost his kingdom, was separated from his mother, persuaded to convert to Christianity and exiled to Britain. There he grew up to be an Anglicized British aristocrat, a favourite of Queen Victoria and well-known as the Black Prince of Perthshire, living for a time at Castle Menzies near Aberfeldy, and then in Elveden Hall, Suffolk. In the process, he would become the first British Sikh.

With his ancestral background, and his political significance to the Sikh nation, it is perhaps not surprising that he has become a figure who can be nostalgically appropriated to reinforce the notion of a great and glorious past. In this chapter, I will focus on the figure of Duleep Singh and his legacy, and examine, firstly, how he was able, in his own lifetime, to mobilize his own nostalgia towards anti-imperial ends and, secondly, how in the years since his death, the nostalgia surrounding his legacy has grown, leading to a number of complex and creative responses to the painful convoluted threads of shared Anglo-Sikh history.

MAHARAJAH DULEEP SINGH: A LIFE OF NOSTALGIA AND REBELLION

When Duleep Singh was first brought to England in 1854, he was too young to have any real sense of who he was, and the significance he had for Sikhs all over Punjab. Quite quickly, he became a favourite of Queen Victoria, whose reaction to Duleep was marked by a fascination with the exotic Orient characteristic of Victorian Britain. Writing in her diaries, Queen Victoria described meeting Duleep for the first time: '[he is] extremely handsome and speaks English perfectly, and has a pretty, graceful and dignified manner. He was beautifully dressed and covered in diamonds.'[2] Duleep's presence in court would become increasingly common, as would his name in court circulars in the newspapers. Two years later, the *Illustrated London News* reported a visit he made to 'different points of interest in' Staffordshire:

> Wearing an elegant silk headdress and massive earrings. . . . His highness, who speaks English with fluency and correctness, expressed himself much satisfied with his visit.[3]

This image of a man clad in oriental finery is what Winterhalter attempted to capture in his painting, and what the owners of the Prince of India restaurant in Stuttgart were attempting to use to indicate an authentic Indian ambience. Brian Keith Axel has analysed in great detail both the artistic significance and political legacy of the Winterhalter portrait. Axel has argued that 'the "ground" on which the image of the maharaja stands is no ground at all' – in the face of the contested nature of Punjab in the 1840s, Winterhalter was clearly not able to position this sovereign-without-a-kingdom in any kind of recognizable, 'real' place. What the viewer is left with is, in Axel's words, 'a male body that, now arrested ambiguously in the space of a colonial frontier, has arrived at the westernmost limit of nineteenth-century Punjab and found, not Afghanistan, but London'.[4] Confined to Winterhalter's canvas, clad in finery that marks him as different, but gives him no agency – he is turbanned in order to mark his Indianness, but he is shorn of the famous Koh-i-Noor, the diamond that had already been taken from him and had become part of the Queen's personal property.

The first few years after his arrival in Britain continued this theme of othering combined with emasculating appropriation, as Duleep was prepared for the unremarkable life of an Anglicized country squire. He was privately educated, and Queen Victoria 'decided that his rank was to be the same as that of a European prince, and as chief of the native princes of India he came next in precedence after the royal family'.[5] Over the next few years, he moved around, living first in various houses in Perthshire, Scotland, before moving to Mulgrave Castle in Yorkshire, and finally settling in Elveden House in Suffolk. As Peter Bance has put it, 'his dashing looks and Indian appearance made him an ideal party accessory'.[6] As in the Winterhalter painting, then, Duleep remained a glorified pet – serving at once to remind the British establishment of their munificence in allowing such an alien creature to live and thrive among them, but also embodying what Axel as called 'an acute act of appropriation – reiterating, renegotiating, and revaluing the surrender of former foes'.[7] In other words, the Winterhalter portrait was designed to serve as a visible marker of the annexation of Punjab.

Duleep Singh may well have passed his entire life thus alienated from his family heritage, except for the fact that in 1861, he was allowed by the British to visit India (though he would never again be allowed to return to Punjab) and reunite with his mother and bring her back to Britain. Maharani Jindan Kaur only survived for two years after moving to Britain, but in that time she took great care to reintroduce him to his family's true heritage. Gradually, Duleep would take greater and greater interest in his birth-right.

The start of the 1880s would find him in the reading rooms of the British Museum, learning about his life, and the processes through which he was deposed from his throne, from the British administrative records covering the annexation of Punjab. Christy Campbell imaginatively re-creates the remarkable impression that Duleep must have made while researching his family tree in the otherwise rather staid surroundings of Bloomsbury:

> Visitors to the British Museum in the spring months of the early 1880s would have seen an unusual figure striding purposefully each morning from his carriage to a particular desk in the great circular reading room. Scholars toiled in the library's daylit quadrants as an Indian gentleman turned obsessively to the so-called 'Punjab Papers' – the collection of correspondence and government documents which dealt with the two Anglo-Sikh wars and the final annexation of the Punjab in 1849. A turbanned servant scribbled furiously beside him, transcribing Prinsep's *History of the Sikhs* and Bosworth Smith's *The Life of Sir Henry Lawrence*. Maharajah Duleep Singh wanted his childhood back. What had happened to him?[8]

It is, of course painfully ironic that in trying to trace the story of his own life, Duleep had to go to the records of the Imperial Government, safeguarded in that repository of colonial knowledge, the British Museum. After Edward Said, it has become almost commonsensical to argue that one of the ways in which colonialism asserts itself is through discursive and epistemological control over the colonized other:

> Knowledge . . . means surveying a civilisation from its origins to its prime to its decline – and of course, it means *being able to do that*. . . . To have such knowledge of such a thing is to dominate it, to have authority over it. And authority here means for 'us' to deny autonomy to 'it' – the Oriental country – since we know it and it exists, in a sense, *as* we know it.[9] [original emphasis]

There cannot be too many more people, however, whose lived experience so directly validates Said's theories of knowledge – the power dynamics of imperialism meant that when Duleep wanted to find out more about his life and its various significances, the only source of knowledge he could access was one that was controlled by Imperial Britain. As Duleep would later go on to realize, the decision to alienate him not just from his kingdom, but from the discursive body that allowed Britain to epistemologically as well as materially own Punjab, was perfectly deliberate. In 1882, he wrote to Queen Victoria thus:

> Had I been aware, My Sovereign, of the true state of things, the knowledge of which was carefully kept from me by the late Sir John Login, a creature of Lord Dalhousie, a very different provision for the maintenance of myself and my children would have been made.[10]

It is perfectly appropriate that Christy Campbell, in his popular account of Duleep's life and legacy, described the drive that moved him to try to learn more about his story as a desire to reclaim his childhood. Having reconnected with his mother and revisited India, Duleep, in the opening years of the 1880s, was getting more and more nostalgic – he was desperate for a sense of rootedness, a narrative that could explain who he was and how he came to be that way. This nostalgic desire for information took him to the British Museum, enabled him to discover how he had lost his kingdom, and gave him the knowledge he needed to campaign for the restitution of his rights. He would begin by campaigning through personal, private as well as open, letters, mostly in *The Times* – when this was unsuccessful, he would start a more active rebellion, reconvert to Sikhism, and attempt to form relationships with Britain's other enemies – the Irish and the Russians mainly, in order to recover his lost kingdom. Ultimately unsuccessful, he would die in Paris and be buried as a Christian, against his express wishes. He remains buried today in Elveden – his grave being one of a few Duleep-related sites that have come to be of great significance in the entangled Anglo Sikh history.

The second half of Duleep's life, then, demonstrates the importance of what might be described as the nostalgic drive – a need for a home, and the deploying of one's memories, one's material and imaginative energies into the reconstruction of a home that once existed but has since been destroyed. Duleep's deploying of his nostalgia also demonstrates how these affective forces can be mobilized to generate an anti-imperial rebellion. Fittingly, today Duleep remains a figure closely associated with nostalgia, and the ways in which he has been represented in culture reinforce the power that counter-colonial nostalgia might have – not just at the height of European Empire, but in the context of the long shadow it casts over today's world.

In 1882, he wrote the first of a series of remarkable letters to *The Times*, the eloquence of which remains potent more than a century after the fact:

> If one righteous man was found in the two most wicked cities of the world, I pray God that at least one honourable, just, and noble Englishman may be forthcoming out of this Christian land of liberty and justice to advocate my cause in Parliament; otherwise, what chance have I of obtaining justice, considering that my despoiler, guardian, judge, advocate, and jury, is the British nation itself?
>
> Generous and Christian Englishmen, accord me a just and liberal treatment, for the sake of the fair name of your nation, of which I have now the honour to be a naturalized member, for it is more blessed to give than to take.[11]

The Times, in its editorial, responded the same day as this letter with a scorn calculated to minimize any sympathies Duleep's letter may have generated:

> It is no doubt the duty of every man to live within his income, and yet if the Maharajah has failed to acquire a virtue rare indeed among Eastern Princes and not too common in the class to which he belongs by adoption, there is no Englishman but would feel ashamed if he or his descendants were thereby to come to want. At the same time it is impossible for the Indian Government, which has claims on its slender resources far more urgent than those of the magnificent squire of Elveden, to guarantee him indefinitely against the consequences of his own improvidence. At any rate, it is safe to warn him against encumbering his personal claims by political pleas which are wholly inadmissible. He is very little likely to excite sympathy for his pecuniary troubles by his bold, but scarcely successful, attempt to show that if he could only come by his own he is still the lawful Sovereign of the Punjab.[12]

The deliberate, scornful undermining of Duleep's claim by *The Times* reflects the panicked response from the British establishment which was only too aware of the incendiary potential any rebellion led by Duleep might have. As I will argue again later, the fact that Duleep's nostalgia-driven rebellion was both very real and very significant is demonstrated by the need felt by Imperial Britain to attack and undermine it at every opportunity. It is also noticeable that *The Times* undermines him by racially othering his perceived shortcomings, in the process robbing him of a legitimate position from which he could claim what was his due. In characterizing his extravagance as an Indian trait, *The Times* is able to both ridicule him as a human being, and to challenge the basis of his claim to his lost kingdom.

Two years after this letter, Duleep would begin writing to Queen Victoria herself, making plain in a series of letters his deeply held grievances, and alerting her as to his plans to reconvert to Sikhism, and to return to India – both highly treasonable acts under the circumstances:

> For Your Majesty's government having branded me disloyal when God knows I was most loyal and devoted to Your Majesty I had no other course open to me except either to turn traitor or continue to submit to the insults repeatedly offered to me by the Administration of India.[13]

The Queen's responses demonstrate her increasing unease at Duleep's attempts to asset himself against her authority:

> My dear Maharajah, as your friend and perhaps the truest you have, I would strongly warn you against those who would lead you into trouble. Do not use threats or abusive language, for it will not be the means of obtaining the impartial hearing of your claims that you desire. Above all I most earnestly warn you against going to India where you will find yourself far less independent and far less at your ease than here.[14]

The Queen's view was at least partly influenced by the advice of her own Viceroy, Lord Ripon:

> Many men, indeed, almost an entire generation, are still alive who remember [Ranjit Singh] who took a leading part in the events which followed his death and it is quite impossible to say what might be the effect of the appearance of the son of their great Maharajah, Christian though he be, in the country of the five rivers.[15]

The British Government had once before in 1861 allowed Duleep to enter India, though they were careful not to allow him to go to Punjab. Now, having been educated about his birth-right by his mother, he posed a much greater threat and the British Government were not about to make the same mistake again. This refusal of permission for Duleep to go back to India suggests that they knew only too well the explosive anti-imperial potential that Duleep's nostalgia for Punjab and his lost kingdom had. Reunited with his people, safely back at home, Duleep may well have been in a position to seriously challenge British authority in the Punjab; alienated from his roots, he remained a powerless, pitiable figure who could be mocked and undermined.

In 1884, Duleep wrote and privately published a book called *The Maharajah Duleep Singh and the Government: A Narrative*, which was an attempt to set out his grievances against the British Government in India. In it he again makes clear his awareness of the reasons why his British guardians were so careful to distance him from any knowledge of his own history:

> The Maharajah had been educated under the auspices of his British guardians. Sir John Login and Colonel Oliphant were Indian officials, and he never fully emancipated himself, until very recently, from the influence which their teaching and counsels exercised over him . . . The Maharajah recently has read the Blue Books and studied the history of his country and the race from which he sprung, and has arrived at a very different view of his rights.[16]

Written entirely in the third person, this book remains an extremely poignant read today, with the knowledge not only of what was destined for Duleep himself, but also for the Sikh nation as a whole. When reading Duleep's words today, one is forced to think not just of the losses he suffered in his own lifetime, but also of the painful fact that, in the two centuries since, the dream of a Sikh nation has remained an unfulfilled aspiration.

In this book, Duleep makes an explicit connection between his grievances caused by British injustice on the one hand, and his deep and painful longing for his home on the other:

> In 1882, the Maharajah again wished to return to India. . . . He longed now more than ever to revisit the scenes of his childhood, where those important events which had influenced his destiny had taken place, though he could not understand their import at the time. The punishment of perpetual banishment is not mentioned in the treaty, and it cannot be matter for surprise if the resis-

tance to his desire has intensified the Maharajah's wish to revisit his native country. There are indeed few impulses of the heart more strong and more laudable than the attachment felt to the land of a man's birth. . . . He now feels doubly expatriated. Having failed in taking root in the land of his adoption he is prevented from even visiting his native country.[17]

Duleep's drive to rediscover his own past, the ways in which he combines national and imperial histories with personal grief, is reminiscent of the connections that Walter Benjamin made between mourning and historical materialism:

a process of empathy whose origin is the indolence of the heart, *acedia*, which despairs of grasping and holding the genuine historical image as it flares up briefly. Among Medieval theologians it was regarded as the root cause of sadness . . . empathy with the victor invariably benefits the rulers. . . . A historical materialist therefore dissociates himself from it as far as possible. He regards it as his task to brush history against the grain.[18]

Benjamin's analysis is helpful for my purposes here not because I am trying to paint Duleep as somehow a model of historical materialism, but because Benjamin helps point to ways in which a particular affective connection with the past can be used to incite rebellion against hegemony. In the specific case of Duleep's life, he is able to combine the 'important events' of British imperial history in India, with his own personal nostalgic connections with his home, in an effort to challenge the centre of absolute imperial power, and its attempt to control the trajectory of his life and that of his country.

Duleep's attachment to 'his native country', and its connections to Benjamin's model of historical materialism, is further reminiscent of Judith Butler's astute observation that loss and mourning has the capacity to help create communities:

Despite our differences in location and history, my guess is that it is possible to appeal to a 'we', for all of us have some notion of what it is to have lost somebody. Loss has made a tenuous 'we' of us all. . . . Loss and vulnerability seem to follow from our being socially constituted bodies, attached to others, at risk of losing those attachments, exposed to others, at risk of violence by virtue of that exposure.[19]

Though Butler is writing in a very different context, I think it is possible to apply her notion of the 'tenuous "we"', the process through which she identifies loss as helping us to attach ourselves to each other, to the ways in which Duleep was able to use his own nostalgia, the loss of home and family and property that he experienced, to build the beginning of an albeit ultimately doomed counter-imperial movement. Butler's tenuous 'we', in other words, might be thought of as a political community, and her insistence on the right to grieve one's losses as a political action of great counter-hegemonic potential.

One of the more interesting aspects of Duleep's nostalgia is that, like many of the other examples I am looking at in this book, this has little to do with conventional modes of nationalism. Even though Duleep refers to his 'native country', his demands, at least at this stage of his political development, have little to do with a rising Indian or Sikh national consciousness. As A. Martin Wainwright has argued:

> Since from the age of fifteen onward Duleep did not reside in India, and since he had no connection with the community of Indian intellectuals living in England, he acquired little if any sense of the national consciousness that was spreading across the subcontinent in the wake of British conquest.[20]

Duleep's consciousness was not primarily determined by either anti-colonial nationalism (though he would, in time, be able to make connections with various nationalist groups in order to plan his rebellion) or by Victorian British Imperial nationalism. He was, rather, motivated primarily by a feeling of rootlessness, a recognition that, for all his material wealth and exotic finery, he did not belong in the British aristocratic class that had apparently adopted him. Suspended between two very different worlds, Duleep's primary drive seems to have been a much more small-scale one – simply a desire for a place to call one's own, a desire to ground himself in a way that the Winterhalter painting denied him. This double alienation felt by the first recorded British Sikh would be familiar to many of us who have since tried to traverse the painful double bind of the postcolonial expatriate – feeling both an affective connection and lingering resentment at the British nation and its role in directing the trajectories of our lives, as well as a paradoxical sense of alienation and belonging in our relationship to our homelands. It is perhaps the British reaction to Duleep's demand to go back home that turned him towards an active anti-imperial position, but it nevertheless demonstrates the political possibilities within this nostalgic drive to return.

In 1885, Duleep found and reprinted two auction catalogues dating from 1850 and 1851. The full, revealing title of this reprinted publication was:

> A Reprint of Two Sale Catalogues of Jewels and other Confiscated Property belonging to His Highness the Maharajah Duleep Singh, which were put up to auction and sold at Lahore, in the Years 1850 and 1851 by the Government of India.

Duleep's aim in publishing these catalogues is made clear in the introduction to this remarkable volume:

> The Title pages to the Catalogues are . . . headed by the expression 'Confiscated Property;' but the Maharajah Duleep Singh contends that the property thus sold was not State property, which was alone, by the operation of the Treaty of 1849, at the disposal of the Government; and it is clear from the general character of the articles specified in the Catalogues, that they were the private property of the Maharajah, and could not properly be described as State property. . . . The word 'confiscate' used in the Treaty is an arrogant expression, singularly illsuited to the relationship in which the infant Maharajah stood towards the British Government.[21]

Duleep takes great pain to tabulate and highlight the approximate amount realized through these sales: 'It would not be very extravagant to put the whole sum realized by the property at half a million of money'.[22] This may be seen as an odd decision. As Wainwright has argued, 'Duleep's willingness to accept a financial solution to the loss of his sovereignty appeared to undermine his argument. For the Maharaja had hardly suffered at the hands of British authorities since the loss of his kingdom.'[23] *The Times*, in its response to Duleep's 1882 letter, made it clear that it felt Duleep's grievances to be economic rather than political:

> His argument concerning his *de jure* sovereignty of the Punjab is manifestly only intended to support his pecuniary claims. If this were settled to his satisfaction, he would doubtless be content, and more than content, to die, as he lived, an English country gentleman, with estates swarming with game, and with an income sufficient to his needs.[24]

What Duleep was attempting to do, however, was to highlight both the personal losses he suffered at the hands of the British and, perhaps more importantly, expose the entire imperial project as, ultimately, driven by economic exploitation by the metropole of the marginal. In *The Maharajah Duleep Singh and the Government: A Narrative*, he writes:

> We wanted the Punjab. We wanted it as a protection to our North-West frontier in India. We wanted its people as soldiers and as subjects. Its revenues would be no less convenient for our exchequer. . . . The revenues have more than answered our expectation, yielding every year a large surplus to be spent in our other territories.[25]

Duleep's recognition of the pecuniary motives of the British Empire was so clear that he is, according to Christy Campbell, on record as referring to Queen Victoria as 'Mrs Fagin'.[26] In the introduction to the reprinted auction catalogues, Duleep notes: 'The principal jewels appear to have been sent to England soon afterwards with the Koh-i-noor'. *The Times* was being quite careful in painting his complaints as merely an attempt to gain more money – in accusing Duleep of an illegitimate greed, *The Times* was trying to efface the illegitimate greed that was the unmentionable *raison d'être* of Empire as a whole.

It is because of this political awareness that Duleep was able to make connections with, and attempt to gain strength from, other anti-imperialist struggles, most particularly from Irish nationalists in Paris, as well as from the Russian Imperial Court. The nostalgia that propelled Duleep to attempt to reclaim his birth-right could easily be understood by other, similarly colonized people. The creation of a common, anti-colonial front must of necessity have been a matter of alarm for the imperial centre, precisely because the potential that nostalgia has to be appropriated into the process of homemaking – and the radically destabilizing potential of the material and discursive home that is constructed as a result. Thus, Duleep used the republishing of the catalogue to set up another, nostalgically driven, less mercenary approach to the losses he suffered as a child. He ends the introduction to the catalogue with this distinctly non-financial claim:

> Independently of the question of money value, it may well be asked what right the British Government could have to dispose of historical heirlooms belonging to the Maharajah, who was its ward, while he was an infant, without even asking his consent, considering the exceptional interest he would have subsequently experienced in the possession of his father's portrait and personal accoutrements when he came to years of responsibility and full maturity. [27]

It would not be too much to say that Duleep is here employing his own nostalgia to set up a counter-imperial value system that challenges the British Empire's practice of viewing these objects only for their monetary value and its inability to recognize the immense symbolic value they would have held for Duleep, as man and monarch.

It is no coincidence that Duleep was expressing his sentiments in such a familial, dynastic fashion. As could perhaps be expected by someone of his background, Duleep's nostalgia was first and foremost for his ancestry – the identity-narrative that most closely fitted a deposed monarch. In Wainwright's words:

> For Duleep's concept of allegiance was neither ethnic nor national. Rather it was dynastic, and it thrived on the personal ties that were possible in an empire that retained the concept of subjecthood to the monarch rather than citizenship of the state. . . . Duleep Singh's rebellion was, therefore, not so much a matter of either nationalism or selfish petulance as it was of dynastic honor. [28]

Thus, in his famous letter to Queen Victoria, he expressed his political and spiritual reawakening in characteristically ancestral terms:

> I did not wish that you . . . should hear from any other source but myself of the possibility of my re-embracing the faith of my ancestors. . . . Your Majesty is

now fully acquainted with the treatment I have received from the Christians who spend vast sums annually to teach the heathen to do justice, love mercy and walk humbly with God and to do unto others as you would wish them to do unto you.

Lord Dalhousie wrote in a bible he presented me the following inscription. 'This Holy Book, in which he has been led by God's Grace to find an inheritance richer by far than all earthly kingdoms, is presented with sincere respect and regard by his faithful friend.' Or, in other words, having deprived me of my inheritance which was in his power to let alone, he hoped as my friend that I may acquire another birthright which was not in his power to bestow.

My Sovereign, such vile hypocrisy of the Christians has made me wish to resort to the faith of my forefathers which is simple trust and belief in the great architect of the Universe.[29]

The incendiary power of these words and of the attempted rebellion that followed cannot be overstated. The Sikh army was one of the few that regularly caused the British problems in India, and the revolutionary potential that Duleep Singh had was clearly understood by the British. This was why he was never again allowed to return to India, even in death, and why the establishment went to such lengths to discredit him – to the point where even today he is often spoken of as little more than an aristocratic playboy. In a series of attacks that implicitly recognized the threat this posed to status quo, *Punch* caricatured Duleep by portraying him as a feckless, stupid half-Irish, half-Indian, indeed half-human monstrosity, a mere puppet in the hands of the big bad Russian bear.[30] In language that, even accounting for historic context, manages to offend, *Punch* describes an imaginary encounter with Duleep in Moscow during which 'the Doo' starts off by pretending to be Irish: 'Why do ye call me out of my name? Shure I am PAT CASEY.' His deception is exposed, however, when the *Punch* correspondent begins to play music and 'the Doo' cannot help but dance:

> Without a moment's hesitation I struck up a plantation song on my banjo, and began to walk round the apartment. The Doo tried hard to restrain himself, but nature once more was too many for him. After a struggle he got up, and joined me in my quaint promenade; and when I indulged in a wild, joyous breakdown, he followed my example.

Punch's rather confused racism is on full display here, as 'the Doo' realizes his disguise has let him down:

> 'Yah! yah! De ole niggar am found dis niggar out! Yah! yah!' returned His Highness, smilingly, speaking his native Hindustani for the first time, in token of submission.

A year later, and *Punch* was still targeting Duleep, in the form of a mock letter from 'Twolip Sing, the Proud and Incapable Foe of England' to an 'Honoured Friend' asking for money:

> Though I have been taking a little money by showing myself dressed up in my 'jools,' as our mutually honoured friends in Dublin would call them, still I haven't yet been able to nobble the Governor here, and as funds are getting low, every rouble is a consideration.[31]

Like the attacks from the British Government in India and in London, and in the pages of *The Times*, it seems clear that behind this line of attack lies the fear of alliances being established by different colonized subjects. What is so dangerous for the readers of *The Times* and *Punch*, and what must therefore be neutralized through this cruel satire, is Duleep's mobilizing of his nostalgic longing for home, and the material objects that represent this home, in order to expose the imperial project for what it was. Presenting him dressed up in his 'jools' allows *Punch* to emasculate Duleep and to therefore undermine not just his rebellion, but also the nostalgic attachment he has to these personal possessions which were taken from him.

A large part of Britain's attempt to discredit him was to highlight the political neutering that was his conversion to Christianity. As early as 1854, Lord Dalhousie had made this awareness of the significance of Duleep's religion manifest:

> The 'night-cappy' appearance of his turban is his strongest national feature. Do away with that and he has no longer any outward and visible sign of a Sikh about him.[32]

This explains the British insistence that he should, against his own wishes, be buried in England, as a Christian. Rendered greedy, effeminate, a lapsed Sikh and therefore an impotent leader of his people, this disproportionate response to what was, on the face of it, a letter-writing campaign demonstrates how much the British feared the prospect of a rejuvenated Sikh rebellion with Duleep as its figurehead.

While most accounts of Duleep's life date his political and religious awakenings to 1882, I would argue that there is evidence that by that point, Duleep had already been mobilizing nostalgia for his lost inheritance for many years. The reference to Sodom and Gomorrah in the letter to Victoria is characteristic – like many other converts, Duleep knew his religious text inside out. In 1865, while living in Auchlyne near Aberfeldy in Perthshire, Duleep's wife Bamba gave birth to a son who died within twenty-four hours, before he could be named. This infant son was buried in the parish church at Kenmore. The inscription on his recently restored grave reads:

> To The Memory of The Infant Son of The Maharajah Duleep Singh, Late Ruler of the Sikh Nation, Punjab, India and the Maharanee, His Wife.

The specific reference to the Sikh nation, suggests the strong possibility, at the very least, that Duleep was already dissatisfied with the course his life had taken, including his childhood conversion to Christianity. Moreover, the royal reference survives even today as a reminder that this unnamed son, had history taken a different course, would have been the rightful heir to the Sikh throne in Lahore. This reference is still visible today in an otherwise unremarkable Christian cemetery, a lingering echo of Duleep's first attack against British imperialism. Even more intriguing is the choice of biblical extracts that survive on the now restored gravestone. The text on the gravestone reads: 'It is not the will of your father which is in Heaven that one of these little ones should perish.' The context of the original quote from Matthew 18:14 suggests that it refers to the promise of eternal salvation through conversion, though the way in which this isolated quote is picked out does rather suggest that Duleep was questioning the way God's will was being interpreted by the authorities who were busy manipulating his life to suit their ends. He was still almost twenty years from initiating active resistance, but the almost blasphemous nostalgia with which he grieves for his dead son should, I argue, be read as harbinger of that rebellion which was to come.

Even in the heyday of his high living, there remain interesting, ambiguous connections to a nostalgically reconstructed Punjab, which, in the context of late nineteenth-century politics was bordering on treason. Living in Elveden Hall, Duleep completely redecorated the building. From the outside, it did not look out of place in that most English of counties. Inside, however, was another matter. On the grand staircase, he proudly displayed August Sheofft's painting, 'The Court of Lahore' – implicitly reminding all his guests who their host was, and what he had lost. Most of the interior was refurbished to match the Mughal-inspired palaces of his childhood. For all of the orientalist interest in the exotic, which obviously drew the British aristocracy to Duleep Singh, it is difficult to believe that this would not have made them at least a little uncomfortable. A decade earlier, on her first meeting with him, Queen Victoria would display a similar discomfort. Writing to Lord Dalhousie, she would claim:

> It is not without mixed feelings of pain and sympathy that the Queen sees this young prince once destined to so high and powerful a position, and now reduced to so dependent a one by her arms.[33]

This 'slight prickling of guilt, like a burr beneath the saddle'[34] in Christy Campbell's words must surely have affected all those who visited Elveden Hall and saw the visual representation of all that Duleep had lost. Duleep's use of nostalgia to expose and critique this guilt, and eventually attempt to foster an active rebellion in solidarity with other victims of British imperialism such as Irish nationalists, provides a useful example of how nostalgia can be mobilized for radical, counter-hegemonic political movements.

NOSTALGIA AND THE LEGACY OF DULEEP SINGH'S LIFE

If Duleep's life provides key examples of the way nostalgia for lost inheritance can be mobilized for radical, anti-imperial and counter-hegemonic purposes, then the importance his legacy has had for British Sikhs since does the same. In the words of Gurharpal Singh and Darshan Singh Tatla:

> A century after his death Duleep Singh continues to excite the Sikh imagination. Today he has become an icon for new generation of British Sikhs, a tangible link with royalty for 'reimagining' the British Sikh experience. In the summer of 1999 Prince Charles opened a permanent statue of Duleep Singh in Thetford, built by the Maraharajah Duleep Singh Centenary Trust to promote Anglo-Sikh heritage. As the British Sikh community seeks to establish a new identity, one which transcends the familiar image of racialised migrants, Duleep Singh's legacy provides an enduring symbol of Sikhs' British attachment as well as the potential for dissonance and ultimate rebellion.[35]

This memorial includes a précis of his life which is clearly intended to educate the viewer about Duleep's importance. It seems deliberately worded to highlight his radical, anti-imperial significance. It refers to that most contested of the material legacies of Duleep's reign, the Koh-i-Noor diamond which, in an interestingly ambiguous act of euphemism, is described as having 'passed to the British authorities'. The memorial acknowledges Duleep's rebellion, and the various ways in which the British undermined and subverted it. In perhaps the most radical element of the text, it finishes with the statement: 'To this day the Sikh nation aspires to regain its sovereignty'. What remains unsaid behind this declaration, and what adds poignancy to Duleep's own repeated description of himself as the last ruler of the Sikh nation, is the trajectory that Sikh nationalism has taken in the intervening years. Punjab was cruelly divided in 1947 between the Muslim-dominated West (incorporated into Pakistan) and the Hindu-dominated East (incorporated into India), and since then the dream of reuniting Punjab under Sikh rule has remained unfulfilled. In 1984, after an armed insurrection movement, then Indian Prime Minister Indira Gandhi launched the infamous Operation Blue Star by sending armed troops into the holiest of Sikh sites, the Golden Temple or Har Mandir Sahib in Amritsar. Four months later, she was killed in retaliation, precipitating the worst anti-Sikh riots since partition. While Duleep Singh could not foresee any of this, the pain of repeated cyclical violence suffered by Sikh communities cannot but be read onto his invocation of the Sikh nation. As was revealed from government records in 2014, Indira Gandhi's government had, in 1984, approached Margaret Thatcher's government asking for help from the SAS – a request which was granted in the utmost secrecy. On 15 January 2014, *The Guardian* revealed that 'Margaret Thatcher gave her Indian counterpart Indira Gandhi Britain's full support in the immediate aftermath of the 1984 Golden Temple raid'.[36] None of this was public knowledge when Prince Charles unveiled the Thetford memorial, but it remains true that, both in Britain and in India, articulating the right to an independent, sovereign Sikh nation remains dangerously counter-statist. Duleep's life and legacy represent a doubled nostalgia – in the 1880s Duleep's own nostalgia helped to challenge and critique 'the colonial magic of the surrender . . . with its celebration of the subjugated body', while in the twentieth and twenty-first centuries, the nostalgia that Duleep represents has again been appropriated to challenge and critique 'the postcolonial conjurings of the nation-state and the diaspora'.[37]

In 2008, Indian author and diplomat Navtej Sarna wrote *The Exile*, a novel based on Duleep Singh's life, the narrative of which performs a similar doubled task of deploying nostalgia – first re-creating the nostalgia that Duleep experienced, and then utilizing the nostalgia that his memory generates to inspire an imaginative retelling of history, Empire, and nationhood. As Sarna makes it clear in the introduction, this is a self-consciously fictionalized version of Duleep's life:

> If one had to reach for the edges of Duleep Singh's story then the answer to my mind, lay in pushing available facts towards the realm of fiction, but pushing them gently, so as not to distort them.[38]

It is beyond my scope here to judge the truth of Sarna's claim that he has not distorted the facts. More interesting for my purposes are the ways in which this narrative, distorted or not, performs interesting, and counter-hegemonic political work in the present, and how this critical resistance is based on a deep-seated nostalgia for Duleep and what he represented. Sarna begins his narrative with an admission of his own sentimental, nostalgic connection to the figure of the Last Maharajah:

> His name has always evoked a predominant feeling of poignancy . . . his story seemed to hold an unusually high emotional quotient, which could never quite be communicated by the cold bare-bones approach of history, weighed down as it is by the bias of those who are in a position to write it.

From the very beginning, then, Sarna is setting out his narrative as a nostalgic rewriting of official history, and he does this through the form of a polyphonic novel. The story is narrated not just by Duleep, but also his trusted servant Arur Singh, his mother's 'favourite slave girl'[39] Mangla, as well as the Logins – who were his guardians after his mother's banishment – and General Carrol-Tevis, an American confidant. These multiple viewpoints help to challenge the bias of the official history writers, and allow for a much more personal, intimate view of the exiled King.

The King's status as an exile is, as the title of the novel suggests, foremost in Sarna's conception of Duleep's life. The novel begins with an epigraph from Edward Said's 'Reflections on Exile', lines that underscore the terrible pleasure-pain of nostalgia that the exile experiences:

> It is the unbelievable rift forced between a human being and a native place, between the self and its true home; its existential sadness can never be surmounted. And while it is true that literature and history contain heroic, romantic, glorious, even triumphant episodes in an exile's life . . . [these] are permanently undermined by the loss of something left behind forever.[40]

In Duleep's case, this loss of his home is the loss of the city of Lahore. In Sarna's depiction of Duleep's death, his final thoughts turn to the city of his birth and the capital of what should have been his kingdom:

> But there are days when, if I shut my eyes, strange colours can still rise in my mind, forgotten words, songs, faces, and the lost caress of the breezes of Lahore. Sometimes, when the light is of a particular shade, especially on late winter afternoons, I see myself in the Lahore fort.[41]

The memories of his servants are used to contrast the communal joyousness of his birth in Lahore with his lonely death in Paris. His birth was marked with magnificent celebrations:

> Then sweets, fruit, milk with almonds and sherbet were brought out for the nobles from the gulabkhana and all over the city, from the Taxali darwaza at one end to the Kashmiri darwaza at the other, the poor sat in long lines and were fed. . . . Guns roared in salute from the walls of the city. At night the lamps that lit up the Roshni darwaza were so bright that anybody looking towards Lahore from miles away in every direction would have known that something special was being celebrated in Ranjit Singh's court.[42]

The sensations of taste and sound and light that marked Duleep's entry into the world are all absent when he is about to leave it:

> His end should not have been as it was – locked up in a cheap hotel room, watching the sun rise beyond the window and slowly reach its height and then descend until the window darkened. That is all he did, often unable to move from his bed, barely able to eat or drink water without assistance.[43]

Lahore and its memories were important to Duleep not just in his final moments. I have already mentioned the measures he took to remind himself and his visitors to Elveden House of his native city and the way it had been taken away from him, and Sarna's version of Duleep is similarly defiant about his own nostalgia:

> I insisted on having the rooms done the way I wanted. I wanted them to remind me of the rooms of my childhood in Lahore. People will say that I, the 'Black Prince' of Suffolk, wanted to recreate Lahore in my drawing room. To feed my fancy, or perhaps to console myself. I did not care then what people said, and I care even less now.[44]

Few cities in the subcontinent lend themselves to nostalgia in the way that Lahore does. In Chapter 6, I look at the way Suhayl Saadi's novel *Psychoraag* intertwines memory of the *Lahori* cityscape with memory of music to create a fictional narrative of the past that one can live in. Here too, Sarna is creating an imaginary version of Lahore – one that Duleep, Sarna himself, and all other Sikhs who have been displaced from Lahore can indulge in. Even before Duleep's tragically short reign had begun, Sarna tells us, 'Lahore was not the place it used to be.'[45]

Sarna not only imaginatively recreates Duleep's nostalgic yearnings for Lahore – the seat of power from which he was separated by the British, but also articulates the loss suffered by the Sikh communities, who overwhelmingly moved to the Indian side of the 1947 border, while their historic capital Lahore remained on the Pakistani side. In the process, Sarna is not just constructing an object of nostalgia for the nineteenth-century regal figure of Duleep Singh, but also an affective connection that can be seen to be just as radical and counter-hegemonic in the twenty-first century. After all, Navtej Sarna in real life is one of the most high-profile diplomatic officers in India and is, at the time of writing, India's Ambassador to the United States. Here he is, however, waxing lyrical about a city that is now technically part of an 'enemy' country, Pakistan, on behalf of a Sikh nationalism that was brutally suppressed by the Indian government in 1984, resulting in some of the worst religious riots India has ever experienced. Sarna's nostalgia for the city of Lahore, whether it was intended to be so or not, has to be read in this context as a challenge to the hegemonic view of the Indian nation-state, its own views of its many minorities, and its foreign policy, all of which it has, often brutally, reinforced.

If Lahore is the most powerful object of nostalgia for Sarna's Duleep, then his mother, Maharani Jindan Kaur, comes a close second:

> Through those years, in the secret recesses of my heart, I yearned for the touch of Bibiji's hands, hands gone now forever, preserved only in the marble cast

that lies at Elveden. She had beautiful hands, my mother, the thin blue veins shining faintly through her lovely transparent skin.[46]

Like Duleep's affective connection to Lahore, this nostalgia can also be used to foster a dangerously radical rebellion. Duleep's reunion with his mother proves to be the catalyst that opens his eyes to the true nature of his oppression:

> It was in those days with Bibiji that I began to learn about what had really happened, about the extent and enormity of my loss, my private estates that had been taken away as if they were State property.[47]

The most important example of this loss of property is, of course, the Koh-i-Noor diamond. In Sarna's imagination, the famous scene during the painting of the Winterhalter portrait, when Queen Victoria allows a young Duleep to hold the diamond again, becomes a similar moment of political awakening, instigated by the nostalgia that this cherished object of his childhood evokes:

> I took it between my thumb and forefinger and held it up to the light. I could not look away from the quiet dazzle. I stood staring at it near the open window and a rush of emotions began to drown me. I realized I had lost everything, I was no longer a king. I was only being made to dress up like one and amuse the Queen's court.[48]

Duleep's nostalgic attachment to the Koh-i-Noor, in Sarna's creation, is so powerful in part because its value for him is about more than the economic. Duleep values the diamond for different reasons than Victoria does, and his alternative value system exposes her worldview for the mercenary, acquisitive approach that it really is:

> Today it matters little to me whether I have it or not. If I had it who knows what I might do with it. Perhaps I would trade it for a few sunny days, a few happy conversations, some justice, a fair enquiry into my case, and certainly for a journey to Punjab.[49]

Sarna's version of Duleep has lost none of his counter-hegemonic potential – he calls Victoria 'Mrs Fagin . . . The biggest pickpocket of them all. The receiver of stolen goods. Stolen kingdoms, stolen jewels'; he undermines his moment of religious conversion by wondering 'if any other Christian in all history has ever been baptized with water from the Ganges, holy to the Hindus'[50]; he is able to reject the British version of History, by declaring of the moment when, as a child, he signed away his kingdom to the British: 'I do not think I understood what was happening'.[51] Through the testimony of Mangla, Sarna is also able to pre-empt the importance that Duleep would go on to have for Sikhs across the world, as Sarna's Mangla both mourns and reveres Duleep and the way he was buried against his wishes in Britain:

> The firanghis will forget who he was, forget his kingdom. They will forget his story, his pain, his mother's broken heart. It will be only a rare son of Punjab who will go all the way to bow before him, to put a flower on his grave, fold his hands and say the Waheguru's prayer for the soul of the Maharajah of Punjab.[52]

Mangla's lament over her dead King and the way his body has, in her eyes, been desecrated by the usurpers of his throne is used here to indict the cruel imperialism of the British and the way they exploited and oppressed Duleep in life and in death,. However, Mangla is also looking forward to a different future, one in which a global Sikh diaspora can occupy the space where Duleep is buried as an equal, where his grave no longer has to symbolize alienation and isolation but can stand in for a globalized, trans-state, Sikh nation. Mangla's vision of Punjabis visiting and paying homage in front of Duleep's grave remains a politically critical moment, given the trajectory of Sikh nationalism in Britain and in India, as I have discussed above.

In 2014, British Sikh artists the Singh Twins painted *Casualty of War: A Portrait of Maharaja Duleep Singh*. Commissioned by National Museums Scotland, it accompanied an exhibition of Duleep's personal possessions at the National Museum of Scotland in Edinburgh. The Singh Twins mobilize a critical nostalgia by depicting events, themes and motifs that are of interest to their own subject-positions as members of the Sikh diaspora, using ancient techniques of Mughal miniature painting. Through this artwork, the Singh Twins are reconfiguring Duleep's and their own political and physical landscape in a deeply nostalgic, and deeply radical, manner. In their painting, Duleep himself is given pride of place – as his portrait occupies by far the largest portion of the canvas. He is portrayed in full royal regalia, recalling closely the Winterhalter portrait. There are however, some notable differences. The Singh Twins artistically return the Koh-i-Noor diamond to Duleep, unlike in the Winterhalter painting; Duleep here is shown with the famous stone on his arm. The non-space that Axel identified as the background of Winterhalter's Duleep is replaced here with a nostalgic backdrop of Lahore. Instead of a glorified pet, adorned as a fashionable toy and bereft of his birth-right, as depicted by Winterhalter, the Singh Twins recognize both his own deeply nostalgic longing for his homeland and the phenomenal anti-imperial force that this represented. Duleep's grave in Elveden – a relic of officially imposed Christianity that was designed to undermine his reputation as an anti-colonial hero, is, through this artwork, re-inscribed with the *khanda* – the emblem of Sikh militancy. This can be seen as the artistic equivalent of Mangla's prediction in *The Exile*. Like in the novel, the artists here realign Duleep's grave in an attempt to begin to redress his pain, rehabilitating him, through their imagination at least, to his rightful place as the Emperor of the Sikh Nation. The Singh Twins replicate the *Punch* cartoon depicting Duleep as a brown-skinned *sahib*, highlighting the concerted efforts of the British establishment to undermine his authority. John Login, the man who was appointed guardian of the boy-king is alluded to – his deeply ambiguous relationship with Duleep rendered through the chains that connect him to Login's grave. The contemporary relevance of these issues is also highlighted – through reference to David Cameron's visits to India, and George W. Bush's statements on Iraq – even in the twenty-first century; the Singh Twins demonstrate that nostalgia for a self-consciously fictional past can be used to generate anti-colonial, anti-imperial and radical points of view. The dates along the middle of the canvas chart this painful history of Sikh nationalism – they span from 1849 (the year Punjab was annexed to the British Empire) to 1947 (the year Punjab was divided) to 1984 (the year of the most painful and sacrilegious attack on the Golden Temple). Through this nostalgically re-inscribed version of history, the Singh Twins are thus conjuring up a new landscape, one in which Sikhism in general, and the British Sikh communities in particular, do not have to feel marginalized and alienated from their own history, but can re-centre their narratives in a creative, radical, deeply counter-hegemonic intervention.

Something of the power of this nostalgia could be felt in the exhibition that this painting was featured in at the National Museum of Scotland. The painting was surrounded by many of Duleep's personal possessions – jewellery that helped inspire the Singh Twins – many of which they included in their painting. These objects were bequeathed to the National Museum of Scotland by Major Donald Lindsay Carnegie, who had bought them from Duleep's eldest son, Prince Victor Duleep Singh, when he had to sell part of his inheritance in order to pay off his considerable debts. Not unlike the Koh-i-Noor, which is today part of the Crown Jewels of the United Kingdom, and therefore on display to millions of tourists in the Tower of London, these jewels, pen cases, and other assorted personal objects remain objects to be looked at by tourists to Britain, and therefore objects which to this day economically benefit the United Kingdom. Indeed, insofar as they represent the glory of the British Empire, it could be said that they have accrued a very different kind of nostalgia through their appropriation and display by and in sites of British establishment like the Tower of London or the National Museum of Scotland. Their incorporation in the work of the Singh Twins, however, helps to redress this balance, and the exhibition incorporating both the jewels and the paintings vividly demonstrated the ways in which these objects and their legacies can still be fought over, can still be used to create competing narratives of opposing nostalgic forces.

In 2015, the multinational video games developer and publisher Ubisoft released the ninth instalment of their best-selling *Assassin's Creed* video games franchise, *Assassin's Creed: Syndicate*. Centred on the twins Jacob and Evie Frye, the game requires the player to challenge and eventually overthrow Crawford Starrick – a cross between Cecil Rhodes and Professor Moriarty – a criminal mastermind who, along with the Templars and the British Indies Company, a thinly veiled reference to the East India Company, is running the British Empire as part of a whole network of criminal activities. In the process, the Frye twins get to meet and work with a number of famous Victorian Londoners – Charles Darwin, Charles Dickens, Alexander Graham Bell, Karl Marx, and Florence Nightingale to name but a few.

One of these figures is Maharajah Duleep Singh, who assists the player in their own quest in return for support for his campaign for the independence of Punjab. The character of Duleep is drawn in a manner that suggests the artists were influenced by a number of different portraits, including Winterhalter's. The writers were also clearly aware of Duleep's life story, and integrated facts from his life into the game, constructing him as a fervently anti-colonial figure. Voiced with great subtlety by British Asian actor Avin Shah, Duleep comes across as a deeply sympathetic figure who passionately believes in the need for Punjab's independence, and the righting of the wrongs committed by the British:

> When the commonwealth seized the Punjab from my people . . . Britain promised to protect me. By robbing me of my kingdom, Parliament acted in violation of the treaty signed with my family. . . . Perhaps it is time to return the Punjab to her people. . . . It is not a matter of money. I cannot stand idle and watch my homeland subjected to the yoke of an outsider's rule. My people are treated as slaves. I will die poor a thousand times over if only to see them free.

Crucially, this anti-imperialism is directly and explicitly connected to a nostalgia for his childhood, a nostalgia which allows him to mourn all the losses that he suffered as a child, personified most importantly in the figure of his mother:

> Children can be quite perceptive. . . . I remember that my mother smelt of cinnamon. And when she cradled me in her arms in the summer heat, I would hold so still that she fell asleep. When I lost my kingdom, it hurt, but truly, when they took my mother away . . . I saw her again two years before she died, the summer long since faded. I miss her. I miss India. I love India because I love my mother.

Duleep's nostalgia and the rebellion that it helps foster leads to the very heart of imperial power in London. Using his assistance, the player is able to invade the Houses of Parliament, Buckingham Palace and the Bank of England – in the process allowing the wish fulfilment of a whole new generation of postcolonial gamers. Duleep's nostalgia for the losses he suffered as a child, and the possibility of the postcolonial gamer's nostalgia for what Duleep's resistance might have led to, can be twinned in this game of complex, alternative histories, multiple timelines and imaginary geographies. Duleep allows the gamer to produce what is at its heart a postcolonial remapping of Victorian London – the first mission Duleep gives the player involves driving prominent politicians such as Gladstone from one part of London to another, while Duleep tries to enlist them to his cause. As one drives the carriage from Belgrave Square, to St James's Park, and onto the Gladstone residence, one cannot help but enjoy the delicious irony of driving through these landmarks of imperial London while, at the same time, in Duleep's words, 'help[ing] disengage the Punjab from British rule'. Duleep Singh's missions in *Assassin's Creed: Syndicate* is a classic example, along with Sarna's novel and the Singh Twins' painting, of the way in which nostalgia of and about Duleep Singh can still be put to counter-imperial political use.

In March 2016, Ubisoft released the last DLC (downloadable content – additional content created for the game), a series of additional stories and playable missions called *The Last Maharajah*. As the name implies, these missions are based on the Frye twins' relationship with Duleep Singh. The DLC missions start with Duleep Singh reluctant to instigate active rebellion against Queen Victoria and the British Indies Company. Henry Green, alias Jayadeep Mir, mentor to the Frye twins, tries to persuade him by taunting him about his humiliating life in London:

> Your highness, you belong to India not here acting the part of the noble foreigner. If your mother could see you now, the last Maharajah of Punjab, basking inside his golden cage!

Duleep is finally persuaded when the Fryes manage to expose the theft of letters from Duleep to his mother, perpetrated by the British Indies Company. These letters, written when he 'was just a boy' prove to be the deciding factor in starting open rebellion. Duleep discovers that 'the British Indies Company have stolen a large sum of wealth from the good people of Punjab', and the Frye twins help him send it back. Finally, in perhaps the most iconic and climactic of Duleep's missions, he targets the object that is most associated with him in the common imagination:

> I propose we steal the Koh-i-Noor diamond. . . . Her Majesty may wear it, but it doesn't belong to her. It was a trophy symbolising the colonisation of India and it deserves to be returned home.

While the Fryes are successful in this daring heist, it turns out to be unnecessary. In a wonderful piece of nostalgia-driven rewriting of history, Henry

Green reveals that his father had swapped the real diamond for a fake one, ensuring that the British imperialists never laid their hands on this most potent of symbols. As in the painting by the Singh Twins, *Assassin's Creed: Syndicate* uses nostalgia to rewrite history from a counter-imperial perspective, indulging a powerfully critical fantasy that carries within it the possibility of a radically redrawn narrative of Anglo-Indian relations.

Duleep in the game is thus allowed to keep his anti-colonial sentiments, while, true to Wainwright's analysis, these sentiments are not appropriated to fit any kind of counter-imperial nationalism. In a fascinating example of radical counter-factuality, Duleep is shown referring to his home interchangeably as Punjab and India. Given the context of the marginalized and oppressed nature of Sikh nationalism in contemporary India that I have outlined above, this indeterminability can be seen to challenge both the greedy exploitation of the British Empire in India, and the postcolonial nation building endorsed by the Indian nation-state. As in the title of Navtej Sarna's novel, the Duleep of the game remains an exile whose memory cannot be easily assimilated into any simplistic nation-building project. As the final words of Brinley Ellsworth, Duleep's one-time friend and later betrayer, demonstrate, Duleep's rebellion may not have been successful, but perhaps for the same reason, the lingering traces of his presence today can still represent a challenge to hegemonic ways of looking at Empire and its afterlives:

> You can't just walk this earth like a free man. You are nothing more than a trophy, a stag's head above the mantelpiece . . . no more than a plaything, a prisoner in a prince's clothing. . . . You will die as you were raised, a trophy of war . . . we will bury you in English soil.

It is impossible to know what proportion of those who played *Assassin's Creed* were able to recognize the way in which Duleep's own nostalgia, and the later nostalgia for him, is employed by the writers and artists of the game. Certainly, if the various chatroom discussions and YouTube video voice-overs and comments are anything to go by, this proportion will not be high. The evidence of rebellion is, however, there nevertheless, visible to those who can read it. Navtej Sarna, the Singh Twins, and Ubisoft have, in their very different ways and very different genres, created a fictional landscape using Duleep's memory that can be used to invoke the possibility of a globalized, trans-state Sikh nationalism that does not have to be silenced by either the neo-colonial British or the postcolonial Indian state.

NOTES

1. Christy Campbell, *The Maharajah's Box: An Imperial Story of Conspiracy, Love and a Guru's Prophecy* (London: HarperCollins, 2001), 66
2. RA *Queen Victoria's Journal*, 1 July 1854

3. *Illustrated London News*, 29 March 1856, 7–8

4. Brian Keith Axel, *The Nation's Tortured Body: Violence, Representation and the Formation of a Sikh "Diaspora"* (Durham, NC, and London: Duke University Press, 2001), 54

5. Edith Dalhousie Login, *Lady Login's Recollections: Court Life and Camp Life, 1820 – 1904* (London: Smith, Elder, 1916), 114

6. Peter Bance, *The Duleep Singhs: The Photograph Album of Queen Victoria's Maharajah* (Stroud, Glos: Sutton Publishing, 2004), 32

7. Brian Keith Axel, *The Nation's Tortured Body*, 46

8. Christy Campbell, *The Maharajah's Box*, 24

9. Edward Said, *Orientalism* (London: Penguin, 2003), 32

10. RA Vic. Add. N2/20, Duleep Singh to Queen Victoria, 15 August 1882

11. *The Times*, 31 August 1882

12. *The Times*, 31 August 1882

13. RA O 10/39, Duleep Singh to Queen Victoria, 10 July 1886

14. RA Vic. Add. N2/180, Queen Victoria to Duleep Singh, 18 September 1884

15. IOR L/P&S/18/D25 *Correspondence relating to the Maharajah Duleep Singh (1849 – 1886) Confidential, Political and Secret Department, India Office, January 1887*, 131

16. Duleep Singh, *The Maharajah Duleep Singh and the Government: A Narrative* (London: Ballantyne, Hanson & Co., 1884), 126–27

17. Duleep Singh, *The Maharajah Duleep Singh and the Government*, 126–27

18. Walter Benjamin, *Illuminations* (London: Pimlico, 1999), 247–48

19. Judith Butler, *Precarious Life: The Powers of Mourning and Violence* (London and New York: Verso, 2004), 20

20. A. Martin Wainwright, "Queen Victoria and the Maharaja Duleep Singh: Conflicting Identities in an Imperial Context," *Ohio Academy of History Proceedings*. Accessed 9 August, 2017, available at: http://www.ohioacademyofhistory.org/wp-content/uploads/2013/04/Wainwright.pdf

21. Duleep Singh, *A Reprint of Two Sale Catalogues of Jewels and Other Confiscated Property Belonging to His Highness the Maharajah Duleep Singh*, 1885, iv–vii

22. Duleep Singh, *A Reprint of Two Sale Catalogues*, vii

23. A. Martin Wainwright, "Queen Victoria and the Maharajah Duleep Singh"

24. *The Times*, 31 August 1882

25. Duleep Singh, *The Maharajah Duleep Singh and the Government*, 128

26. Christy Campbell, *The Maharajah's Box*, 69

27. Duleep Singh, *A Reprint of Two Sale Catalogues*, vii–viii

28. A. Martin Wainwright, "Queen Victoria and the Maharajah Duleep Singh"

29. RA Vic. Add. N2/176

30. "An Interview with a Singh-ular Individual". *Punch*, Saturday, 11 June 1887, 277.

31. "Singh Song: A Letter for Duleep Year". *Punch*, Saturday, 21 January 1888, 33

32. J.G.A. Baird, *Private Letters of Marquess of Dalhousie* (London: William Blackwood and Sons, 1911), 325

33. RA Vic. N14/74

34. Christy Campbell, *The Maharajah's Box*, 62

35. Gurharpal Singh and Darshan Singh Tatla, *Sikhs in Britain: The Making of a Community* (London and New York: Zed Books, 2006), 45

36. Rajeev Syal and Phil Miller, 'Margaret Thatcher Gave Full Support over Golden Temple Raid, Letter Shows', *The Guardian*, 15 January 2014

37. Brian Keith Axel, *The Nation's Tortured Body*, 68

38. Navtej Sarna, *The Exile* (New Delhi: Viking, 2008), xi

39. Navtej Sarna, *The Exile*, xiii

40. Edward Said, *Reflections on Exile and Other Essays* (Boston: Harvard University Press, 2002), 138

41. Navtej Sarna, *The Exile*, 6

42. Navtej Sarna, *The Exile*, 14

43. Navtej Sarna, *The Exile*, 8

44. Navtej Sarna, *The Exile*, 180

45. Navtej Sarna, *The Exile*, 55
46. Navtej Sarna, *The Exile*, 163
47. Navtej Sarna, *The Exile*, 170
48. Navtej Sarna, *The Exile*, 153
49. Navtej Sarna, *The Exile*, 151
50. Navtej Sarna, *The Exile*, 146
51. Navtej Sarna, *The Exile*, 103
52. Navtej Sarna, *The Exile*, 13

Chapter Two

A Teacher, a Factory Worker, and a 'Battered' Housewife

Rebellious Nostalgias, Nostalgias of Rebellion

Altab Ali was a Bangladeshi textile worker living and working in Tower Hamlets, East London. On 4 May 1978, aged just twenty-five, he was killed in a racially motivated attack on his way back from work, near the corner of Adler Street and Commercial Road, close to Aldgate tube station, and within a stone's throw of the famous curry houses of today's Brick Lane. His killers were two seventeen-year-old boys, Carl Ludlow and Roy Arnold, as well as an unnamed sixteen-year-old. When asked for their reasons, the unnamed boy replied: 'For no reason at all. . . . If we saw a Paki we used to have a go at them.'[1]

Blair Peach was a teacher and anti-fascist activist, originally from New Zealand, but living and working in the East End of London. On 23 April 1979, he was killed during a demonstration against a planned National Front rally in Southall Town Hall, in West London. After years of denial, the Metropolitan Police finally admitted in 2010 that it could 'reasonably be concluded that a police officer struck the fatal blow'.[2] There was, however, insufficient evidence to bring charges against any individual police officer.

These deaths galvanized the British Asian communities in a way that hadn't happened before, and, I argue, their stories have been nostalgically mobilized to represent the process through which British Asians are able to reclaim an alternative narrative of history as important and defining, thus constructing distinctive models of British Asian identity.

The third person I am looking at in this chapter was and is very different. Kiranjit Ahluwalia was, for ten years, married to a cruel and violent man.

Throughout her marriage, she had suffered physical and emotional violence including rape, food deprivation and other forms of abuse. One night in 1989, after a particularly severe violent attack during which he attacked her with a hot iron, Ahluwalia retaliated by setting him on fire. He died in hospital ten days later, and she was charged, and later convicted of his murder. Three years later, however, her conviction was overturned, she was awarded a retrial, and her guilty plea of manslaughter on grounds of diminished responsibility was accepted by the court. The activism and advocacy that helped secure her release also helped to shed light on the issue of domestic abuse, and allowed for a change of the law, leading to the release of other women who were in a similar position.

These three figures – the 'battered wife', the teacher and the factory worker – obviously constitute a diverse and rather odd group. While they represent very different aspects of British Asian history and are separated from each other by temporal, racial, gendered, national and class boundaries, they have been, I argue, in their very different ways, crucially important in the construction of a distinctively British Asian history. The ways in which their lives have been used over the years demonstrate the ways in which nostalgia can be exploited to generate resistance and rebellion, the ways in which the articulation of a proud demand of the right to belong can aid the nostalgic process of homemaking. Memories of these acts of resistance and rebellion then get further appropriated through the nostalgic recollections of subsequent generations, becoming in turn another marker of belonging.

In my approach to the ways in which moments of British Asian resistance are commemorated, I am indebted to Peter Glazer's work on US commemoration of the Spanish Civil War, and his analysis of the ways in which 'the performance of radical nostalgia can serve valuable ends, re-infusing lost histories with credibility, substance and emotional resonance.'[3] Writing of specific acts of commemoration that honour the involvement of American anti-fascists in the Spanish Civil War, Glazer posits that 'nostalgic veterans' commemorations of the war have the potential to preserve and transmit a radical history and its tenets'[4] because these commemorations are just as counter-hegemonic in the present, as the actions they celebrate were in the past. Glazer's analysis of radical nostalgia for the Spanish Civil War applies equally well to my own analysis of diasporic nostalgia as well:

> Radical nostalgia's desire to find meaning in the past must be contextualized. If the specific histories celebrated by commemorative nostalgia have been stigmatized and undercut by dominant cultural forces . . . then its reconstruction in historicized commemorative ceremonies could be necessary and liberatory.[5]

Influenced by Glazer's approach to memories of specific acts of resistance, then, in this chapter I examine specific moments of British Asian rebellion centred upon three individual figures. I argue that their legacy can help to identify a specifically British Asian radical nostalgia that can then be deployed to help construct a space to belong, and a space from which one can continue the fight against racism and sexism. Like Glazer's account of Spanish Civil War commemoration, I posit that these moments of resistance, and their tellings and retellings, become political not just in the historical context in which they occurred, but that they retain their political valency in the present, and in the future that might one day be.

'THE WRATH OF THE ASIAN': ALTAB ALI, ASIAN DUB FOUNDATION AND CLAIMING TOWER HAMLETS

The small park adjoining Adler Street, Tower Hamlets, was once the site of the old fourteenth-century white chapel, St Mary Matfelon. In 1998, it was renamed Altab Ali Park, in honour of the man who had been murdered close to it. Across the entrance to the park, there is a sculpted arch commemorating Altab Ali and all the other victims of racist violence. There is a quote from a poem by Bengali poet and Nobel laureate, Rabindranath Tagore: 'The shade of my tree is offered to those who come and go fleetingly'. Altab Ali Park commemorates both the life and death of Altab Ali the man, and the wider movement that culminated, ten days after his death, into a seven-thousand-strong march from Whitechapel to Hyde Park. The predominant slogan of the Asian Youth Movements that grew out of the deaths of people like Altab Ali, 'Here to stay, here to fight' shows how nostalgia can take on an active, assertive form. Along with a yearning for the lost home that one has left behind, there is the equally powerful yearning to construct the lost home in the here and now.

This multivalent nature of the home that is mourned and reclaimed in the same moment is of particular interest when studying the space that is Altab Ali Park. Along with the architectural and artistic details that memorialize anti-racist movements, Altab Ali Park also includes a replica of the Shaheed Minar, or Martyrs' Memorial – erected in Dhaka to commemorate the single most iconic event in Bangladesh's struggle for liberation from Pakistan. On 21 February 1952, in Dhaka, East Pakistan, the army opened fire on protestors demanding the right to study in their own language, Bengali, as opposed to the official language, Urdu, leading to the death of several student protestors. The Shaheed Minar in Dhaka, and therefore its replica in Altab Ali Park, memorializes the struggle for Bangladesh's liberation and the process of homemaking that that involved. Altab Ali Park is, then, doubly nostalgic. In the same moment, it marks a longing for and a reconstruction of two separate, but linked homelands – the one over there in Bangladesh, and the one over here in London. Equally significantly, in both cases, it identifies specific instances of resistance and rebellion as part of the process that allows these homes to be created and reclaimed. The resulting space evokes multiple, pan-national homes – it quotes a line from a Bengali, Hindu poet Rabindranath Tagore, who had links across both Indian and Bangladeshi Bengal and who penned the national anthems of both countries. The line itself, 'The shade of my tree is offered to those who come and go fleetingly' speaks to the power of the concept of home, and the radical temporal structure of the polyvalent home of the diaspora. The object of this nostalgia, then, cannot be easily reduced to a simplistic narrative of nationhood or nationalism – rather it points out the radical potential of nostalgic affective connections that exist between people and the places that they might call home.

The power of the space can be seen in the way it remains a contested site. Michael Keith has pointed out how:

> In 1997, almost twenty years after the murder, the sign that confirms the name of the park continued to be painted over with a black spray can of paint. On no fewer than seven occasions in that single year the municipal authorities would paint in the name of the park only for the black paint to cover it up. . . . In each case the 'graffiti' – if it can be called such – involves only the erasure of presence.[6]

Graffiti, as I have argued elsewhere,[7] exists in order to turn a wall into a sign. By writing or painting on a wall the graffiti artist draws attention to the materiality of the wall as a physical entity – attempting at the same time to both transcend and reinforce the space that the wall encloses. In the process, the wall is textualized, a process which reflects the contested nature of the wall. This is definitely the case with the graffiti in Altab Ali Park, which reflects the contested nature of that space, and the contested nature of the area surrounding Brick Lane as a whole. In an area that has seen waves of immigration, and also seen its fair share of far-right politics – from Oswald Mosley's British Union of Fascists in the 1930s, through the National Front of the 1970s, to the British National Party and the English Defence League today – it is perhaps not surprising that Altab Ali Park remains such a contested site. The walls and signs in and around Altab Ali Park, then, are also regularly used as the canvas for political messages, as this area of London continues to generate and mobilize a nostalgic narrative of anti-fascist and anti-racist movements – originating from the famous Battle of Cable Street in 1936, through the protests that followed the murder of Altab Ali in 1978, to the anti-EDL and anti-BNP protests in the twenty-first century.

In Monica Ali's famously controversial 2003 novel *Brick Lane*, Altab Ali Park is again configured as a contested site:

> Out of the estate and onto Commercial Road, past the clothes wholesalers, up Adler Street and left onto the brief green respite of Altab Ali Park where the neat, pale-faced block of flats had picture windows and a gated entrance, from which the City boys could stroll to work. Nazneen ran down the slope and caught the green man at the crossing on Whitechapel.
>
> A row of police vans covered the mouth of Brick Lane. Behind them a legion of policemen stood with arms folded and feet turned out.[8]

In a scene reminiscent of old black-and-white photos of the demonstrations demanding justice for Altab Ali, Naazneen is prevented from walking down the street because of 'disturbances'. Tower Hamlets remains, Monica Ali reminds us, a front in a battle that is not quite over. Tower Hamlets might have become famous as Banglatown, Ali suggests, but the Bengali communities, their curry houses, grocery stores, mosques and community centres are still dominated by the 'pale-faced' flats and the white city boys, and the police whose record of institutional racism and brutal violence during antiracist demonstrations place them squarely on the side of the white establishment.

It is in this context that the nostalgic reconstruction of a dual home – one back there and one here and now – has to be read. This is why the establishment of community centres such as the Kobi Nazrul Centre – a general-purpose performing arts and cultural venue on nearby Hanbury Street – is so crucial. Named after the second most important Bengali poet (after Tagore), this was one of the first Bengali community spaces to gain recognition in Tower Hamlets. Like Tagore, Nazrul, who achieved fame as Bengal's rebel poet, represents a radical, pan-national Bengali identity. In choosing to name the community centre after him, then, the organizers were clearly evoking a particularly radical nostalgic force. In its persistent presence, these community spaces come to represent the home that is being constructed, and whose origin stories are being nostalgically preserved. Homemaking is a long-drawn, continuous process, and the home it constructs is more often than not polyvalent and heterogeneous.

Altab Ali's legacy has now become part of the heritage of the local communities – a relic of the fights that had to be fought in order to earn the right to call this place home. In her book, *On Brick Lane*, Rachel Lichtenstein discusses the park – a space which 'has become a contemporary meeting place for the Bengali community and a starting point for political marches against racism and the war in Iraq'.[9] Many of her correspondents refer to their memories of the protests that followed Altab Ali's death – Stephen Watts, for example:

> He talked about the many demonstrations he has taken part in over the years, particularly in the 1970s, supporting his Bengali neighbours in their fight

against racism: 'I marched with thousands of others to Downing Street after the murder of Altab Ali. It was one of the first significant events in a long-term struggle to successfully change the atmosphere of Brick Lane.'[10]

In 2012, Ansar Ahmed Ullah and Steve Silver co-edited a pamphlet under the auspices of the public service trade union UNISON. Called *Commemorating Altab Ali Day 4 May: Against Racism and Fascism*, this pamphlet tells the story of how the increased attacks on the Bengali communities throughout the 1970s led to a deeply politicized generation of activists who were prepared to fight for their right to call this place their home. The pamphlet makes a clear connection between the legacy of militant anti-racist and anti-fascist activism, and the process of homemaking:

> From the 1970s–1980s Bengali community politics moved away from preoccupations with political struggles in Bangladesh to activism in the UK. . . . By now this was not an immigrant community but a community of British Bengalis in the UK.[11]

An example of the cultural legacy of Altab Ali, the movement his death inspired and the nostalgia that was part of both the original movement and its own cultural memory, is the 1995 album *Facts and Fictions* by the British Asian band, Asian Dub Foundation (ADF). This music can be read as an often nostalgic appropriation of many diverse historic, musical, and literary inheritances in order to articulate a right to belong, a creative and political exercise in homemaking.

It may seem odd to attempt to read nostalgia in the work of ADF. After all, their music, and the various subgenres of New Asian Dance Music to which they are often linked, is more often celebrated for its hybridity. Indeed, as Ketu Katrak has pointed out, 'the Asian Dub Foundation is criticized for not being "Indian enough"'.[12]

On the other hand, other scholars, most notably Sanjay Sharma and John Hutnyk have critiqued this reading through what Hutnyk has called 'hybridity-talk'[13] as a deliberate conservative attempt to marginalize the truly radical nature of this music. Even here however, I would argue that the role played by nostalgia has not been fully explored. In a sense, this is not surprising, as the relationship between ADF and nostalgia is ambivalent at best. In the track 'PKNB', for example, they seem to be attacking a particular brand of conservative nostalgia that harks back to an idyllic, racially homogenous past in order to reinforce anti-immigration politics:

> 'Things were good in the good olden days' they say
> 'Jobs in the factories' (economic slaves!)
> 'We kept our doors open right throughout the day'
> (But the poverty was such that there was nothing to nick anyway!)[14]

The juxtaposition of conservative phrases with the bracketed responses is designed to expose the falsehoods that conservative nostalgia reinforces in order to generate anti-immigration sentiments. The song is then lyrically performing the demand it makes in its refrain: 'Gotta separate the facts, yes the facts from the fiction'. It is easy to see why this type of politics is seen to have little to do with nostalgia. Ignoring the nostalgic elements present in this music, however, does a disservice both to the music and to the ambiguous affect of nostalgia.

The song that links the music most directly to Altab Ali's story is 'TH9':

> In this time there is no justice or peace
> In this time there is no trust in the police
> Quddus Ali saw no justice or peace
> Altab Ali saw no justice or peace
> Stephen Lawrence saw no justice or peace
> Too many people still waiting for release [15]

Quddus Ali was attacked by a racist gang in Watney Market, Shadwell, on 8 September 1993, when he was only seventeen. The attack left him in a coma, disabled and brain damaged. The next day, there was a vigil held for him outside Whitechapel Hospital, where Quddus was in intensive care. A week later London elected its first ever BNP councillor in Millwall. There was a protest march on 4 October, starting from Altab Ali Park, about a ten-minute walk away from the Dean Swift, the pub outside of which Quddus Ali was beaten up.

As a result, it makes perfect sense that when ADF wrote a song about Quddus Ali, they referred to Altab Ali, as well as the perhaps more high-profile case of Stephen Lawrence, whose murder the same year that Quddus Ali was attacked led to the Macpherson Report that famously labelled the Metropolitan Police as 'institutionally racist'. In other words, ADF are not just citing a long list of racially motivated attacks, but also referencing the anti-racist protests that followed these attacks and the legacy of which has helped members of the south Asian communities to make a home in Britain:

> Now is the time
> For us to hit and run
> 'Cos we're second generation
> but we're not second class
> Now the wrath of the Asian will hit you like a blast [16]

This music which, as Kalra, Hutnyk and Sharma have described as a space 'where politics and music were meshed in a deliberate political and cultural programme' [17] becomes through these lines fundamentally about homemaking. It is this process of homemaking that, for me, connects the music of ADF to progressive nostalgia – it might not always remember the past fondly, or sentimentally, as commonsensical views of nostalgia might require, but it does mobilize certain narratives of past in order to construct spaces of belonging. Along the way, there are moments of celebration, where past resistance can be eulogized in order to generate similar movements in the present.

This can be seen more fully in the video to another of the tracks on this album, 'Rebel Warrior'. The video opens with shots of a young man running through an industrial wasteland. Shot around the remnants of what was once London's thriving docklands, but predating the subsequent gentrification that has once again transformed the area, the black-and-white shots depict a desolate, almost lifeless landscape. These shots are then intercut with a shot of sunrise, with the musicians standing in a row, looking up at the sunlight. The intercutting continues, as this landscape of urban squalor is contrasted with shots of children playing in an archetypal East London council estate. The voiceover begins, a reading of a poem by Nazrul, as the camera focuses on what seems like ashes. Magically, the ashes are reconstructed into a photograph of Nazrul, the same photograph which features on the album cover, striding on a map of the Indian subcontinent.

By physically reconstructing Nazrul's image from the ruins of a desolate urban London, ADF are then constructing a home for the Asian communities, or more correctly, articulating the right for British Asians to call this place right here their home. Nazrul's poem sampled in this song is a defiant call to arms, a refusal to surrender in the face of imperialist oppression. The anti-colonial politics that Nazrul represented manifested itself in the desire to make a home in the subcontinent, by fighting for independence. In the 1990s, the anti-racist politics that ADF represent manifests itself in the desire to fight for a home here.

In fact, ADF are actually doing much more than sampling Nazrul's poem. The entire song is a loose translation of the original Bengali poem, presented in a sharply contemporary setting. As in the original, whose message was based on a call for Hindu-Muslim unity in the face of Western colonial aggression, ADF's version brings together a number of very different musical traditions – from a Punjabi Bhangra drummer, through rap, hip-hop and reggae, in order to create a syncretic Asianness that is 'neither essentializing nor dissolutive into a deconstructive play on difference',[18] in Sanjay Sharma's words. The syncretism is, however, deeply political, as visually depicted in the video with the band singing and dancing under and around a statue of Robert Clive, commander-in-chief of British India, and the man usually credited (blamed) for securing India for Britain. Through this music video, then, ADF are rejecting a narrative of colonial nostalgia that seeks to rewrite history, painting the British Empire in a better light, and serving to further alienate British Asians today. Instead, they are projecting a narrative of alternative, or radical nostalgia, where the history of resistance and rebellion is valorised and used to reconstruct one's home.

> Check my anger, it's real
> Ain't no token
> I'll be satisfied only when your back's been broken
> It's my burning ambition to burn down your empire
> Man I'll be building you a funeral pyre
> The fire in my eyes
> If looks coulda kill
> I won't be satisfied until I've had my fill.[19]

Clive's presence in the background is given equal weight to a tableau of Bollywood film posters, principally for the 1995 blockbuster *Karan Arjun* starring Shah Rukh Khan and Kajol, two actors who, as I discuss in Chapter 5, come to represent the archetypal Bollywood version of the diasporic love story. The juxtaposition of Clive's statue with the film poster does more than suggest that they are equally important. It also implicitly suggests a remapping of Empire and movement, as the journey of the colonialist oppressors to south Asia gets replaced with the story of the reverse journey of the south Asian diaspora, moving to the UK in order to establish their own home in the heart of the former Empire. In the process, it also replaces the imperial nostalgia of Britain with another, counter-imperial and oppositional nostalgia of the British Asian.

Nazrul and Bollywood, from different parts of India, and from different positions on the cultural spectrum, serve a similar function here. Both of these intertextual references are used to imagine a moment when such resistance will no longer be necessary – in other words, when this place will truly become home. Calling this place home, then, is a performative utterance that is coloured by a nostalgia for a future, looking forward to and simultaneously helping to create a discursive and material home that can be imagined and fought for in the present:

> I am the rebel warrior
> I have risen alone with my head held high
> I will only rest
> When the cries of the oppressed
> No longer reach the sky
> When the sound of the sword of the oppressor
> No longer rings in battle
> Hear my war cry!

The repetition of the 'when', then, is deeply radical as it allows the musicians, and the audience to collectively imagine the radical potentiality that exists in this 'when', in the nostalgia of the imagined home. This nostalgia is visible in an online article reviewing ADF's 'TH9'. Published on the website cybersylhet.com, Emdad Rahman's article 'My Friend Quddus Ali: 12 Years On' narrates the Watney Market attack that inspired the track. Rahman's account poignantly begins with his memories of Quddus Ali:

> I grew up with Quddus Ali. Living a stones [sic] throw away from him, we spent approximately 10 years together in primary and secondary school. A slight, quick witted and sharp lad, Quddus was always the one who was sleek and thin enough to squeeze through the school gates to retrieve the ball from the road behind each time one of our flat footed mates decided to hoof the ball through the posts rugby style.[20]

This nostalgic account of their shared childhood in Tower Hamlets is contrasted with the brutality of the attack:

> The 17 year old student from Tower Hamlets college was viciously beaten by a gang of eight racists on Commercial Road in Whitechapel. . . . They clearly intended to kill him. The attack was overtly racist.

Rahman intersperses lines from the song in his accounts of the attack and its aftermath – the official cover-up and the effect this has had on the family and the community. The juxtaposition of traumatic accounts of violence with a nostalgic sense of home is continued in the site as a whole. Named after Sylhet, the province of Bangladesh where the largest proportion of the Tower Hamlets Bengali population originate, the Bengali subtitle of this bilingual site is: 'Surma's waves online'. This is a reference to the main river that flows through Sylhet, the Surma and, in conjunction with the coconut trees that form part of the site's logo, is clearly intended to create a nostalgic sense of rootedness – which, as the primary focus on British Asian matters attest, can transcend both the homelands left behind and the home being constructed here. This then is the true power of the nostalgia that is visible in ADF's music. It is not a nostalgia that harkens back to an idyllic, purified past back home in Bangladesh, nor a nostalgia that sanctifies a simple, romanticized multiculturalism here in Britain. It is rather a nostalgia that can celebrate conflict and anger and resistance – a nostalgia that can make space for the rebellions and the setbacks, both the violence and pain, and the fightback that was needed in order to be able to claim both Nazrul and Hanbury Street as home, the fightback that made it clear that one had the right to live, love and belong near both the Surma River and Watney Street Market.

'A VILLAGE IN PUNJAB': BLAIR PEACH AND THE REBELS OF SOUTHALL

If Altab Ali's death sparked a movement that helped in this homemaking process, then Blair Peach's death is certainly no different. Happening within a year of each other, these deaths and the many other incidents of racist violence galvanized the politically aware from many different communities into a broad-based anti-racist and anti-fascist movement. The Anti Nazi

League, Rock Against Racism, the Asian Youth Movements, and the Southall Black Sisters all date from this period, and all in their various ways display the effects of radical nostalgia, both in the way they organized political action at the time, and the ways in which the collective memory of political action has since become a part of the narrative through which communities of colour in Britain tell their own histories.

Clement Blair Peach was thirty-three when, on 22 April 1979, he went to take part in a demonstration against the National Front in Southall. Southall was then, as it is now, an area with a high south Asian population. Despite this, the authorities had granted the National Front permission to hold a political rally in the Town Hall. Tens of thousands of anti-fascists joined a counterdemonstration, and the Metropolitan Police called in the infamous Special Patrol Group. The demonstration became violent, and Blair Peach was knocked unconscious at the junction of Beachcroft Avenue and Orchard Avenue. He died in hospital the following day. Clarence Baker of the Southall-based reggae band Misty in Roots was severely injured and had to be hospitalized. The inquest into Blair Peach's death controversially returned a verdict of death by misadventure and it was not until 2010 that the Metropolitan Police finally admitted that he had indeed been struck down and killed by a police officer. There were multiple demonstrations in the days after Blair Peach's death – his body lay in repose at the Dominion Cinema hall in Southall, which was visited by eight thousand people. Three years previously, a young student named Gurdip Singh Chaggar had been stabbed to death on the street outside this same Dominion Cinema hall – famous for screening Bollywood films and thus at the very heart of Southall's Asian community.

As in the case of Altab Ali in East London, these deaths helped to galvanize the community in organized resistance. Groups like Southall Asian Youth Movement and Southall Black Sisters were formed to fight against the increased presence of the National Front and allied groups. Fights with fascist gangs were getting more and more frequent. In 1981, the band The 4 Skins were performing at the Hambrough Tavern pub in Southall. The audience was mostly 'skinheads' – code for the supporters of National Front and other far-right groups. The Southall Youth Movement organized a fightback involving activists and other members of the local Asian communities. With the police attempting to protect the racists, the violence turned into a three-way battle, in which the whole pub was burnt down.

In October 2013, rapper Swami Baracus released an independent mixtape album called *The Recipe*, a track of which was dedicated to Blair Peach. Called 'Stand Strong (Ode to Blair Peach)', the words make the connection between resistance to racism and homemaking clear:

What do you really know about the area you were born and raised in?
How do you represent something without knowing about the history, culture, politics and struggles of the people?

I want to tell you where I'm from, and for that I only really have one question:
Who killed Blair Peach? My town still needs to know.[21]

The words make a causal connection between the history of activism in Southall (it mentions the Southall Youth Movement and Southall Black Sisters) through the response to Blair Peach's death and the way in which Swami Baracus defines himself: 'where I'm from' and 'my town'.

This is by no means the first musical response to Blair Peach's death, however. In 1979, the same year he was murdered, Jamaican born dub-poet Linton Kwesi Johnson released a song called 'Reggae Fi Peach'. The song uses Blair Peach's death as a rallying call that makes it clear what the stakes are: 'Is England becoming a fascist state? / The answer lies at your own gate'.[22] Like ADF or Swami Baracus, Johnson was, through his music and poetry, creating a pan-national counter-hegemonic, anti-imperialist landscape which all colonized people could call home. In an international arc of anti-fascism, a Jamaican poet was eulogizing a teacher from New Zealand who had died while demonstrating in solidarity with Indians. In 1996, the Basque band Negu Gorriak would cover this song in their own version 'Reggae Peachentzat'. Negu Gorriak, active from 1990 to 1996, were an underground Basque band, whose music came out of the Basque Radical Rock movements of the 1980s. Singing only in Euskera, their music was deeply politically committed to the Basque cause, often including protest songs about police brutality and corruption and the Spanish government's colonial relationship to the Basque country. Their use of 'Reggae fi Peach' thus reinforces the point that a nostalgically reconstructed tradition of militant activism can be transported across nationalist borders and resurrected, both in a spirit of solidarity and in order to aid other, different homemaking projects. When the socialist theatre company Belt & Braces staged Dario Fo's play *Accidental Death of an Anarchist* in 1979, the accompanying theatre programme cited a number of incidents of police violence, including Giuseppe Pinelli's death in Milan on which the play was based, as well as police brutality in the context of the Troubles in Ireland. Under the heading 'For those who think it doesn't happen here', the programme included a detailed account of the Blair Peach case, a reprint of a Paul Foot article originally published in *Socialist Worker*.[23] This creation of an alternative, radical heritage can thus be used to both nostalgically recover lost and marginalized voices, and also to generate support for similar contemporary radical struggles. The homemaking process which nostalgia allows provides a home not just for specific racialized or colonized groups, as in the case of Southall or Tower Hamlets, but also a discursive, cultural and material home for an international anti-fascist, anti-racist and anti-capitalist movement.

In 2014, the Asian Health Agency and digital:works launched a Heritage Lottery–funded project to produce a documentary telling the history of the

Southall Youth Movement. Called *Young Rebels: The Story of the Southall Youth Movement*, the film was produced by young people from the communities – in most cases the children and grandchildren of those actively involved in anti-racist politics of the 1970s. The testimony of one of these young people, Aashish, demonstrates the link between commemorating a legacy of anti-racist politics, and the nostalgic process of homemaking and belonging:

> I was born and raised in Southall, this is my town, this is where I've grown up, this is where my parents taught me everything I know and this is where I went to school. My parents told me many stories about riots that happened in Southall in the late 70s and early 80s and the atrocities that my community, the Asian community, had to face at the hands of groups like the National Front.[24]

Young Rebels features interviews with people who, through their activism, helped to form the Southall Youth Movement. Very carefully rooted in Southall, formed after a public meeting in the famous Dominion Cinema, this organization was probably the one most directly responsible for the anti-racist fightback after the murders of Gurdip Singh Chaggar and Blair Peach, and in response to all the other racist attacks that had made Asian life in Southall almost untenable. Fighting racism in local governments, the education system, on the factory floor, and on the streets, the young activists of the Southall Youth Movement helped to consolidate and stabilize Asian life in Britain, and, in the process, prove inspirational for similar movements elsewhere in Britain.

At one point in the film, a group of men, now middle-aged or older, sit around a table sharing their memories about how they occupied and eventually took over a London bus in order to drive through police lines. These men are old friends – Suresh Grover, Balraj Purewal and Sunil Sinha, all founding members of the Southall Youth Movement, as well as Poko from Misty in Roots – and they sit around a table bearing witness both to the level and scale of oppression, and the courage of the fightback. There is something very powerful about this scene in which older men fondly reminisce about the activism of their youth, fully aware of the importance of the activism at the time, and the stigmatization that it caused, as they jokingly brag about having their photograph appear on the front page of *The Guardian*.

Perhaps unsurprisingly for a Heritage Lottery–funded project, the impetus is to capture a community history – a deeply nostalgic process of recovering a great and glorious past. As one of the other young producers, Prabhjot, says, the film is 'about keeping a bit of history going'. The website for the parent group that ran this project, an independent local alliance called Inspire Southall, reinforces this nostalgic approach to history:

> The communities of Southall once inspired a whole generation to struggle against racism nationally. We remained united despite suffering, at first hand, bussing of school children, low wages and discriminatory practices by employers, provocative fascist marches into the town, police violence and government indifference.
>
> It is Southall where the first Asian and Caribbean workers took action to secure their future, where the Youth Movement was born, where Asian and Caribbean women began to organize for their rights, where pioneer Bhangra bands were formed, and where the first temples were built.[25]

However, this same website also demonstrates the counter-normative, radical potential such nostalgic retellings can have:

> The current Government is now eroding these hard won gains. Drastic economic cuts to public services and benefit are already affecting the African, Caribbean and Asian communities disproportionality. For the first time, in many decades, there is now the bleak and dangerous prospect of another generation of young people being condemned to a life on the margins, excluded from mainstream society and possibly suffering rates of discrimination in employment, education, housing, health and criminal justice worse than their parents.

In other words, the nostalgic recovering of a lost or marginalized history can be used to reinforce a tradition of resistance, which can then be used to fuel future resistance. The narrative of history thus created may well be romanticized and idealized, but it does not necessarily have to be conservative. This can be seen in Jagdish Banger's testimony from the film. A Southall Youth Movement activist from the 1970s, he recalls the important role played by the then newly established Indian Youth Club:

> We'd go to [the Indian Youth Club], we'd learn photography. We'd learn the history of where our parents were [from]. We'd know about the Gurdwara, the temples. We'd learn about things like music, there was a music room – we'd learn how to record digital sounds, in them days, you know, recording studios and everything. Misty in Roots were born and brought up there – big, major Jamaican band now. We used to go, pass the time – any advice we need, if we were picked on at school . . . it was a place where we could go as a unity and sit, get to know everybody.

Jagdish's testimony is paired with a photograph from the Indian Youth Club as it looked in the 1970s. On the wall, there are two posters – the first advertising 'New Indian Cinema', and the second a photograph of Malcolm X.

In linking a legacy of resistance to homemaking, these narratives are not then being used to reinforce any particular brand of nationalism – the home being constructed cannot be easily aligned to any one nation. Rather, the resulting home becomes a diverse, ambiguous, often unstable space that can transcend racial, religious, national and generational divides. Instead of conventional accounts of nostalgia which seek to link it inextricably to a first-generation connection with the homelands, this view of nostalgia suggests that the generational divide is not as big as might be expected and that, moreover, the home that is being nostalgically recovered is not necessarily the same as that which was left behind during migration. To say this is not to say that these divides within and between generations did not exist – generally speaking, and as can be seen in the testimonies featured in *Young Rebels*, the second-generation activists from the Asian Youth Movements saw themselves as more radical and more militant than the early generations of the Indian Workers' Associations. Nor is this reading of nostalgia meant to minimize the real and important political differences that existed between various groups of the newer generations – from the Asian Youth Movements through Southall Black Sisters to Rock Against Racism and the Socialist Workers Party. My point is not to say that these differences do not matter, though exploring the precise nature of these is beyond the scope of this book. The point is that, for all their many differences, they all to a greater or lesser extent constructed, and then became part of, a nostalgically driven tradition of anti-fascist, anti-racist and anti-capitalist activity. It is this long heritage of radical activism that has helped to create a rooted homeliness in the here and now of the various British Asian communities. As the mission statement of Inspire Southall puts it: 'The reality is that race equality legislation and policies were secured after decades of campaigning by communities such as Southall, and by families affected by violent and institutional racism'. In a more personal, but equally political reaction, Jagdish remembers his feeling at the burning down of the Hambrough Tavern:

> You know what, my heart was pounding thinking 'Shit, this is it man!' . . . Because we were standing ground. . . . It's a proud moment. We stood up for ourselves, saying: 'This is Southall and it's full of Indians'.

Young Rebels is, then, a deeply nostalgic film that looks back with obvious pride at a history of activism that has helped to make what Southall is today. The film highlights the role played by the entire community in the fightback. Sukhdev Aujla recalls the demonstration that followed Blair Peach's death:

> History is a witness that Southall at that time organized the biggest demonstration, with more than 10000 people. That day I believe the media from across England and Europe descended on Southall to find out and to understand from where all these young people had come and who had organized them.

Similarly, Jagdish remembers the community's response to the National Front presence at The 4 Skins gig at the Hambrough Tavern:

> All we could see is this community of people, Indians, just forwarding towards the Hambrough Tavern . . . and you know what, every shopkeeper was just shutting shop and walking towards that way. . . . We're not gonna let this go, everybody was at it.

The leaflet accompanying the DVD depicts a similar portrait of community solidarity:

> In a remarkable show of solidarity, many residents smashed down their own front walls and passed bricks to the Asian youth and gave refuge to those injured.

According to this narrative, it is active resistance that brings together the community, providing the cohesiveness needed to turn this space into home. As Jagdish puts it:

> National Front had to put their hand up. Especially after 1981, they did not dare show their faces in Southall.
>
> Southall changed after that, it got much more confident of who they were, and what it was about.

This decades-long struggle is also depicted in Nikhil Advani's 2011 film *Patiala House*. Publicized as a mainstream Bollywood sports drama, in the mould of the more famous *Bend It Like Beckham*, it is my contention that this film is more interesting than it might at first appear. The plot is set in Southall and involves the Kahlon family. The protagonist, Parghat (Akshay Kumar) is a second-generation British Sikh whose life's ambition is to play cricket for England. His father Gurtej (Rishi Kapoor) is a prominent local activist who, scarred by the racist attacks he experienced in the 1970s, maintains a rigid anti-assimilationist stance and refuses to allow his son to pursue his ambition.

The film opens on young Parghat's birthday party, in an archetypally British-Indian living room. The comfort of familiar language, food, and customs is rudely broken as a stone thrown by a group of white skinheads shatters the window among shouts of 'Go home!' In his first act of resistance, Gurtej picks up that most Indian of cooking utensils, a pressure-cooker and storms after them. The next sequence shows Gurtej's attempts to fight racism in order to create a more stable life for Southall's Asian communities. The film intercuts 'real' and 'fake' documentary footage, and still-shots of various anti-racist and labour movements in Southall over the years. Some of the documentary footage is the same that was used in the *Young Rebels* documentary, and that is repeated on British news every time incidents like Blair Peach's death are revisited. Specific real-life incidents such as a seven-week-long strike at the Woolf's Rubber factory in 1965 are alluded to. Comparing real-life photos from the race riots that marked Southall with shots from the film clearly shows how the filmmakers were influenced by the radical history of the Asian communities of Southall.

While Blair Peach himself is not mentioned, there are indirect allusions. The Dominion Cinema, where his body was taken and outside of which Gurdip Singh Chaggar was killed, no longer exists, so the filmmakers substituted it with the Himalaya Palace instead. The footage of rallies and political speeches outside the Himalaya Palace building bears a remarkable resemblance to the archival footage and black-and-white photographs of similar events in and outside the famous Dominion Cinema.

Gurdip Singh Chaggar's death becomes, in the fictionalized version of the film, a murder of an elderly lawyer, Virender Singh Saini. Mirroring a traumatic experience that many British Sikhs had to go through, the Kahlon family decides to cut Parghat's hair in order to shield him from racist attacks. The song that accompanies this traumatic moment reveals the fears of homelessness and rootlessness that afflicted the British Asian communities and helped to fuel the anti-racist struggles: 'The soil has become an outsider / In this unknown city'.

As Parghat narrates his community's and his father's history, in order to explain his father's anti-assimilation stance, his voiceover expresses a clear causal link between the nostalgia evoked by the old footage and the apparent success of the community in the present:

> Slowly, they made their own school, their own pharmacy, their own Gurdwara, they created everything. It was as if Southall was no longer a part of England, but had become a village in Punjab. And my father, the Headman of Southall.

In Chapter 4, I examine some of the consequences of thinking of Southall as a 'village in Punjab', but for my purposes here it is enough to note that the process which allows the British Asian inhabitants of Southall to think of it as connected to Punjab, to think of it as belonging to them, has active political resistance at its heart. There is then a twin nostalgia here – the nostalgia to reconstruct a home that helps to galvanize the resistance against racism and fascism in the 1970s and 1980s, as well as the nostalgia for those rebellious moments today, which can also manifest itself in resistance against the descendants of the National Front today – whether it is the British National Party, or the English Defence League.

It is true that the narrative of the film posits Gurtej's rigid stance as outdated: 'Times changed, but Father didn't', in an effort to maintain a generational divide. However, this does not, for me, take away from the huge emotional resonance that comes from being able to claim ownership of the place that is Southall. The protests that took up the cry of 'Here to stay, here to fight' led directly to the transformation of places like Southall and Tower Hamlets into the multicultural, multi-faith spaces of diaspora that they are today. As I will discuss further in Chapter 4, the persistence involved in occupying a place, insisting on staying and fighting, is a powerfully counter-hegemonic act that helps to create and maintain a home in which one belongs. Nostalgic memories of these past acts of resistance then continue to be important because they can help to inspire and sustain current and future acts of rebellion as well.

'BETTER THAN NO CAUSE AT ALL': KIRANJIT AHLUWALIA AND THE NOSTALGIC COMMUNITIES OF SISTERHOOD

It is easy, the radicalism of the Asian Youth Movements and ADF notwithstanding, to overestimate the liberatory role played by the homemaking process in Southall and Tower Hamlets. Homemaking does not necessarily work in the same way for everyone, and certainly not everyone is able to claim the same new home. It is noticeable, for example, that *Young Rebels*, as discussed above, features no interviews with female activists of the Southall Youth Movement. Southall Black Sisters, which was created in 1979 after Blair Peach's death, is mentioned in passing, but nobody from that organization is interviewed at all.

As may be surmised from this absence, the relationship between the Southall Black Sisters and the anti-racist left has often been a difficult one. In the words of one of the founders of SBS, Rahila Gupta:

> Both black women and men who continue to be involved exclusively in the anti-racist struggle see feminism as the Trojan horse of the anti-racist struggle and believe that campaigning against male oppressors in our communities is tantamount to betraying the anti-racist struggle.[26]

While the intricacies of the ideological and personal divisions across these various organizations are far beyond the scope of my argument here, what interests me is the possibility of radical nostalgia of a different form that exists within the continuing activism, and the historic victories of the Southall Black Sisters. In this section, I will look at the case of Kiranjit Ahluwalia, and the activism and advocacy of Southall Black Sisters in her case, as a story that, not dissimilar to that of Blair Peach and Altab Ali, can be used to generate a progressive, critical nostalgia of its own.

Kiranjit Ahluwalia, a British Sikh woman, was convicted of murdering her husband in 1989, and served more than three years of a life sentence, before her conviction was overturned after the court was presented with new evidence:

> She had not been aware she could plead guilty to manslaughter on the grounds of diminished responsibility, and that she had been suffering from severe depression when she killed her husband.[27]

Southall Black Sisters agitated for Ahluwalia's release, through a mixture of public protests and legal challenges. On 29 June 1992, they organized a public meeting in Crawley, at which Rahila Gupta read out a speech written by Ahluwalia, in which she delivers a moving and damning indictment of the patriarchal culture that has oppressed her for so long. It would seem, then, that this is a rejection of the kind of nostalgia that I have been discussing in this book – it certainly is far from the nostalgia of Duleep Singh that is arguably bound up with particular notions of Sikh nationalism, for example:

> My culture is like my blood coursing through every vein of my body. It is the culture into which I was born and where I grew up which sees the woman as the honour of the house. In order to uphold this false 'honour' and glory, she is taught to endure many kinds of oppression and pain, in silence. . . . This is the essence of my culture, society, religion. Where a woman is a toy, a plaything – she can be stuck together at will, broken at will. Everybody did what they wanted with me.[28]

Ahluwalia's case gathered significant public interest, which inevitably played a part in the court's decision to overturn her conviction. As well as in the mainstream press, her story was featured in the radical feminist press, from *Spare Rib* to *Women Against Fundamentalism*. In the October/November 1992 issue of *Spare Rib*, her release is announced with a banner headline saying 'Free at Last', accompanied with a black-and-white photograph of her and her legal team facing the media after her release. Looking at the photograph today, it creates an effect not dissimilar to the photographs of the antiracist demonstrations discussed above. Dressed in a white shirt and dark jacket, and surrounded by microphones, with an enormous smile on her face, Ahluwalia seems to be embodying the freedom that she has only just won. For a movement that does not enjoy very many successes, this is, clearly and radiantly, a success story. Activist groups like Southall Black Sisters need success stories like these – both for the publicity that they generate at the time and the memory of the good times that helps sustain them during the many defeats. As Rahila Gupta puts it in *From Homebreakers to Jailbreakers: Southall Black Sisters*:

> This collection of essays was meant to mark our twenty-first anniversary, a reflective pause to look into the future through the prism of the 1st decade of the last millennium, but in true SBS style (lack of resources) we have got there just a little too late. It is not easy for activists to sit down and record their work, but in this age of information overload you need to record in order almost to prove that you exist.[29]

In 2006, Indian director Jag Mundhra made a film based on Ahluwalia's life, called *Provoked: A True Story*, starring Aishwarya Rai as the title character; Nandita Das as Radha Dalal, a composite character inspired by two of the founders of SBS, Rahila Gupta and Pragna Patel; and Robbie Coltrane as Lord Edward Foster, the barrister who helps to secure Ahluwalia's release. The film charts Ahluwalia's story, beginning with the night she attacks her husband, through her life in prison, culminating in her release. It is my contention that the film deploys a particularly critical nostalgia in telling Ahluwalia's story and, through this nostalgia and its celebration of a success story, is doing important counter-hegemonic political work.

The cinematic version of Ahluwalia is shown as occupying a deeply ambivalent position with respect to her cultural heritage. On the one hand, she has been abused for many years by a violent man, a victimization that was facilitated and supported by a conservative patriarchy based around notions of shame and honour. On the other hand, as one of the few south Asians in the prison, she is immediately and consistently racialized – from guards and prisoners failing to pronounce her name, to the expectation that she can take off all of her clothes in front of a guard, through the inability/unwillingness of the prison system to cater to her dietary needs. The moment when the guard asks her to take off all her jewellery, including the *mangalsutra*, which is a symbol of her marriage, is particularly revealing. While the necklace symbolizes her marriage to a violent, abusive husband, Kiranjit is still depicted as hesitant – unable to live with the violence that the institution of marriage exposed her to, but also not yet willing to jettison the culture that, in her own words, 'runs through her blood'. Her description of her life back home in India carries this similar ambivalent sense:

> I was born in the village of Chak kalal in Punjab. I was the youngest of nine children, and the most loved. My father died when I was only few months old. My mother died of cancer when I was sixteen. [My mother] wanted me to become lawyer . . . [but] my husband did not allow . . . but my family say, get married, have children, be proper Indian woman.

The real-life Ahluwalia embodies this ambivalence as well. While bravely resisting the oppressive patriarchal structures that her 'culture' has manifested itself in, she still marks herself out as Indian. When Julie Bindel meets her in prison in 1991, she asked if Bindel could bring some 'red chilli peppers' because, she said, 'English food has no taste'.[30]

One way of charting the trajectory of the film, and Kiranjit's ambivalence, is to see the development of the central character through her rejection of a conservative home that has been made for her, in favour of a home that she can make for herself. The film depicts and celebrates this process of homemaking, in the process evoking a complex, counter-hegemonic nostalgia that is centred around the deeply political, hugely radical notion of sisterhood.

The first, most obvious example of the construction of a community of sisterhood is the Southall Black Sisters themselves. The Southall Black Sisters are presented as the archetypal activist group – always short of funds and support, and usually fighting a losing battle, but passionately committed to the good fight. They are introduced in the film during a visit from the bailiffs as they lose their photocopier and fax machine due to lack of money. The precariousness of their existence is presented as part of the challenge they pose to the establishment: 'Banks aren't notoriously fond of non-profit groups. It kind of goes against their belief system.'

What they do have, however, is each other and their shared belief that 'a lost cause is better than no cause at all'. The activists of the Southall Black Sisters are presented as riotously, flagrantly counter-normative – they get drunk in pubs, they smoke while sitting on the top of cars, and when needed, Radha has no hesitation in conning Kiranjit's mother-in-law (who cannot read English) into believing that there is a court order forcing her to allow her grandchildren to visit their mother in prison. Throughout Kiranjit's trial, the activists occupy the visitor's section of the courtroom, loudly denouncing the procedures as biased against the defendant. The cinematic recreation of the famous Crawley meeting, where Kiranjit's speech is read out by Radha, is another example of an active construction of a sisterhood. This political solidarity is presented through the voiceover. The camera follows Kiranjit as she is writing her speech in prison; the speech begins in Aishwarya Rai's voiceover, but as the camera moves to the actual meeting, Rai's voice changes to Nandita Das's – an aural representation of the solidarity of sisterhood that transcends prison, and manages to construct a common home for women who are free and women who are behind bars. Much like the resistance movements outlined above, the film depicts the Southall Black Sisters' resistance and political activism and advocacy as a process of homemaking. The raising of awareness, the letter-writing campaigns, the public meetings and demonstrations, the printing and circulating of posters and leaflets, the campaign of ring-arounds and fundraising – all of this does not just help to secure Kiranjit's release, but it also creates a space for her and other 'battered women' like her, as well as their activist sisters, to belong in. When patriarchy has destroyed any possibility of comfort in a home that was made for men, to suit men's interests, the process of fighting patriarchy also becomes a process of homemaking for these women.

If the Southall Black Sisters represent sisterhood outside the prison, then there is also a parallel community construction at work inside. While in prison, Kiranjit becomes friends with a group of women – Jackie (Deborah Moore), Lula (Maxine Finch), Gladys (Julie T. Wallace) and most importantly Ronnie (Miranda Richardson). These are, in Ronnie's words, her 'friends . . . sisters, in Her Majesty's Resort'. The construction of this community of sisterhood is what allows Kiranjit to find a space for herself, perhaps for the very first time. When Radha asks her how she feels in prison, she says, 'I feel free.' Kiranjit's undermining of the distinction between prison life and outside life mirrors the real-life Ahluwalia's speech at the Crawley meeting: 'I have come out of my husband's jail and entered the jail of the law. But I have found a new life, in this legal jail.' The political connotations of the sentiment are only too obvious – when patriarchy regulates a woman's life, the distinction between home and prison seems slightly academic. Southall Black Sisters may take understandable pride in the label 'Homebreakers', but part of what gives them their subversive power, as well as maintaining their presence as a supportive, solace-giving organization, is their ability to remake a home together, on one's own terms, once the decision to break the home that was handed down to one has been taken.

One of the scenes in which the film cinematically connects the fictionalized version of the Southall Black Sisters with the real group of women, is the one where Radha first visits Kiranjit in prison, offering to help her with her case. Radha is carrying a copy of *Against the Grain*, the volume that was released to mark the tenth anniversary of Southall Black Sisters, and which was revealingly subtitled 'A Celebration of Survival and Struggle'. The volume charts the trajectory of the group which, by 1989, had already become multigenerational, through sections called 'Legacy', 'Inheritors' and 'Successors'. As the introduction makes clear, for Southall Black Sisters, the need to celebrate their tenth anniversary was experienced as a defiantly political desire:

> We were anxious that the tenth anniversary of the group should not go unmarked. We have little to celebrate these days so opportunities must be seized.[31]

The insistence on celebrating a history of resistance is part of the homemaking process that I am discussing in this book. Evidence of this celebration can be seen in the film through the passion of the struggle and the joys of success, all of which help to create spaces in which women can belong.

What is truly liberatory is the ability of woman to come together, form communities of resistance – sisterhoods to fight back with – and the narrative of the film demonstrates the fact that this active, assertive homemaking can take place both within and outside prison. In a particularly poignant scene of sisterhood, Ronnie and Kiranjit are playing Scrabble, and Kiranjit has formed 'big word, sholder [sic]'. Ronnie points out Kiranjit's mistake. 'U! I need u?' asks Kiranjit. 'Yeah, you need me. Don't worry, I'm there', reassures Ronnie.

In the process, however, the film lays itself open to charges of simplification and sentimentalism in its depiction of prison life. Kiranjit's cellmate Ronnie is almost impossibly kind-hearted – when she is first introduced, she has smuggled food for her, even though she has yet to even meet her. Soon after, when Kiranjit is targeted by the bully Doreen, Ronnie chooses to pick a fight, knowing that she will be punished with solitary confinement as a result. When Kiranjit asks her why, her response is, 'I guess I've just always hated a bully'. Ronnie is a stereotypical stock working-class character – rough around the edges, but with a heart of gold. Versions of her can be seen in many other British films, such as *Brassed Off*, *Kinky Boots* and *The Full Monty*. In the words of comedian and author Marc Blake, these films follow a similar pattern: 'Find a dispossessed group of people, give them a hobby and an unrealistic goal, and see them triumph against the forces of oppression.' *Provoked* does not follow this template precisely, but it does arguably provide the same model of 'chirpy period working-class people that can be seen in these other films.'[32] Even Doreen, the prison bully, is converted through the power of Kiranjit's speech.

While Blake is correct in identifying a tradition of representing the working class in British comedies, rather than the films he cites, a closer parallel to *Provoked* might be *Made in Dagenham* or *Pride* – two other films which, like *Provoked*, portray moments of victory for resistance movements – striking female factory workers in the former case, and miners and gay rights activists in the latter. Writing about *Made in Dagenham*, Jonathan Moss has critiqued what he sees as the depoliticization of the victories that films like these demonstrate:

> Since the 1990s there have been a number of popular films concerned with working-class lifestyles as a depoliticised subject of fascination, such as *The Full Monty* (1997) or *Billy Elliot* (2000). In these other 'feel-good' films, experiences of class inequality are presented in ways that create an illusion that hard work is rewarded, and inequality and adversity can be overcome by ordinary individuals. These films' production coincided with the decline of class as a collective political identity, as people have increasingly sought to assert their 'ordinariness' and distance themselves from the political implications of 'class'. *Made in Dagenham* also exemplifies this phenomenon, as the producers self-consciously depoliticised the strike in a bid to achieve a sense of nostalgia and also to appeal to the values of ordinary people.[33]

Moss's criticism echoes that of Blake, who also identifies nostalgia as a problem with this genre of films:

> Nostalgia is a feature of the British film industry. . . . There is a perceived golden age, always thirty-fifty years ago, where manners, common sense and policing by consent existed, immigration was not an issue and one 'knew one's place'.[34]

This critique of nostalgia is so commonplace that it can leave some very problematic fundamental assumptions behind the unchallenged arguments. Moss's argument seems to imply that 'appeal[ing] to the values of ordinary people' is necessarily apolitical, while Blake's position seems to only recognize the nostalgia of those who do consider immigration to be an issue. Where this leaves the nostalgia of the dispossessed, assuming they do have the luxury of nostalgia, is not quite clear.

In fact, and of course, the reverse is true. Depicting a community constructed by and for the dispossessed is a deeply and fundamentally political act. It is true that *Provoked* differs from *Made in Dagenham* in that the former depicts an actual moment of success, while the latter manufactures a success story for what Moss describes as the 'feel-good' factor. In both cases, however, the narrative can, and I argue, should be read as a deliberate, self-conscious, and supremely radical deploying of the nostalgia of the marginalized – a people who have been othered based on class, race, gendered, or regional terms – and a nostalgia which constitutes the homemaking process, whereby these othered people can find a space to belong on their own terms. When the mainstream can feel so alienating, so oppressive, when one's actual home is more debilitating than prison, this imaginative construction of a community within which one is accepted, within which one can find solace and support to aid one's activism, has to be seen as a powerfully counter-hegemonic action.

In her essay 'Walls into Bridges: The Losses and Gains of Making Alliances', Rahila Gupta describes Blairite Britain as an alienating, dispiriting place for progressive politics:

> Although the time and energy costs of alliance-building are high, a significant by-product of the process is the creation of a political culture based on inclusivity rather than exclusivity. This is critical in our fragmented times, when to talk of a feminist movement or anti-racist movement is to see things through rose-tinted glasses.[35]

I do not wish to critique Gupta's assessment of the political situation in Britain as she saw it in 2003. What I do want to think about, however, is what might be at stake, politically speaking, to insist on seeing things through rose-tinted glasses. Frequently derided as falsifying the reality of a situation, retreating to a familiar, comfortable version of reality that suits one's assumptions, and that one finds comforting, refusing to change oneself and one's point of view to adapt oneself to a changing world – this could serve as a definition of the commonsensical, hegemonic view of nostalgia. As such, it may well lie at the foundation of the suspicion that much of scholarship has for the concept of nostalgia and for any progressive political currency it might have.

It is also, however, undeniably true that there is a connection between seeing things through rose-tinted glasses and Radha's belief in *Provoked* that 'a lost cause is better than no cause at all'. A nostalgia-induced belief in rose-tinted glasses that insists on the utopian belief in a unified feminist or anti-racist movement is easy to deride and dismiss, but as Peter Glazer puts it: 'What better way to encapsulate the concept of an engaged progressive politic than as the attempt to integrate utopia and reality?'[36] The various commemorative texts I have looked at in this chapter provide evidence to support Glazer's argument, and a reminder that we dismiss the progressive potential of nostalgia at our peril.

To be sure, nostalgic homemaking brings with it problems of its own. As this chapter has shown, the home that one community or group makes for itself may prove to be oppressive for another. There is a lot about the nostalgia that leads Southall to be described as 'a village in Punjab' that the Southall Black Sisters will find problematic, or offensive, or even actively dangerous.

Having said that, and for all of the problems associated with nostalgic homemaking, there is still an urgent need to recognize the progressive, subversive potential that nostalgia can have, when it can be mobilized to provide support for the lonely, help for the dispossessed, and somewhere to belong for the marginalized. The homes that the marginalized groups create using this nostalgia can be many and various, and they may well impose new oppressions of their own, but they all share a common, powerful characteristic – in their very existence, these homes represent a challenge to the centre, the centre that refuses to recognize the legitimacy of the margins.

NOTES

1. David Widgery, *Beating Time: Riot 'n' Race 'n' Rock 'n' Roll* (London: Chatto & Windus, 1986), 16
2. Paul Lewis, "Blair Peach: After 31 Years Met Police Say 'Sorry' for Their Role in His Killing", *The Guardian*, 27 April, 2010. Accessed on 10 August 2017, available at: https://www.theguardian.com/uk/2010/apr/27/blair-peach-killing-police
3. Peter Glazer, *Radical Nostalgia: Spanish Civil War Commemoration in America* (Rochester, NY: University of Rochester Press, 2005), 7
4. Peter Glazer, *Radical Nostalgia*, 255
5. Peter Glazer, *Radical Nostalgia*, 261

6. Michael Keith, *After the Cosmopolitan? Multicultural Cities and the Future of Racism* (London and New York: Routledge, 2005), 144

7. Anindya Raychaudhuri, "'Just as Good a Place to Publish': Banksy, Graffiti and the Textualisation of the Wall", *Rupkatha Journal on Interdisciplinary Humanities*, 2.1, 2010

8. Monica Ali, *Brick Lane* (London: Black Swan, 2003), 468

9. Rachel Lichtenstein, *On Brick Lane* (London: Hamish Hamilton, 2007), 40

10. Rachel Lichtenstein, *On Brick Lane*, 123

11. Ansar Ahmed Ullah and Steve Silver, *Commemorating Altab Ali Day 4 May: Against Racism and Fascism* (London: UNISON and Altab Ali Foundation, 2012), 6–11

12. Ketu H. Katrak, "Changing Traditions: South Asian Americans and Cultural/Communal Politics", *The Massachusetts Review*, 43.1, Spring 2002, 85

13. John Hutnyk, *Critique of Exotica: Music, Politics and the Culture Industry* (London: Pluto Press, 2000)

14. Asian Dub Foundation, "PKNB", *Facts and Fictions* (Nation Records, 1995)

15. Asian Dub Foundation, "TH9", *Facts and Fictions* (Nation Records, 1995)

16. Asian Dub Foundation, "TH9"

17. Virinder S. Kalra, John Hutnyk and Sanjay Sharma, "Re-Sounding (Anti)Racism, or Concordant Politics? Revolutionary Antecedents" in Sanjay Sharma, John Hutnyk and Ashwani Sharma (eds) *Dis-Orienting Rhythms: The Politics of the New Asian Dance Music* (London and New Jersey: Zed Books, 1996), 145

18. Sanjay Sharma, "Noisy Asians or Asian Noise" in Sanjay Sharma et al. (eds) *Dis-Orienting Rhythms*, 44

19. Asian Dub Foundation, "Rebel Warrior", *Facts and Fictions* (Nation Records, 1995)

20. Emdad Rahman, "My Friend Quddus Ali: 12 Years on", Cybersylhet.com, 14 June 2008. Accessed on 10 August 2017, available at: http://www.cybersylhet.com/index.php?option=com_content&view=article&id=86:my-friend-quddus-ali-12-years-on&catid=34:the-way-it-is&Itemid=61

21. Swami Baracus, "Stand Strong (Ode to Blair Peach)", *The Recipe* (2013)

22. Linton Kwesi Johnson, "Reggae Fi Peach", *Bass Culture* (Island Records, 1980)

23. Tony Mitchell, *Dario Fo: People's Court Jester* (London and New York: Bloomsbury, 1986), 259. I am grateful to Tony Mitchell for giving me more information about this production, and for helping me to track down its programme and other publicity material. His view, expressed to me in personal correspondence on 20 May 2015 that this production took 'a "scattershot" approach to UK political injustices' is very insightful, not least in giving me insight to the legacy of Blair Peach's murder in British politics.

24. http://www.tmg-uk.org/young-rebels-the-story-of-southall-youth-movement/ (Accessed on 10 August 2017)

25. http://www.tmg-uk.org/current-community-projects/southall-inspires/ (Accessed on 10 August 2017)

26. Rahila Gupta (ed.), *From Homebreakers to Jailbreakers: Southall Black Sisters* (London: Zed Books, 2003), 3

27. Julie Bindel, "I Wanted Him to Stop Hurting Me", *The Guardian*, 4 April 2007. Accessed on 10 August 2017, available at: https://www.theguardian.com/world/2007/apr/04/gender.ukcrime

28. Kiranjit Ahluwalia and Rahila Gupta, *Provoked: The Story of Kiranjit Ahluwalia* (New Delhi: HarperCollins, 2008), 112

29. Rahila Gupta (ed.), *From Homebreakers to Jailbreakers*, 3

30. Julie Bindel, "I Wanted Him to Stop Hurting Me", *The Guardian*

31. Southall Black Sisters, *Against the Grain* (London: Southall Black Sisters, 1990), 3

32. Marc Blake, *Writing the Comedy Movie* (London and New York: Bloomsbury, 2016), 219–20

33. Jonathan Moss, "'We Didn't Realise How Brave We Were at the Time': The 1968 Ford Sewing Machinists' Strike in Public and Personal Memory", *Oral History*, 43.1, Spring 2015, 46

34. Marc Blake, *Writing the Comedy Movie*, 220

35. Rahila Gupta (ed.), *From Homebreakers to Jailbreakers*, 263

36. Peter Glazer, *Radical Nostalgia*, 23

Chapter Three

Aloo-gobi, Mangoes and a Small Aubergine

Food, Foodscapes and Nostalgia

The 2013 film *Jadoo* by British Indian director Amit Gupta tells the story of the Chandana family – two brothers who used to work as chefs together until a falling out results in them opening competing restaurants across the road from each other on the Golden Mile in Leicester. Shalini, the daughter of the older brother, Raja, is engaged to Mark, a white British doctor. She wants her father and uncle to cook at her wedding, so persuades them to enter the 'Kings of Curry' competition, in the process of which they are reconciled with one another. When Raja finds out that his daughter is marrying a white man, his waiter Kirit consoles him (unnecessarily, as it turns out) by saying: 'As long as they have an appetite, God has blessed everyone with the potential to be Indian!'

Whether it is true or not that Indians have a distinctive appetite, it is the case that there is a particular appetite for Indian-food films, whether produced in India or in the diaspora. The former category includes *Ramji Londonwaley* and *Salaam Namaste* (both from 2005) and *Break ke Baad* (2010). The latter category includes the aforementioned *Jadoo*, as well as *The Hundred-Foot Journey* (2014) and *Today's Special* (2009). All of these films, in their different ways, connect their protagonists' culinary abilities to their success as immigrants.

Ramji Londonwaley, for example, tells the story of an unsophisticated and naïve village cook from Bihar, India, who arrives in London and in spite of numerous difficulties – during which time he has to live and work illegally, take part in a fake wedding and evade the clutches of British immigration officers – still manages to win a cooking competition which would allow him to live and work in Britain. The central characters of both *Salaam Namaste* and *Break ke Baad*, Nick and Abhay respectively, move to Australia and accidentally discover that they are very good chefs. Nick is a failed architect who loses his first job – that of designing a restaurant, only to be hired by his client to be the head chef of the same restaurant. Abhay is working as a taxi driver when he realizes that all his colleagues love his homemade lunches. He quits his job, starts up a lunch cart and apparently within no time at all, has found investors, allowing him to open his own restaurant. His brand of food is called, with appropriate symbolism, 'Ghar ka khana' or 'Food from Home'. *The Hundred-Foot Journey* tells the story of the Kadam family, who set up an Indian restaurant in rural France, and whose son Hassan eventually becomes a Michelin-starred chef. *Today's Special* tells the story of Samir, a second-generation Indian American, and the son of a restaurateur in the Little India of Jackson Heights, New York. When his father falls ill, Samir gives up his ambition of working as a chef in Paris and instead takes over his father's restaurant. With the help of Akbar, a chef-turned-taxi-driver – who can 'make a Murgh Masala that will haunt you like a lost love', Samir turns the failing restaurant around, in the process turning it into the best place for Indian food in the city, according to a review in the *New York Times*.

On the one hand, it is undeniably true that these films chart a narrative of neo-liberal success, a deeply problematic story of the model immigrant, which reinforces hierarchies of race, class, nationhood and empire in many ways. However, it is my contention that to read these stories simply in this manner would be to misunderstand their complexity, and to underestimate the ways in which they also tell the story of an imaginative recreation of a reality, a way of questioning hegemonic hierarchies in favour of new, imaginary value systems.

Kirit's claim in *Jadoo* that everyone has the potential to be Indian hides behind it the unspoken desire for validation. It also suggests the possibility that the representation of this desire is not supposed to be read literally. The key word here is surely 'potential'. In a world marked by hierarchies of value across symbols and objects of different cultures, this vision of everyone becoming Indian can be read as an attempt to recalibrate and subvert hegemonic hierarchies for a more egalitarian, imaginary reality. We are not expected to believe that all these people can so easily achieve such great success in the United States, Britain, France or Australia; rather, these films allow us to explore and exult in the possibility of a world where such inevitable validation might be a possibility, where the hierarchies that prevent such success might no longer exist.

These hierarchies can be seen explicitly in *The Hundred-Foot Journey*. The physical distance between Maison Mumbai and Le Saule Pleureur may only be slight, but the hundred feet of the title symbolizes a gulf between upscale French and devalued Indian cuisine. 'Curry is curry, is it not?' as the snobbish owner of Le Saule Pleureur, Madame Mallory, rhetorically asks. The eventual success of Maison Mumbai suggests an equivalence between Michelin-starred food such as 'frog's legs and escargot' on the one hand, and 'murgh masala with cashew-nuts and cardamom, and saag-aloo and daal' cooked with the 'secret family spices', on the other. Similarly, Samir is a Manhattan chef who never cooks Indian food at the start of *Today's Special*, but by the end he has achieved fame not because he is based in a fashionable Manhattan restaurant, but in an Indian restaurant in Jackson Heights. The lights of Manhattan may have signified for Samir's father the quintessentially American belief that 'any dream can come true', but Samir's success suggests the possibility that the gulf between Manhattan and Jackson Heights may not have to symbolize 'only his failure', in the words of Samir's mother.

The ease with which these hierarchies can be overcome, the ease with which Tandoori Palace and Maison Mumbai become the next big thing in rural France or New York, hints towards the magical. The magic in Akbar's cooking in *Today's Special* is alluded to from the very beginning. It can be seen in the serendipity of Samir's first meeting with Akbar in his taxi – this fantastical character who was once a chef in the greatest restaurant in Mumbai, but before that he ran an orphanage in Delhi, and before that he was in a circus. He knows the characteristics of all the spices – 'Cumin is a saucy wench'; 'Coriander seed – like a young girl walking through a lemon grove by the ocean'; 'Cloves and Cinnamon . . . like your crazy aunt and uncle, very noisy, very funny, very opinionated' and 'Turmeric – the golden spice that makes everything glow.' Through the magic of Akbar's hands, and his spice bowl, these characteristics are imparted into the food that he cooks in the kitchen of 'Tandoori Palace'.

If *Today's Special* hints at the magical qualities possessed by spices, Chitra Banerjee Divakaruni's novel *The Mistress of Spices* takes it much, much further. Tilo, the central character and the titular mistress, runs an Indian grocery shop in Oakland, California. From her shop, she deploys the magic of spices in order to solve the problems of the diasporic south Asian population. She tries to protect them from violence, helps them get work, find husbands and have babies, using her secret knowledge:

> I know their origins, and what their colours signify, and their smells. I can call each by the true-name it was given at the first, when earth split like skin and offered it up to the sky. Their heat runs in my blood. From *amchur* to *zafran*, they bow to my command. At a whisper they yield up to me their hidden properties, their magic powers.[1]

She is their confidante, their support. They come to her not just for 'cheap coarse rice, *dals* on sale, a small bottle of oil, maybe some *atta* to make *chapatis*,² and so on. They come to her because of her magic, magic that she wields to make the unfamiliar world around them less hostile, more comforting. The shop is a storehouse of memories from the homeland they have left behind:

> If you stand in the centre of this room and turn slowly around, you will be looking at every Indian spice that ever was – even the lost ones – gathered here upon the shelves of my store.³

Jadoo might be named after the restaurant that the Chandana brothers used to run together, but, as the start of the film makes clear, it is also a Hindi word for magic. The word also suggests (to me at least) the magic of memory. In most of northern India, for example, the word 'Jadoogher' – literally 'Magic House', refers to that most important site of memory, the museum.

Like museums, grocery shops and restaurants both have this magical ability to conjure up the forgotten, the left behind. The ability to cook, serve, and eat the food of one's home, the food of one's memories, can be used to dream up a world where one can be accepted for who one is, in the valuing of one's way of life as desirable, even though (or rather because) it deviates from hegemonic notions of mainstream and alternative, successful and unsuccessful, desirable and unwanted. As Chitra Banerjee Divakaruni puts it in *The Mistress of Spices,* this nostalgia for one's own food gives expression to the

> longing for the ways they chose to leave behind when they chose America. Their shame for that longing, like the bitter-slight aftertaste in the mouth when one has chewed *amlaki* to freshen the breath.⁴

In other words, food carries within it the possibility of memory – Hassan's mother in *The Hundred-Foot Journey* tells him, as she teaches him how to cook: 'You cook to make ghosts, spirits that live on in every ingredient.' It is this power that food has to evoke nostalgia for one's home that makes it so crucial to diasporic life. When Akbar first cooks in Samir's restaurant in *Today's Special*, his customers burst into tears at the taste. As one of his customers puts it: 'It's delicious. Reminds me of my grandmother cooking back home.'

Memory of food thus helps to reduce the distance between the home one has left behind and the home one is making for oneself in the here and now. This is 'the mysterious power of memory' that Walter Benjamin identified – 'the power to generate nearness'. Food, and the memory of food, is the ultimate symbol of home, the *sine qua non* of 'what is homey about home',⁵ to use Benjamin's wonderful phrase. Having one's food validated is therefore the same as having one's home validated, removing the necessity of having to choose between what one has left behind and what one has created in this new life. When, in its ability to reduce the distance between the here and now and the back there and then, memory is able to invoke the essential hominess of the lost home, it moves from the general rubric of memory to the particular specificity of nostalgia. Food – the taste and smell of it, the sense-experience and its memory – is particularly good at stimulating dreams of the home, as Marcel Proust and Salman Rushdie, in their very different ways, discovered long ago.[6]

JHUMPA LAHIRI AND THE PIRACY OF FOOD

On 1 April 2000, Indian American author Jhumpa Lahiri published an article called 'Indian Takeout' for the magazine *Food & Wine*. In it, she talks about her parents' piratical habits of smuggling food from India on their periodic visits from the diasporic life in the United States. She says:

> Throughout my childhood I was convinced my parents were running the modern equivalent of the ancient spice trade. They didn't exactly plunder this food; they bought it in the bazaars of Calcutta, where my mother was born and to which we returned as a family every couple of years. The destination was Rhode Island, where we lived, and where, back in the Seventies, Indian groceries were next to impossible to come by.[7]

The aim of this food piracy was, in Lahiri's own eloquent words, 'not only to satisfy our hunger but to make Calcutta seem not so very far away'. As in the cinematic examples I examine above, and as in Lahiri's own creations, the role played by food in evoking memories of home, memories that possess the 'great art of making things seem closer' cannot be overestimated.

Lahiri describes, with a longing that is almost painful, her memories of her family's 'food suitcase':

> an elegant relic from the Fifties with white stitching and brass latches that fastened shut with satisfying clicks. The inside was lined in peach-colored satin, had shirred lingerie pockets on three sides and was large enough to house a wardrobe for a long journey.

In the Lahiri family, however, it became 'a portable pantry', one that carried within it as many of the senses and sensations of home as possible. On every visit to Calcutta,

> My parents created lists on endless sheets of paper, and my father spent days in the bazaars, haggling and buying by the kilo. He always insisted on packing the goods himself, with the aura of a man possessed: bare chested, seated cross-legged on the floor, determined, above all, to make everything fit. He bound the Food Suitcase with enough rope to baffle Houdini and locked it up

with a little padlock, a scheme that succeeded in intimidating the most assiduous customs inspectors. Into the suitcase went an arsenal of lentils and every conceivable spice, wrapped in layers of cloth ripped from an old sari and stitched into individual packets.

The food suitcase is reminiscent of the Kadam-family spice case in *The Hundred-Foot Journey*. It used to belong to the mother of the family, but after she is killed in the fire that destroys everything the family has and forces their move to Europe, her son Hassan inherits it. For Hassan, the case and the spices within it evoke all his memories of his home, the lessons of food and life that his mother taught him, and simultaneously the possibility of success and acceptance in a hostile and unfamiliar new life in Europe.

It is not just the food suitcase or spice cases that has this apparently magical power to evoke memories. Lahiri's parents brought with them other objects that performed a similar role:

My parents also bought utensils: bowl-shaped iron *karhais,* which my mother still prefers to ordinary pots and pans, and the areca-nut cracker that's now somewhere in the back of the silverware drawer, and even a *boti,* a large curved blade that sits on the floor in Bengali kitchens and is used instead of handheld knives. The most sensational gadget we ever transported was a *sil-nora,* an ancient food processor of sorts, which consists of a massive clublike pestle and a slab the size, shape and weight of a headstone. Bewildered relatives shook their heads, and airport workers in both hemispheres must have cursed us.

Speaking on the BBC radio programme *A History of the World in 100 Objects*, chef, author and actress Madhur Jaffrey talks about a similar familial tradition:

It [grinding spices] is a fundamental act, both of cooking and of living, and living with a family and passing on, at least in India. When I left India, which was a long, long time ago, my mother gave me certain utensils to take with me and they were all heavy, I remember that. There was a wok, a grinding stone, and a huge mortar and pestle. So those are what I left with and I have all of them and I use my mortar and pestle to this day.[8]

Both Lahiri and Jaffrey make it clear that the value they and their families place on the objects is not dependent on practicality or even functionality. The mortar and pestle are heavy and difficult to transport across continents. They are not the most practical things to own for a presumably peripatetic diasporic subject. They are, however, supremely important because of their inherent, intrinsic hominess – the way they can make the gulf between the past and the present disappear.

In *Today's Special*, this role is played by Akbar's spice-mixing bowl. When Samir first calls Akbar in to help him with his father's restaurant, Akbar brings this bowl to mix the *masala* in. As he is preparing his first dishes in the Tandoori Palace restaurant, he teaches Samir the importance of spices:

> *Masala* is the soul of Indian food. And food is the soul of India. . . . Of course you can't really tell until it's in the oil. The *masala* is the symphony, and the oil is the orchestra. The greatest chef in the world taught me that . . . my mother.

The spice bowl is so much more than just a utensil. Later on, when Akbar leaves New York for Akron, Ohio, he leaves his spice bowl with Samir. Armed with this magical object, Samir is finally able to create the correct spice blend that will be able to reproduce the tastes of home and ensure the success of his family and their restaurant.

In *Jadoo*, this role is played by the Chandana-family recipe book, created by Raja and Jaggi's mother, and torn in two when the two brothers fight and start up separate restaurants. Their reconciliation and reunion is symbolized visually by the reuniting of the two halves of this treasured family heirloom. Even here, however, the nostalgia that makes these objects seem so valuable is much more complex than one would assume. The two brothers, even when cooking together, took responsibility for different parts of the kitchen – Raja cooked starters, and Jaggi the main courses. When they decided to separate, the book was torn up along these lines, with Raja getting the recipes for the starters, and Jaggi the mains. It should be borne in mind, however, that dividing a meal into a starter and a main course is a distinctly European, non–south Asian tradition. The nostalgia that makes these objects what they are, then, cannot be simplistically translated into an authentic image of the homeland – it is always already made more complicated by memories, experiences and values of diasporic life.

This importance of food-objects can also be seen in Jhumpa Lahiri's characters as well. Like her parents, Mrs Sen, the eponymous character from one of the short stories in *The Interpreter of Maladies*, has carried a *boti*, this distinctively Bengali blade, all the way from home. She uses it instead of a knife to chop vegetables, fish, and meat as she cooks her own food in her new American life:

> Instead of a knife she used a blade that curved like the prow of a Viking ship, sailing to battle in distant seas. The blade was hinged at one end to a narrow wooden base. The steel, more black than silver, lacked a uniform polish, and had a serrated crest, she told Eliot, for grating.[9]

The comparison with the bow of a ship is no accident – like Lahiri's parents' food suitcase, and like the Kadam-family spice case, the blade manages to symbolize at once both home and travel, evoking the memory of home, and the pain of homelessness at the same time. Mrs Sen is able to use the blade to re-create the food that she remembers from home, but in the process, her solitary life in her kitchen reminds her of all that she has left behind. As she uses her blade while looking after Eliot, she tells him about the community that it reminds her of, and the companionship that she has lost:

> 'Whenever there is a wedding in the family,' she told Eliot one day, 'or a large celebration of any kind, my mother sends out word in the evening for all the neighborhood women to bring blades just like this one, and then they sit in an enormous circle on the roof of our building, laughing and gossiping and slicing fifty kilos of vegetables through the night. . . . It is impossible to fall asleep those nights, listening to their chatter.' She paused to look at a pine tree framed by the living room window. 'Here, in this place where Mr Sen has brought me, I cannot sometimes sleep in so much silence.'[10]

Lahiri charts Mrs Sen's experiences in the United States through her relationship with food:

> One evening when Eliot's mother came to pick him up, Mrs. Sen served her a tuna croquette, explaining that it was really supposed to be made with a fish called bhetki. 'It is very frustrating,' Mrs Sen apologized, with an emphasis on the second syllable of the word. 'To live so close to the ocean and not to have so much fish.' In the summer, she said, she liked to go to a market by the beach. She added that while the fish there tasted nothing like the fish in India, at least it was fresh. . . . 'In the supermarket I can feed a cat thirty-two dinners from one of thirty-two tins, but I can never find a single fish I like, never a single.'[11]

The reference to cats will be repeated. When Mrs Sen is able to visit the fish market and asks for her fish to be cleaned but with the heads left on, the fishmonger assumes it is because she has a cat at home. The fish Mrs Sen buys might seem to her as quintessentially American (and therefore not Bengali) but by virtue of the same fish, she becomes racialized – and the bus driver asks Eliot to open a window to get rid of the smell of the fish, supposing that Mrs Sen – dressed in a sari and carrying a bag of fish, would not be able to speak English.

When she does manage to get the fish home, it is a prized delicacy, in spite of its Americanness, and Mrs Sen takes great care while cutting it so that she can make it last for three meals. The food produced, however, does not live up to the memories of the food eaten back at home. Mrs Sen announces that she is going to make 'a very tasty stew with fish and green bananas' but has to immediately qualify her ambitions: 'Only I will have to do without green bananas.'[12] American food, including the Bengali food produced using American ingredients, is, like American life, being constantly compared to Bengali food and Bengali life and found wanting. The few positive experiences for Mrs Sen, are only positive insofar as they approximate similar experiences back home. When Mr and Mrs Sen take Eliot to a restaurant to have clam cakes, Mrs Sen puts 'a good deal of Tabasco sauce and black pepper on hers'. Her question. 'Like pakoras, no?'[13] is not answered by either her husband or Eliot. Eliot has no knowledge of what pakoras are, and her husband apparently has little sympathy with her loneliness, her homesickness and her desperate longing for familiar tastes from home.

Mrs Sen is hardly the only one of Lahiri's characters to display this nostalgia for food. Ashima, from *The Namsake*, is first seen trying to satisfy a craving for Bengali street food:

> On a sticky August evening two weeks before her due date, Ashima Ganguli stands in the kitchen of a Central Square apartment, combining Rice Krispies and Planters peanuts and chopped red onion in a bowl. She adds salt, lemon juice, thin slices of green chili pepper, wishing there were mustard oil to pour into the mix. Ashima has been consuming this concoction throughout her pregnancy, a humble approximation of the snack sold for pennies on Calcutta sidewalks and on railway platforms throughout India, spilling from newspaper cones.[14]

From the very beginning of the narrative, Ashima's identity is bound up with the food she cooks. The process of getting to know her husband is marked out through the meals she cooks for him:

> Eight thousand miles away in Cambridge, she has come to know him. In the evenings she cooks for him, hoping to please, with the unrationed, remarkably unblemished, sugar, flour, rice, and salt she had written about to her mother in her very first letter home. By now she has learned that her husband likes his food on the salty side, that his favourite thing about lamb curry is the potatoes, and that he likes to finish his dinner with a small final helping of rice and dal.[15]

Ashima's life in the United States and the way she negotiates the conflict between her American and Indian identities is also depicted through her attitudes towards food. At her son Gogol's birthday party, she is effortlessly able to cook for forty guests:

> As usual, his mother cooks for days beforehand, cramming the refrigerator with stacks of foil-covered trays. She makes sure to prepare his favourite things: lamb curry with lots of potatoes, luchis, thick channa dal with swollen brown raisins, pineapple chutney, sandeshes molded out of saffron-tinted ri-

cotta cheese. All this is less stressful to her than the task of feeding a handful of American children, half of whom always claim they are allergic to milk; all of whom refuse to eat the crusts of their bread.[16]

The overwhelming, overflowing quantities of Indian food cooked and consumed at numerous Indian parties is contrasted with the small culinary concessions she has to make to the American way of life and her children's demands:

> In the supermarket they let Gogol fill the cart with items that he and Sonia, but not they, consume: individually wrapped slices of cheese, mayonnaise, tuna fish, hot dogs. For Gogol's lunches they stand at the deli to buy cold cuts, and in the mornings Ashima makes sandwiches with bologna or roast beef. At his insistence, she concedes and makes him an American dinner once a week as a treat, Shake 'n Bake chicken or Hamburger Helper prepared with ground lamb.[17]

By living out the contradictions of American and Indian influences, Ashima is able to embody a particularly subtle and complex form of integration – the process through which the immigrant is able to construct a distinctively diasporic way of life. One of the many axes along which the narrative of *The Namesake* can be plotted is Ashima's journey from alien immigrant to diasporic statelessness. At the start of her time in America, in a particularly poignant section, Ashima compares her immigrant status to that of pregnancy:

> Though no longer pregnant, she continues, at times, to mix Rice Krispies and peanuts and onions in a bowl. For being a foreigner, Ashima is beginning to realize, is a sort of lifelong pregnancy – a perpetual wait, a constant burden, a continuous feeling out of sorts. It is an ongoing responsibility, a parenthesis in what had once been ordinary life, only to discover that that previous life has vanished, replaced by something more complicated and demanding. Like pregnancy, being a foreigner, Ashima believes, is something that elicits the same curiosity from strangers, the same combination of pity and respect.[18]

Almost in spite of herself, however, Ashima has begun to adjust and is soon in a position to help other immigrants on their journey to diaspora. Again, this advice is presented in terms of food and cooking:

> The wives, homesick and bewildered, turn to Ashima for recipes and advice, and she tells them about the carp that's sold in Chinatown, that it's possible to make halwa from Cream of Wheat. The families drop by one another's homes on Sunday afternoons. They drink tea with sugar and evaporated milk and eat shrimp cutlets fried in saucepans.[19]

Ashima does indeed produce hybrid cuisine: from Indian street food with Rice Krispies, to Bengali sweets with ricotta cheese. However, this hybridity is marked as a success or failure only in terms of how close it can get Ashima to her homeland in Calcutta. Hybridity is never Ashima's goal; it is an unintended by-product of her desire to replicate the food of her past in her present. The memory of this food is, once again, able to make the past and present seem closer than it actually is. By the end of the novel, when Ashima is able to fully inhabit her diasporic subjecthood, she has transcended the gap between India and America, and managed to bend geography to suit her own life:

> Ashima has decided to spend six months of her life in India, six months in the States. It is a solitary, somewhat premature version of the future she and her husband had planned when he was alive. . . . In spring and summer she will return to the Northeast, dividing her time among her son, her daughter, and her close Bengali friends. True to the meaning of her name, she will be without borders, without a home of her own, a resident everywhere and nowhere.[20]

Ashima might be a more successful immigrant than Mrs Sen – she is certainly presented as more adaptable and given more agency in terms of the ability to create a life for herself, but this life is just as centred around food, food-memories, and the desire to re-create those memories in the present. When Ashima's son Gogol brings a girlfriend back home for the first time, Ashima, entirely characteristically, welcomes her through cooking an elaborate meal:

> Along with the samosas, there are breaded chicken cutlets, chickpeas with tamarind sauce, lamb biryani, chutney made with tomatoes from the garden. It is a meal he knows it has taken his mother over a day to prepare.[21]

As if this was not enough, she offers 'to pack them some extra cutlets and samosas for the road', and before they leave 'there is tea, and bowls of payesh made in honour of his birthday'.[22]

Food in the diaspora continues to symbolize community, and one can be nostalgic for the same community in the way one is nostalgic for the home that has been left behind. As an adult, Gogol cannot help comparing the fashionable dinner parties his girlfriend Max's parents have to the much less organized ones his parents had when he was a child:

> How different they are from his own parents' parties, cheerfully unruly evenings to which there were never fewer than thirty people invited, small children in tow. Fish and meat served side by side, so many courses that people had to eat in shifts, the food still in the pans they were cooked in crowding the table. They sat where they could, in the different rooms of the house, half the people having finished before the other half began.[23]

Her hybrid food may help to make her own life limitless; she may well have apparently come to terms with her diasporic identity, but the nostalgia for the food of her memories remains strong. When she thinks of returning to live in Calcutta, her thoughts still turn to the culinary differences between her life in India and her life in America:

> She will return to a world where she will not single-handedly throw parties for dozens of people. She will not have to go to the trouble of making yogurt from half-and-half and sandesh from ricotta cheese. She will not have to make her own croquettes. They will be available to her from restaurants, brought up to the flat by servants, bearing a taste that after all these years she has still not quite managed, to her entire satisfaction, to replicate.[24]

For both Mrs Sen and Ashima, then, what marks their relationship with the food they produce and consume is not a sense of hybridity – a desire to use available ingredients in a new manner to create new dishes – but rather a deep-felt sense of nostalgia for the food and the life they left behind, and a desire to use the best of available ingredients to approximate the tastes from home, with the acceptance that the actual tastes may be forever irreproducible.

NOSTALGIA AND ITS DISCONTENTS – THE GENDERED NATURE OF FOOD PRODUCTION

The kind of nostalgia for food that I have discussed above has attracted criticism from a number of different quarters. Anita Mannur, for example, has argued with reference to Mrs Sen that her 'obsessive need to prepare a fully Bengali dinner must be read in light of her position as an immigrant woman wedded into a system of Bengali heterosexual patriarchy.'[25] For Mannur, this nostalgic re-creation is a reactionary force that is 'blind in some ways to the structural inequities and forms of difference that might structure the past.'[26] In other words, Mannur believes nostalgia is a necessarily backward-looking (in all senses of the word) gesture because it 'can lead to the creation of distorted fictions, which imagines cuisines as discrete, immutable, and coherent expressions of unfaltering national essences.'[27] For Mannur, then, the nostalgia of the immigrant communities leads them to become 'invested in an image of the homeland as an unchanging and enduring cultural essence and are often singular about the ontological coherency of their national cuisines, despite the fact that memories are fragmentary [and] partial.'[28]

In her suspicion of Mrs Sen's or Ashima's attachment to food from the homelands, Mannur can be said to be replicating the scholar from Sujata Bhatt's poem 'Chutney':

> The diaspora women who thought Culture
> meant being able to create
> a perfect mango chutney in New Jersey
> were scorned by the visiting scholar[29]

This is doubly ironic because Mannur begins her book by quoting from this poem but does not seem to have recognized that the poet's sympathies are much more with the 'diaspora women' than with the 'visiting scholar' and her scorn.

This scorn is hardly limited to scholars either. One of the commonest targets for affectionate mocking in the ground-breaking British Asian sketch show *Goodness Gracious Me* is the figure of the Indian mother. She is obsessed with feeding people, sometimes literally at gunpoint; she is equally obsessed with her children's (usually her son's) success at everything from education and his career, to his sexual prowess; and finally, she is obsessed with thrift – insisting that there is no point buying anything because she 'can make it at home for nothing.' She recites a list of fairly random ingredients in order to be able to reproduce the object in question, and her lists always end with 'and a small aubergine'. These Indian mothers would, one senses, understand only too well the importance of making 'a perfect mango chutney'.

If the mocking in *Goodness Gracious Me* is mostly kind, it is arguably much less so in the work of British Indian film director Gurinder Chadha. A useful example is her 2002 film *Bend It Like Beckham*. This charts the attempts of Jess (Parminder Nagra), a Londoner from a diasporic Sikh family, to escape from parental pressures to get married and become a solicitor in order to be able to follow her dream and become a footballer. Jess's family represents an interestingly hybridized identity – they are immigrants from India via East Africa; they live near Heathrow Airport, the frequent overflying planes visually demonstrating their status as living in the margins of state and nationhood. Through their language, clothing and food, Jess and her family are identified as part of a characteristically London-ized Sikh population. However, this hybridity is not without its own set of hierarchies. Throughout the film, having to cook Indian food is represented as the traditional life that Jess needs to escape from: 'Indian girls aren't supposed to play football', as Jess explains to her teammates. Jess's abilities at that quintessentially British game, football, are what allow her to transcend a particularly racialized domesticity – as the tagline for the film puts it, 'Who wants to cook Aloo Gobi, when you can bend a ball like Beckham?' Jess's mother, Mrs Bhamra (Shaheen Khan) provides the example of the life that Jess does not want to lead – the life of Indian domesticity, which is presented as uniquely oppressive and patriarchal. In response to this patriarchally enforced set of hierarchies, Jess sets up hierarchies of her own, ones that the audience is actively encouraged to accept. As Jess puts it, 'Everyone can make Aloo Gobi, but how many people can bend a ball like Beckham'. As in the tagline quoted above, the act of cooking Indian food is presented as necessarily less important, and less skilled, than being able to play football. Indeed, if we, the audience were to be in any doubt of the oppressive nature of cookery, we are shown how Jess's body is physically scarred as a result of a childhood cooking accident.

It should also be noted that while Jess's actions (and her football team the Hounslow Harriers as a whole) are presented as liberating, this does not stop Jess from judging other women's behaviour. She consistently sets herself, in deceiving her parents and playing football, as different from, and better than, her friends who are 'sleeping around with boys . . . [they] aren't going to end up marrying'. As Jess is the character with whom the audience is encouraged to identify the most, this does result in a clear message that Jess's rebellion is praiseworthy because she does not challenge those other, perhaps more serious gendered norms of behaviour having to do with sexual activity.

What is more relevant for my purposes here, however, is that Jess's rebellion consistently takes place at the expense of her mother, and of the other older members of the community. Older Punjabi women are presented as the object of humour, to be mocked because of their inability or unwillingness to allow their daughters to follow their dreams. Near the climax of the film, the racialized nature of this patriarchy is made even more obvious as Jess prepares to take a free-kick to win the match for her team. In her imagination, the line of defenders is transformed into a line of Indian women who have all been instrumental in stopping her from playing football. Notably, when she does get permission from her family to go and play, it comes from her father (Anupam Kher) and not her mother. It is her father who allows her to go and play football on her sister's wedding day, and it is her father again who allows her to go to the United States to become a professional footballer. His recognition of her footballing talents, matched with his realization of his own mistakes in allowing racism to stop him from playing cricket, allows him to arrive at an understanding that his wife, her mother, is denied. At the very end, even after her husband's permission has rendered her own objections irrelevant, Mrs Bhamra is still insisting on the importance of food: 'At least I have taught her full Punjabi dinner, the rest is up to God.' And both Jess and her father are still laughing at her for it.

The fact that Jess has to fight her family to be able to play is repeatedly put down to her Indianness. To be fair, the film does present evidence of Western patriarchy as well, in the form of Jess's best friend Jules's mother (Juliet Stevenson) who is equally unhappy at having a football-playing daughter (Keira Knightley). However, the similarities only go so far. When Jules's mother accepts her daughter's passion, this acceptance is shown through her attempts to learn the offside rule using bottles of olive oil, vinegar and teriyaki sauce – a level of acceptance that Mrs Bhamra is constantly and consistently denied.

The trope of the mockable Indian mother is a particularly common one and, I would argue, a particularly pernicious staple of British Asian comedy. As Christine Geraghty has argued with reference to another of Gurinder Chadha's mothers – Mrs Bakshi in *Bride and Prejudice*:

> The claustrophobia, femininity, and warmth of family life is reinforced not just by the emphasis on the family in Bollywood films but also by references to the stereotype of the Indian family used as the basis of comedy in BBC radio/television programs. This affects, in particular, the role of Mrs. Bennet/Bakshi as the Indian mother who is obsessed with marrying off her daughters and defending the family's social status.[30]

I am not, of course, denying that the family is one of the most significant institutions of patriarchy. It would be foolish to deny the sexist nature of housework, or to deny that the burden of cooking falls disproportionately on women. It is, however, true that there is something problematic in the suggestion that Indian domesticity and the nostalgia for home-cooked food that fuels it, in and of itself, represents a more pernicious form of patriarchy than usual. This belief that nostalgia reinforces rather than challenges existing hierarchies – whether gendered, racial, regional or national – helps to explain the scorn that Sujata Bhatt articulates and that films like *Bend It Like Beckham* epitomize. The implication that 'cooking full Punjabi dinner' is necessarily and inevitably an example of patriarchal oppression robs women like Mrs Bhamra of their agency – their desire and their ability to nostalgically recreate the food and the life of their homelands. Without glossing over the sexism inherent in domestic work for one minute, I think there also needs to be a recognition of the ways in which food production, food consumption, and the nostalgia that can be identified in both can be a way of constructing, preserving, and above all valuing, a matrilineal heritage which can, under certain circumstances, be hugely valuable in allowing women of different generations to exercise their own agency.

'THE OLD SECRETS YOUR MOTHER'S MOTHERS KNEW': NOSTALGIA FOR FOOD AND A MATRILINEAL INHERITANCE

If Mrs Bhamra and Mrs Bakshi represent the stereotype of the ridiculous Indian mother, whose agency is undermined through the politics of the narrator, then an alternative can be found in another of Gurinder Chadha's Indian mothers – Mrs Sethi from *It's a Wonderful Afterlife*. Mrs Sethi is a widow living in Southall who is trying and failing to find a match for her daughter Roopi. Angered by the ways in which her community is judging her daughter by their own conventional, patriarchal standards, Mrs Sethi takes revenge by murdering everyone who has insulted her daughter. Turning to the apparent tools of patriarchy – cooking instruments and utensils – she murders her victims one after another – the first man is force-fed to death, the second victim is hit on the head with a rolling pin, the third is suffocated with *chapatti* dough, while the fourth is stabbed with a kebab skewer. When her victims come back to haunt her, however, she is unrepentant, making it clear that in murdering them, she was avenging the patriarchal oppression that she recognized was affecting her daughter's life:

> That's why I did it. You said my daughter is too fat for you. And you said she is too ugly for your cousin's sister's son. And you! You said she's not good enough for your nephew Tej. So you broke her engagement, made some mischief and broke her heart. You all rejected her without even knowing her. You can't be nice to her even in death. She is all I can ask for in a daughter. She is loving, dutiful, considerate – and still no one will have her. She deserves to have a good husband and a good family. And you all got what you deserve.

Mrs Sethi is able to directly and explicitly weaponize food – using her nostalgic attachment to her own food as a tool to fight the patriarchal oppression that she and her daughter are experiencing. Moreover, this is not the only example of food being used as a weapon in this film, either. When Roopi's best friend, Linda, is humiliated by her fiancé at their engagement party, there ensues a parody of the famous prom scene from *Carrie*. Instead of pig's blood, Linda is covered in tomato chutney, and she then uses her telekinesis to turn all the food into weapons. Food and utensils fly through the air, hitting all the guests indiscriminately, as (much like Carrie herself) Linda's rage against patriarchy becomes almost uncontrollable. Reviews[31] of this sequence have suggested that this parody is trivializing and nonsensical. It may well be a send-up, but I think the underlying point about the possibility of using an affective attachment to food to express rather than undermine female agency is deeply serious.

Jadoo similarly depicts the possibilities of female agency that exist within the affect of food nostalgia. Shalini, in collaboration with her aunt, works to bring the feuding families together. Through it all, she strategically deploys the family memories of her grandmother as a way to force her father and her uncle to talk to each other. The connection between Shalini and her grandmother, which is what helps her to reunite her family, is presented as a connection of taste:

> The recipe for the cauliflower took my grandmother twenty years to get right. I tasted it and told her it was perfect. I was six and it is one of my happiest memories.

The same *aloo-gobi* dish that in *Bend It Like Beckham* serves as a symbol of patriarchal oppression is, here, a symbol of a distinctively matrilineal connection. Notably, when her father, a professional chef, tries to recreate this dish, he fails. 'It's not the same, is it?' he asks, and Shalini agrees. It takes the granddaughter, rather than the son, to remember that the grandmother's recipe 'had a little mango powder, *amchur*', in it. It is this connection, this knowledge of food and family recipes, this appreciation of the importance of food-memories that connects grandmother and granddaughter and allows for the survival of the family as a harmonious unit. Raja compliments Shalini on her exceptional 'memory and taste' – as if the two are the same, which, in a way they are. As an experienced chef, Raja knows only too well the importance of interpreting a recipe: 'What is a pinch of *zeera*? God has made all of our hands and hearts different' – and it is Shalini's ability to identify and value the differences between dishes that marks her out as a true inheritor of her grandmother's skills.

The importance of hands and hearts is commented on in *The Mistress of Spices* as well. The familiar Bengali phrase '*hater gun*'[32] (literally 'quality of one's hands'), originally referring to the subjective qualities of cooking, is used by Chitra Banerjee Divakaruni to refer to the magic that the mistresses wield – 'the hands that call power out of the spices'. Tilo uses her hands to try to insulate her clients from the hostile world they live in. She tries to rescue Lalita from a joyless marriage to an alcoholic husband, to protect Jagjit from being bullied at school, to help bring Manu and Daksha closer to their parents and in-laws. The spices have the magic, but it is only Tilo who is allowed to exert control over them.

Behind the magical realism of Banerjee Divakaruni's novel, I think, is the alternative value system that nostalgia can help to create. The magic that she describes is the magic of the mundane, the elevation of the ordinary, the neglected, into something valuable. This is what the spices in her store represent:

> Most ordinary, for that is the nature of deepest magic. Deepest magic which lies at the heart of our everyday lives, flickering fire, if only we had the eyes to see.[33]

Like the '*hater gun*', this magic has a definite gendered angle, and Tilo, like Ashima, represents the importance of female companionship, the appreciation of female solidarity – the need for women to share stories and secrets, survival strategies with which to combat the hostility of both patriarchy and diaspora. This is the true magic of spices – knowledge, memories, experiences, handed down from generation to generation, a true matrilineal heritage – 'the old secrets your mother's mothers knew'.[34]

Even when one is deprived of this female support network, one can still use food nostalgia as resistance. I have written above of the longing that Jhumpa Lahiri's Mrs Sen expresses for fish, and how her busy husband is unable to understand either her need for fish or the loneliness that provokes it. Mr Sen insists that she needs to learn how to drive because afterwards, 'everything will improve'. She, however, is not so sure: 'Could I drive all the way to Calcutta? How long would that take, Eliot? Ten thousand miles, at fifty miles per hour?'[35] His solution is the logical, rational one because he is not able to understand that Mrs Sen's attachment to food has nothing to do with logic or reason.

At the start of the story, Mrs Sen orders fish from the market, and Mr Sen goes to pick it up. Then as he gets busier, he thinks she should be able to make do with 'the chicken in the freezer'.[36] Later, she will take Eliot on the bus, in an attempt to assert her own independence. At the end, receiving little or no help from her husband, she will drive Eliot there, and in the process, crash the car. Like the impractical heavy utensils which Lahiri's parents brought all the way from India, Mrs Sen's attachment to whole fish is an impediment for Mr Sen and his meetings and office hours. It is inconvenient, impractical, irrational – and therefore a marker of Mrs Sen's own resistance against the patriarchy that prizes her husband's decision to move to America, and everyone's assumption that she would necessarily be happy in her new life. In maintaining her attachment to fish, Mrs Sen is also maintaining her attachment to the life she has left behind:

> Mrs. Sen said she had grown up eating fish twice a day. She added that in Calcutta people eat fish first thing in the morning, last thing before bed, as a snack after school if they were lucky. They ate the tail, the eggs, even the head. It was available in any market, at any hour, from dawn until midnight. 'All you have to do is leave the house and walk a bit, and there you are.'[37]

It is the choice of cooking and eating fish, much more than the practical, rational choice of learning how to drive, that helps to eliminate the distance between the American supermarkets where she cannot get the things she wants and the Calcutta markets of her memory. Like the blade I discussed above, the fish represents home, community, a connection that is so valued precisely because it is absent. It is also, not incidentally, a specifically female memory and experience and, as such, it represents an imaginative fightback against patriarchal rationality. The blade, and the Bengali fish that it cuts in Calcutta, represents female community, female solidarity against patriarchal oppression. The blade, and the American fish that it cuts in America, represents the lack of this female support network, as Mrs Sen has been removed from the female community that she belongs in through the patriarchal-capitalist forces of marriage, and (male) employment-related migration.

While it is true that processes of food production and consumption can often be marked by a nostalgia that is sometimes matrilineal in origin and therefore coded as female, this is certainly not always the case. If the food-nostalgia of Tilo, Mrs Sen and Mrs Bhambra can be read as resisting both the patriarchy of the diasporic family and the patriarchy of the white Euro-American outside world, this should not negate the similar food-nostalgia of Samir, Akbar, or the Chandana brothers, which demonstrates the fact that food-nostalgia does not have to be gendered at all.

If Mr Sen does not seem to experience nostalgia for fish in the way his wife does, the same cannot be said for Ashok Ganguly in *The Namesake*. On the contrary, fish features in the rituals of everyday life in the whole Ganguly family. As Gogol grows up, his development is presented in culinary terms:

> Gogol has already been taught to eat on his own with his fingers, not to let the food stain the skin of his palm. He has learned to suck the marrow from lamb, to extract the bones from fish.[38]

Like Mrs Sen, Ashima also takes great care to replicate the food of her homeland as much as possible, but, like Mrs Sen and like Lahiri's parents and their food suitcase, it does not compensate for the aura of food brought back from India. Like Lahiri's parents, Ashok and Ashima are pirates. After every visit to India, 'the chanachur is poured into Tupperware and the smuggled mangoes eaten for breakfast with cereal and tea'.[39]

Nostalgia for mangoes comes close to matching the nostalgia for fish and is equally capable of being mobilized as resistance. Illicitly eating contraband mangoes in America is, in and of itself, an act of rebellion against the regulations governing the ways in which space can and cannot be used. An even more direct example of weaponizing nostalgia can be seen in 'Sunshowers', a 2004 single by British Tamil musician M.I.A., from her debut album *Arular* (2005). Like much of M.I.A.'s music, 'Sunshowers' is an explicitly political song:

> 'Sunshowers' is about how in the news the world is being divided into good and evil with this axis of evil and terrorism thing, so the song is asking how can we talk about gun culture and other issues while Blair is preaching that if someone hits us, we should hit back twice as hard.[40]

A reference in the lyrics to the PLO and M.I.A.'s refusal to censor it meant 'Sunshowers' was banned by MTV, demonstrating the seriousness of the political challenge that her music represents. What is particularly interesting for my purposes here is that M.I.A explicitly connects the radicalism of the PLO to a much simpler, perhaps more mundane, act of consuming food: 'I salt and pepper my mango shoot spit out the window . . . / Like P.L.O. I won't surrendo.'[41] The video is directed by Rajesh Touchriver and shot in the lush green jungles of south India – a perfect backdrop to a nostalgia for an almost clichéd south Asian childhood. M.I.A. is surrounded by girls and young women – visually suggesting the importance of a specifically female community. To quote from another of her songs, nostalgia for a childhood spent on tree tops eating mangoes can, it seems, help to create an environment where 'Bad girls do it well'.[42] 'Doing my thing', M.I.A. seems to suggest, can unite marginalized groups fighting against oppression, whether it is a Sri Lankan child trying to reclaim an idyllic childhood not blighted by civil war, or oppressed Palestinian peoples waging a violent insurrection to try to achieve national independence. Girls sitting in trees, eating mangoes and spitting, can be thought of as somehow equivalent to international insurgent warfare.

M.I.A. continues this connection between food-nostalgia and political resistance in a later single, 'Mango Pickle Down River' which she produced in collaboration with the Indigenous Australian group The Wilcannia Mob. According to the lyrics of the song, acting 'kinda strange' possesses the same radical force as the children who sit in the trees of 'Sunshowers' and eat mangoes. Here, the subversive force comes, as the title of the song suggests, from a similarly nostalgic invocation of 'fish and mango pickle'.[43] Acting 'kinda strange' is, in a normatively regulated world, in and of itself an act of resistance, and one that, for M.I.A., is partly constituted by overturning hierarchies of mainstream and alternative memories, experiences, tastes and preferences. On the face of it, Tilo, Samir, Akbar, Mrs Sen, Ashima and M.I.A.'s international community of rebel children have little in common – but they actually all know one crucial fact: the memories of food from one's past are a powerful thing, and can be put to use in the present to do important and serious political work.

MEMORIES OF FOOD

Madhur Jaffrey talks about the importance of taste-memories in her food-related memoir, *Climbing the Mango Trees*. Even though she is probably most famous around the world as a chef, she still connects her culinary ability to her decision to leave India and become a diasporic subject:

> When I left India to study in England, I could not cook at all but my palette had already recorded millions of flavours. From cumin to ginger, they were all in my head, waiting to be called to service.[44]

Like M.I.A, Jaffrey's taste-memories too are dominated by that specific experience familiar to so many who have had a south Asian childhood – mangoes with spices. Jaffrey remembers that she, along with her siblings and cousins,

> like flocks of hungry birds, attacked the mangoes when they were still green and sour. As grown-ups snored through the hot afternoons in rooms cooled with wetted, sweet-smelling, vetiver curtains, the unsupervised children were on every branch of every mango tree armed with a ground mixture of salt, pepper, red chilies and roasted cumin. The older children on the higher branches peeled and sliced the mangoes with penknives and passed the slices down to the smaller fry on the lower branches. We dipped the slices into our spice mixture and ate; as our mouths tingled, we felt initiated into the world of grown-ups.[45]

Again, like the examples I have discussed above, Jaffrey uses food-nostalgia to reinforce the memory of all sorts of rebellions – from childhood resistance against adult regulation to the vindication of powerful women who live on in her memories – the 'tiny, sweet melons posted to us from Lucknow by my father's second-youngest sister, Saran Bhua'[46]; the *daulat-ki-chaat*, a winter specialty made by 'the Lady in White' who was, even by then 'one of the few women left in the whole city of Delhi who can make this'[47] and Jaffrey's grandmother whose 'homemade lime pickle . . . Black with age and with black pepper, cloves and cardamom' which was a 'magic potion' that helped relieve nausea on the 'hairpin bends' along the road to the Himalayan hill-station of Simla.[48]

Most of all, though, is the figure of her mother, who would pass on the utensils that Jaffrey carried around with her throughout her diasporic life. Her mother, who, until her dying day, had saved with pride 'several silver medals she had won in school for top scholastic honours' but who was forced to leave at the end of her primary education because 'it was not thought necessary for girls to study too long'.[49] Her mother, Bauwa, cooked 'all the traditional Hindu festival foods' like *papris* and *puas*, 'not just ordinary things but extraordinary creations'.[50] And she would pass on her 'desire to excel' to her children through the food she fed them:

> Every now and then, Bauwa would pop a bit of food from her plate into our mouths. Perhaps at that witching hour, when it was neither night nor day, my mother was quietly passing on an ancient tradition from her generation to ours.[51]

Climbing the Mango Trees is not the only example of a cross between a recipe book and a food memoir, either. In 2006, Sandeepa Mukherjee Datta launched a blog called *Bong Mom's Cookbook*, which led to a book of the same name, published in 2013. In a manner very similar to Jaffrey's book, Mukherjee Datta uses both her blog and her book to explicitly valorize cooking as an important matrilineal legacy. In her blog, for example, she discusses the influence the women in her family have had on her:

> I start this blog as an acknowledgement to my Ma, Dida, mom-in-law and all the mashis-pishis, kakimas-jethimas who fed me well, fed me good all my years in India. This will be a humble collection of Bengali recipes and the food I cook representing Bengali Cuisine as I know it. . . . I want to pass on my legacy of Bengali food to my two little daughters and all the other little ones out there who growing up in a foreign land will find a way to connect to their Bangla roots through the smell and taste of Bangla cuisine.[52]

She writes very movingly about her mother's cooking, validating its importance and desirability when compared with other, more normatively valuable forms of cooking and eating:

> My Mother's forte is the simple unassuming everyday Bengali meal which she cooks everyday. Even if there is two vegetables, a dal, a fish curry; all in their cold corning ware whites stacked up in the refrigerator, she cooks. I shout at her asking her to stay away from the kitchen, to relax; but at the end of the day, there is always a pyrex bowl resting on the counter, still warm and smelling better than Dior. And it doesn't even contain goat cheese. Or heavy cream. Or even a hint of saffron. But there is a very good *Methi Begun* – fenugreek greens cooked with eggplant. And my Mother made it. And that is all that matters.[53]

This sense comes through in her book as well, where she again acknowledges the matrilineal inheritance that is part of her birth-right:

> I gather their recipes from my mother, my husband's mother, a friend's mother – in short, all Bong motherhood – and re-create them in my far off kitchen, along with the stories and memories they bring with them. . . . This is my story, but it might well be yours and maybe even yours.[54]

The comments on her blog posts from her readers suggest that this belief is not misplaced. Shayma writes:

> I love the concept of writing smthg down which you can pass on to your daughters. I started my blog a few weeks ago bec I had learnt how to cook from the women in my family, but unfortunately, they never wrote anything down. I think it's a lovely idea to document everything for your children. This winter when I am in Karachi, I hope to get my mother-in-law's recipes which she has scrawled in a notebook.[55]

Sumana, another reader, writes:

> thank you for taking us back to familiar scents and tastes and sharing our heritage so we won't have to wait for mashis and pishis and kakimas and jethimas to give us a taste of home[56]

Sumana is referring to the various Bengali words to describe the different female relations in an extended family and is therefore setting up a similarly powerfully matrilineal inheritance that can be valued on its own terms. This set of inherited memories, experiences, and sensations possess the same magical quality that I have been describing throughout this chapter, the 'great art of making things seem closer':

> I get solace in cooking, the comfort of the spices sputtering in the oil, the waft of the jeera & tejpata as they turn brown, the rich yellow of my musuri'r dal gives me peace, makes me calm and in this far off land makes me connect to my home.[57]

Similarly, an anonymous contributor to the blog writes that 'the fragrances and flavours of Indian cooking are just one way of connecting with home'[58] while Marie Rose says that she 'too grew up in Kolkata' and therefore is 'very sentimental about Bengali food and street food'.[59] Mita writes that:

> I grew up in Orissa in a bangali household and now I'm a bit of a wanderer based in UK with two boys, a husband and a dog. Cooking bangali seems to calm the soul at the end of a long day.[60]

Ketu Katrak, among others, has noted how nostalgic culinary narratives can help to manage memories of the 'homeland', and through acts of reading and eating, one can perform imaginary acts of returning. Of her own journeys, she writes:

> my own memorybanks about food overflowed only after I left India to come to the United States as a graduate student. The disinterest in food that I had felt during my childhood years was transformed into a new kind of need for that food as an essential connection with home. I longed for my native food as I dealt with my dislocation from the throbbing Bombay metropolis.[61]

For Mukherjee Datta, Katrak, and for so many women, the act of buying and cooking traditional food is a common way of reconnecting with one's 'homeland', as this extract from *Bong Mom's Cookbook* demonstrates:

> When the parents are here we eat a lot of fish. Almost everyday. Mostly it is the sweet water familiar fish from back home which we get from our Bangladeshi grocers. *Rui, Ilish, Koi, Pabda*. . . . The fish feeds my nostalgia perfectly and makes my Mother think a six month stay in the US is not exactly same as living in Mars. At least '*maach paoa jaay*' [fish is available]. . . . Once my parents have gone back to their own surround where they can buy fresh fish everyday and watch Star Jalsa, my daughters and husband revert back in auto-pilot to filet of Tilapia and Salmon from the American Superstores. None of them care for the fish my parents and I had happily devoured. A name

dropping of *Rui*, *Ilish* or *Koi* does not light up their eyes or palate. I try to live in the past waiting for next year.[62]

The proliferation of readers' comments on this post and throughout the blog suggests that Mukherjee Datta is certainly not alone in her affective relationship with food. As Dayeeta Roy writes, half in Bengali and half in English: 'Sandeepa, this cooking really reminds me of home, childhood days. You put the rice on, I'm on my way.'[63]

Mukherjee Datta's blog and book thus helps to create the female-centred community that Mrs Sen so sorely lacked in her new life in the United States. The interactions between author and readers through the comments on the blog demonstrate the way food can help to provide support and solace that is so comforting in an unfamiliar, and often unfriendly, world.

This ability that food has to create and valorize a distinctively female community, a prized female lineage and tradition, is also referred to in Anneeka Ludhra's cookbook *Dadima's: Celebrating Grandmother's Wisdom through Indian Cooking*. As Ludhra writes in her introduction:

> This book is about traditional Indian recipes, which were shared with me over a period of time by very experienced dadimas. They all have a passion for cooking, and feeding their immediate and extended families and friends. These dadimas welcomed me into their homes and hearts, and it was an absolute privilege to learn from them. They shared with me their culinary journeys and knowledge of Indian cooking, and they talked to me about significant moments in their lives. These dadimas all stated how the process of participating in my book research was a first time for them in talking through their food journeys and associated life events. . . . My dadima was the inspiration for the concept behind this book. Passionate about cooking for her family, she is the ultimate Mother Nature figure. She does not work in a Michelin-star restaurant, or appear on television, but in her very special way, she is our family's celebrity chef. My dadima's traditional cooking is a precious family heirloom, her dishes have stood the test of time, and are now being enjoyed by her great-grandchildren. Most importantly, her cooking contains years of rich stories and life experiences, which include hardship, resilience, faith and hope. Her food is so much more than just great food – it is full of love, wisdom and kindness.[64]

This then is what nostalgia for food recognizes – the fact that the value of food lies in something more than nutrition or even delicacy. It lies in the familial, intergenerational connection that food helps to establish, and the way these connections can allow the imagining of a new, reoriented geography. This new geography may sometimes be seen to replicate or reinforce existing social hierarchies (as in the gendered nature of housework), but it also contains within it the possibility of an alternative value system. As tastes and memories are handed down from generation to generation, it perhaps opens up the potential for rewritings; official histories and narratives can be dispensed with for new, half-forgotten stories. Memories of tastes and recipes can bring generations closer together, replicating Walter Benjamin's model for memory. When, as in the case of the diaspora, these generations are separated by space as well as time, these memories are able to 'generate nearness'[65] in a manner that can enable the questioning of normative value systems. The nostalgia that values food even though (perhaps because) it takes hours to cook, the nostalgia that elevates the impractical pestle and mortar into an icon to be cherished thus creates the possibility of jettisoning the conventionally valuable for the unreasonable, the illogical and the restorative.

NOTES

1. Chitra Banerjee Divakaruni, *The Mistress of Spices* (London: Black Swan, 1997), 3
2. Chitra Banerjee Divakaruni, *The Mistress of Spices*, 14
3. Chitra Banerjee Divakaruni, *The Mistress of Spices*, 3
4. Chitra Banerjee Divakaruni, *The Mistress of Spices*, 4
5. Walter Benjamin, "The Great Art of Making Things Seem Closer" in Michael W. Jennings, Howard Eiland and Gary Smith (eds) *Selected Writings 1927 – 1930* (Cambridge, MA, and London: Harvard University Press, 1999), 248
6. Laurent Milesi, "'Promnesia' (Remembering Forward) in *Midnight's Children*; or Rushdie's Chutney versus Proust's Madeleine" in Michael Syrotinski and Ian Maclachlan (eds) *Sensual Reading: New Approaches to Reading in Its Relations to the Senses* (Lewisburg, PA: Bucknell University Press; London: Associated University Presses, 2001), 179–212.
7. Jhumpa Lahiri, "Indian Takeout", *Food & Wine*, 1 April 2000. Accessed on 15 August 2017, available at: http://www.foodandwine.com/articles/indian-takeout
8. Neil Macgregor, "Episode 4: Bird Shaped Pestle", *A History of the World in 100 Objects* (BBC Radio 4, 2010). Accessed on 15 August 2017, available at: http://www.bbc.co.uk/programmes/articles/1mN4trKyMx0Blv6cm6qTBT9/episode-transcript-episode-6-bird-shaped-pestle
9. Jhumpa Lahiri, *The Interpreter of Maladies* (Boston and New York: Mariner Books, 1999), 114
10. Jhumpa Lahiri, *The Interpreter of Maladies*, 115
11. Jhumpa Lahiri, *The Interpreter of Maladies*, 123
12. Jhumpa Lahiri, *The Interpreter of Maladies*, 133
13. Jhumpa Lahiri, *The Interpreter of Maladies*, 129
14. Jhumpa Lahiri, *The Namesake* (Boston and New York: Mariner Books, 2004), 1
15. Jhumpa Lahiri, *The Namesake*, 10
16. Jhumpa Lahiri, *The Namesake*, 72
17. Jhumpa Lahiri, *The Namesake*, 65
18. Jhumpa Lahiri, *The Namesake*, 49–50
19. Jhumpa Lahiri, *The Namesake*, 38
20. Jhumpa Lahiri, *The Namesake*, 275–76
21. Jhumpa Lahiri, *The Namesake*, 148
22. Jhumpa Lahiri, *The Namesake*, 149
23. Jhumpa Lahiri, *The Namesake*, 140
24. Jhumpa Lahiri, *The Namesake*, 276–77
25. Anita Mannur, *Culinary Fictions*, 161
26. Anita Mannur, *Culinary Fictions*, 32
27. Anita Mannur, *Culinary Fictions*, 29

28. Anita Mannur, *Culinary Fictions*, 31
29. Sujata Bhatt, *The Stinking Rose* (Manchester: Carcanet, 1995), 29
30. Christine Geraghty, *Now a Major Motion Picture: Film Adaptations of Literature and Drama* (Lanham, MD: Rowman & Littlefield, 2008), 41
31. Tim Robey, "It's a Wonderful Afterlife, review", *The Telegraph*, 22 April 2010. Accessed on 15 August 2017, available at: http://www.telegraph.co.uk/culture/film/filmreviews/7620660/Its-a-Wonderful-Afterlife-review.html
32. Chitra Banerjee Divakaruni, *The Mistress of Spices*, 31
33. Chitra Banerjee Divakaruni, *The Mistress of Spices*, 51
34. Chitra Banerjee Divakaruni, *The Mistress of Spices*, 3
35. Jhumpa Lahiri, *The Interpreter of Maladies*, 119
36. Jhumpa Lahiri, *The Interpreter of Maladies*, 124
37. Jhumpa Lahiri, *The Interpreter of Maladies*, 123
38. Jhumpa Lahiri, *The Namesake*, 55
39. Jhumpa Lahiri, "Indian Takeout"
40. Mark Binelli, "Guerilla Goddess", *Rolling Stone*, 29 December 2005. Accessed on 15 August 2017, available at: http://www.rollingstone.com/music/news/m-i-a-guerilla-goddess-20051229
41. M.I.A., "Sunshowers", *Arular* (XL/Interscope Records, 2005)
42. M.I.A., "Bad Girls", *Matangi* (N.E.E.T./Interscope Records, 2013)
43. M.I.A. (with The Wilcannia Mob), "Mango Pickle Down River", *Kala* (XL/Interscope Records, 2007)
44. Madhur Jaffrey, *Climbing the Mango Trees: A Memoir of a Childhood in India* (London: Ebury, 2006), x
45. Madhur Jaffrey, *Climbing the Mango Trees*, viii
46. Madhur Jaffrey, *Climbing the Mango Trees*, 11
47. Madhur Jaffrey, *Climbing the Mango Trees*, 8
48. Madhur Jaffrey, *Climbing the Mango Trees*, 98–99
49. Madhur Jaffrey, *Climbing the Mango Trees*, 31
50. Madhur Jaffrey, *Climbing the Mango Trees*, 32
51. Madhur Jaffrey, *Climbing the Mango Trees*, 49
52. Bong Mom, "Welcome to My Cookbook", *Bong Mom's Cookbook*, 7 October 2006. Accessed on 15 August 2017, available at: http://www.bongcookbook.com/2006/10/welcome-to-my-cookbook.html
53. Bong Mom, "Methi Begun – the way my Ma makes it", *Bong Mom's Cookbook*, 19 February 2012, accessed on 15 August 2017, available at http://www.bongcookbook.com/2012/02/methi-begun-way-my-ma-makes-it.html
54. Sandeepa Mukherjee Datta, *Bong Mom's Cookbook: Stories from a Bengali Mother's Kitchen* (Noida, India: Collins, 2013), 4
55. Shayma, comment on "Welcome to My Cookbook", 9 November 2009, 7 October 2006, accessed on 15 August 2017, available at: http://www.bongcookbook.com/2006/10/welcome-to-my-cookbook.html
56. Sumana, comment on "Welcome to My Cookbook", 27 April 2012
57. Bong Mom, "Welcome to My Cookbook"
58. Anonymous, comment on "Welcome to My Cookbook", 26 July 2007
59. Marie Rose, comment on "Welcome to My Cookbook", 20 August 2008
60. Mita, comment on "Welcome to My Cookbook", 7 November 2009
61. Ketu Katrak, "Food and Belonging: At 'Home' and in 'Alien-Kitchens'" in Arlene Avakian (ed.) *Through the Kitchen Window* (Boston: Beacon Press, 1997), 270
62. Bong Mom, "Tel Koi – Tale of Fish", *Bong Mom's Cookbook*, 17 May 2012. Accessed on 15 August 2017, available at: http://www.bongcookbook.com/2012/05/tel-koi.html
63. Dayeeta Roy, comment on "Tel Koi – Tale of Fish"
64. Aneeka Ludhra, *Dadima's: Celebrating Grandmother's Wisdom through Indian Cooking* (Sheffield: RMC Media, 2016), 17
65. Walter Benjamin, "The Great Art of Making Things Seem Closer", 248

Chapter Four

'Straight from the Village'

Diasporic Public Spaces and the Heterotopias of Nostalgia

On 9 September 2013, 632 branches of what since 1995 had been Lloyds TSB bank were rebranded as TSB bank, resurrecting a name that had existed since the 1800s. The remaining branches were renamed Lloyds, as one of the conditions of the 2009 governmental bank rescue package was finally met, and one of the big four UK banks was broken up. Reports from the time predicted that 'immediate impact for customers will be relatively low-key' and that 'few will notice much change beyond a new brand-name above the branch door.'[1]

This may well have been the case for the vast majority of branches, but things were slightly different in one west London suburb. On 30 September 2013, the Lloyds TSB branch on Southall High Street reopened as Lloyds bank, an event which was marked by a street party, Southall style. The party featured music from Kudos and Jazz Drumline and comedy from Brij Mohan Comedian, and the ribbon was cut by bhangra and R&B singer and musician Juggy D. A video of the day was uploaded to YouTube by harjapbhangal, who comments in his own video: 'Normal banks open their doors and let their customers in. When a bank opens in Southall, this is how it is done.' In the title to his video, he describes the party as 'in true Punjabi style'.[2]

In the video, bank staff (in their official uniforms) and a multi-ethnic, multi-religious body of customers can be seen dancing together to the beat of the *dhol*. The branch itself has been decorated with balloons in the corporate colours of the new Lloyds bank. *Jalebis* and *laddoos* – south Asian sweets typically used at celebratory events have been distributed, as people participate in a variety of ways – eating the sweets, dancing, laughing at the comedian (dressed somewhat incongruously as an Indian policeman) or simply recording the whole thing on their mobile phones. At one point, an elderly white woman tries to approach the bank, seemingly confused by what is happening. She is told that Southall is celebrating the divorce of Lloyds and TSB. Not obviously any less confused, she laughs and walks away, visibly othered in her whiteness. Perhaps a little unfairly, her presence and her slightly nervous laughter becomes the symbol of the mainstream, the normal against which the rest of Southall can define itself as different.

A few months later, on 29 January 2014, when comedian Mark Steel visited Southall for the fifth series of his BBC Radio 4 show *Mark Steel's in Town*, he commented on this video, and what a bank opening of this kind says about Southall and its community identity:

> Something else that is puzzling to the outsider is if you've learnt about Indian culture from watching Bollywood films, you expect to walk into Lidl and see two hundred people dancing at the checkout. But then I heard about the Lloyds bank here and that is almost what happened. Because after Lloyds split from TSB, the branch closed for a while and then it reopened, but instead of opening in the normal way a bank might reopen with the manager opening the door and saying 'Well, welcome all of you, it is nice to be open again' there was a street-party. . . . That's brilliant for a reopening for a branch of Lloyd's![3]

Both Mark Steel and harjapbhangal stress the difference in the way a bank opens in Southall, with the way a 'normal' bank would open anywhere else in Britain. This opening of a branch on Southall High Street, then, comes to represent the essential alterity, the otherness of Southall – it is not like other normal places in Britain. It is my contention in this chapter that this otherness of a place like Southall can be read through the lens of diasporic nostalgia.

In this chapter, I look at cultural representations like this video to examine how Southall, and other places like it, represent the possibilities that exist in the different ways in which places can be lived in, occupied, manipulated and rearranged to change their meaning. As Henri Lefebvre has argued, 'each living body *is* space and *has* its space: it produces itself in space and it also produces that space.'[4] The performance of the street party can thus be thought of as a microcosm of the way particular narratives of Southall are performed every day, and an example of how Southall can be made to mean different things through these performances.

DIASPORIC HETEROTOPIAS

These narratives of places like Southall that are performed through specific acts like the opening of a bank, the ways in which the space within it can be altered through these performances and the different ways in which different bodies can occupy these spaces can all be read as effects of a nostalgic attachment to home and a consequent attempt to imaginatively recreate the lost home in the present. Diasporic nostalgia helps to remake these places; to give them new and different meanings; to undermine existing normative connections, values and regulations; and to replace them with imaginative new ones

In fact, Southall and other places like it can be described as examples of what Michel Foucault famously called 'heterotopias':

> There are also, and probably in every culture, in every civilisation, real places, actual places, places that are designed into the very institution of society, which are sorts of actually realised utopias in which the real emplacements, all the other real emplacements that can be found within the culture are, at the same time, represented, contested, and reversed, sorts of places that are outside all places, although they are actually localizable.[5]

It is this contested nature of heterotopias that interest me most, and it is this contestation that leads to Jay Miskowiec translating this same passage from Foucault as 'something like counter-sites'.[6] There is a lively debate about the accuracy or otherwise of the different translations of Foucault's work, but for my purposes here, the concept of the 'counter-site' is particularly useful, containing as it does within it the possibility of resistance, the counter-hegemonic.

Southall, or Leicester or Bradford or Tower Hamlets in the United Kingdom, or Lexington Avenue or Jackson Heights in New York, or Harris Park, Sydney, for example, can be seen as similar 'counter-sites', spaces that disturb the normal or natural order, spaces which have 'the ability to juxtapose in a single real place several emplacements that are incompatible in themselves'.[7] Thus, Southall in London can open a bank 'in true Punjabi style'; Jackson Heights can 'prove an authentic slice of South Asia in New York City's largest borough',[8] while Belgrave Road in Leicester 'brings an incense-rich whiff of the East to the East Midlands'.[9]

It is important to note that these reviews of these spaces are exactly as simplistic as they sound – there is very little authenticity of any kind to be found in Southall or Leicester or Jackson Heights, New York. To criticise them for being inauthentic is, however, to miss the point. Authenticity is not what is important about them, or why they attract such a large south Asian population that is diverse, multi-faith, and multicultural. What is important about these spaces, and why they generate such affection and attachment across national and regional borders, is that they allow for the imaginative recreation of home. London or Leicester or New York become different places, different cities, because they contain these spaces, and this magical transformation has nostalgia at its heart.

Chapter 4

HOME AND THE WORLD: INSIDE/OUTSIDE

The ability that heterotopias like Southall have to allow the reconstruction of a home can be seen in the character of Kulwinder, in Balli Kaur Jaswal's 2017 novel *Erotic Stories for Punjabi Widows*. Out on a walk, she remembers her own journey to Southall:

> The smell of sweet fried jalebi rose from a cart nearby. . . . She knew what the rest of London thought of Southall – she'd heard all of their comments when she and Sarab decided to move here from Croydon. *Village people who built another Punjab in London – they're letting all types of people into this country these days.* 'Best choice we ever made,' Sarab had declared when they unpacked their last box. Kulwinder agreed, her heart almost bursting with happiness from the comforts of their surrounds – the spice markets, the Bollywood cinema, the gurdwaras, the samosa carts on the Broadway.[10]

Southall, in this narrative, is constituted of a number of different sensations – all equally familiar, and all equally capable of summoning up the emotions of home. Like the food-memories I discussed in the previous chapter, it is here the sense-experience of Southall that helps to provide Kulwinder the familiar comfort she needs. It is this imaginative connection, through the familiarity of senses that allows Kulwinder to nostalgically connect the home she has left behind to the home that she can resurrect in the here and now.

In Amit Gupta's 2013 film *Jadoo*, Mark is nervous about meeting his British Indian future father-in-law for the first time. Seeking advice about how he should behave, he goes to his friend Vinod. Vinod warns Mark that most mixed-race marriages 'don't work out' because of the in-laws – 'just that generation, traditional, straight from the village.' When Mark appears confused because 'her Dad's from Delhi', Vinod clarifies – 'Talking about Leicester . . . dark place.'

The joke works on a number of different levels. There is a gentle mocking of the London metropolitan elite's mistrust of provincial England. There is perhaps a slightly more direct mocking of a British tendency to define India as a place of backward villages, the colonializing and orientalizing impulse to define the colonized other as primitive. Perhaps most obviously, however, there is an implicit recognition, as there was in Mark Steel's stand-up routine about Southall, of the essential alterity of Leicester. Leicester is being reconstructed not as a town in the East Midlands but as part of an essentially imaginary world where it is in fact directly connected to India.

If this example from *Jadoo* uses humour to depict this heterotopian nature of Leicester, Nikhil Advani's *Patiala House* performs a similar gesture in a more serious manner. The opening monologue of protagonist Pargat depicts the transformation of Southall from a space of racial hostility and alienation to a space that is marked by its Asian homeliness. Pargat says, 'It was as if

Southall was no longer a part of England, but had become a village in Punjab. And father, Headman of Southall.' I discuss this film in both Chapters 2 and 5, in the context of resistance in Southall and Bollywood representations of diaspora, respectively. Here, however, I am more interested in the ways in which *Patiala House*, but also *Jadoo* to a lesser extent, portrays this homeliness as helping to procure the heterotopian identity of Southall and Leicester. I am interested here in the use of nostalgia to transform British Asian spaces into heterotopias of home.

Kulwinder's meditations on Southall are reminiscent of Gaston Bachelard's work on the importance of the home and the concept of homeliness. Like Bachelard's house, Southall, too, 'shelters day-dreaming . . . protects the dreamer . . . allows one to dream in peace'. As Foucault writes about Bachelard:

> The enormous work of Gaston Bachelard and the descriptions of the phenomenologists have taught us that we are living not in a homogenous and empty space but, on the contrary, in a space that is laden with qualities, a space that may also be haunted by fantasy. The space of our first perception, that of our reveries, that of our passions harbors qualities that are all but intrinsic . . . these analyses, though they are fundamental for contemporary reflection, are concerned primarily with internal space.[11]

Foucault is correct when he identifies an inside/outside dichotomy in Bachelard's work. As Bachelard puts it, 'Memories of the outside world will never have the same tonality as those of home and, by recalling these memories, we add to our store of dreams'.[12] However, I believe that these heterotopias of nostalgia work by subverting the inside/outside dichotomy, so that Southall as a whole can become one's home. The poetics that Bachelard finds in the architecture of a house can be extended to these public spaces so that whole neighbourhoods can perform a similarly protective function. Southall, and places like it around the world exist as testament to perhaps the most powerful connection there is – the connection to home and the desire to reclaim a home of the past that has been lost. This is what makes these places heterotopic – the ways in which the concept of home can be inscribed and re-inscribed onto them, fundamentally changing their meaning. In extending Bachelard's argument to the outside as well as the inside of the physical home, I am reading the ways in which diasporic heterotopias are performed as helping to transcend not just the hegemonic borders that are supposed to police the private/public dichotomy, but also the geographic and metaphorical borders between the home that was left behind, and the home that needs to be rebuilt in the present.

This strategy can be seen at work in Shaad Ali's 2007 film *Jhoom Barabar Jhoom*. The film tells the story of Rikki Thukral and Alvira Khan, two British Asians who meet at Waterloo Station in London while waiting for delayed trains. Something about this Waterloo Station, however, is out of the ordinary. The film opens on a mysterious, fantastical character called Bulla Man (played by the most iconic Bollywood actor of all time, Amitabh Bachchan) as he sings and dances his way through Waterloo Station. Rajinder Dudrah has written very perceptively about this sequence, and what it says about the fluidity of diasporic identity:

> The film opens at Waterloo Station and joining Big B [Bachchan] right from the outset and throughout his song and dance sets, he is accompanied by everyday Westerners and specifically non-brown-skinned folk, who upon his 'click finger' instructions all dance in sync with him and in accompaniment. . . . The camera moves with and around the ensemble: it swirls, it tracks and is highly mobile moving in and out of dance choreography as it is staged across the concourse area and the platform spaces of the railway station. Big B literally invites us into the film and the generic entertaining world of Bollywood cinema.[13]

Dudrah is completely correct in his analysis of the relationship between Bachchan's iconic star status, and the way the film makes knowing use of him as a celebrity. Here, however, I am more concerned with the way this sequence specifically, and the film more generally, reconstructs Waterloo Station as a heterotopic site, a 'counter-site' where normal rules and regulations do not apply, or at least do not apply in the same way.

One of the most important aspects of Bachchan's backing dancers in this sequence is that they are not just multi-ethnic, but they are, as Dudrah points out, 'everyday Westerners'. They are everyday London commuters, dressed in everyday clothes. In other words, this is not just an example of the fantastical song-and-dance routine that characterizes much of the industrial cinema produced in Bombay and known around the world as 'Bollywood'. Dudrah is perfectly correct when he describes *Jhoom Barabar Jhoom*'s use of Bollywood entertainment conventions as 'deliberate and knowing',[14] but I think there is something else happening here as well. The decision to clothe Bachchan's backing dancers in 'everyday' clothes hints at the possibility that these dancers should be read as everyday commuters in the specific place that is Waterloo Station, rather than imaginary subjects that are being constructed by cinematic fantasy.

This distinction is crucial because while imaginary geographies are obviously of central importance to Bollywood cinema and the ways in which it can help to create a distinctively diasporic identity, the disruption that *Jhoom Barabar Jhoom* causes to the geography of Waterloo Station is of a different order entirely. In the next chapter, I analyse how Bollywood diasporic representations can be described as utopian, in the Foucauldian sense. *JBJ*, however, reconstructs Waterloo Station not as a utopian space of abstraction, but as a specific, rooted place – a heterotopia. In Foucault's conception, utopia and heterotopia are connected and can, as here, be seen to perform similar roles, but they are still different entities:

> Utopias afford consolation: although they have no real locality there is nevertheless a fantastic, untroubled region in which they are able to unfold: they open up cities with vast avenues, superbly planted gardens, countries where life is easy, even though the road to them is chimeral. Heterotopias are disturbing, probably because they shatter or tangle common names, because they destroy 'syntax' in advance, and not only that less apparent syntax which causes words and things (next to and also opposite one another) to 'hold together'.[15]

Where my analysis differs from Foucault, however, is that I believe both utopias and heterotopias can be disturbing because the counter-hegemonic imaginary homemaking that I am charting here can make itself felt in both the abstract spaces of utopia and the concrete places of heterotopia. When the song 'Bol na halke' in *Jhoom Barabar Jhoom* uses cinematic cutting to indicate a proximity between Waterloo Station and a symbolic Indian railway station, the film is using diasporic nostalgia to create an imaginary, utopian space where diasporic subjectivity can be unhesitatingly expressed and experienced. The cinematic cutting generates nearness in a way that is fundamentally utopian, as it is not interested in the specificity of location. When the same film, using its title song, 'Jhoom barabar jhoom', creates a flash mob dance on the main concourse of Waterloo Station, it uses a similarly diasporic nostalgia to turn Waterloo Station into a heterotopic place. Both are examples of homemaking in the sense in which I am using it in the book, and both of them are constructing this homeliness by using nostalgia to connect what was back there and back then to the geography of the here and now. The former does it by imagining new spaces, the latter does it by emplacing, to use Foucault's term, new norms and values within existing places – Southall, Leicester, Jackson Heights or, indeed, Waterloo Station. The meanings that these places accrue, the connections that people inhabiting them have are being changed in the process. In this chapter, I am more concerned with the way heterotopian places can be represented in culture as objects and vehicles of nostalgia, while in the next chapter, I will look in more detail at cinematic representations of nostalgic utopian spaces, and how these can help mobilize nostalgia in different ways.

This distinction is connected to the now well-established distinction between space and place. In the words of Marc Augé:

> The term 'space' is more abstract in itself than the term 'place', whose usage at least refers to an event (which has taken place), a myth (said to have taken place) or a history (high places). It is applied in much the same way to an area.... It is thus eminently abstract.[16]

My use of the word 'place' is similar to Augé's, and like him, includes within it 'the possibility of the journeys made in it, the discourses uttered in it, and the language characterizing it'.[17] It describes, in short, specific locations, the ways in which bodies inhabit them, and the ways in which meaning is constructed out of this specificity. The diasporic heterotopias I am examining in this chapter might be numerous, and located in different cities across different continents, but they are nevertheless specific and identifiable. They are important as sites of nostalgia because they are not abstract spaces, but they are places that exist and whose existence can be conceptualized in certain particular ways.

The importance of the heterotopias of nostalgia that I am discussing here, then, is that they are specifically located, they are material places that can be experienced in multiple but precise ways. Ashok and Ashima Ganguly in Jhumpa Lahiri's *The Namesake*, for example, go to Lexington Avenue. On a trip to New York, Gogol and his sister

> were allowed out of the car only once they got to Lexington Avenue to eat lunch at an Indian restaurant and then to buy Indian groceries, and polyester saris and 220-volt appliances to give to relatives in Calcutta. This, to his parents, was what one came to Manhattan to do.[18]

Even a film like *Bend It Like Beckham*, which is not especially sympathetic to diasporic nostalgia and its homemaking efforts, portrays Southall as distinctive and different to the rest of the United Kingdom. When Jess and her sister Pinky go shopping in Southall for wedding clothes and '*dhania*, four bunches for a pound', the camera swirls in and around the people on Southall High Street; there is a montage of high-angle shots looking over the bustling activity, contrasted with close-ups of people shopping for vegetables, buying and eating *jalebis*, and manequins in shop windows dressed in Indian clothes. The disorientating camera technique helps to remind the film's (White) audience that firstly, this is Southall, and secondly, Southall is not just another London suburb. In establishing its difference from just another London suburb, the camera also authenticates it as specifically and definitely Southall.

Jhoom Barabar Jhoom introduces the audience to Southall through long panning shots of temples, gurdwaras and mosques, as well as shops, restaurants, pedestrians and shoppers. The soundtrack is a wonderfully effective layered combination of Hindu, Sikh and Muslim prayers – the reading of the Guru Granth Sahib, and the Islamic *azaan* or call to prayers. Through the narrative of the film, the audience is introduced to specific Southall landmarks – Jalebi Junction Restaurant, Southall Gurdwara, the Himalaya Palace cinema building, the Glassy Junction Pub – which anchors the self-aware fantasies of the film in the specificity of this most important place of British Asian identity.

What *Jhoom Barabar Jhoom* does for Southall, *Jadoo* does for Belgrave Road, Leicester. Known as the Golden Mile, it is where both of the Chandana brothers' restaurants are located. It is where Shalini goes to buy cooking utensils, sweets, and bridal clothes. It is also where Shalini and her brother find out the secrets of the community. When Shalini and her brother go to buy sweets, the shopkeeper Abdul explains that Leicester is not necessarily devoid of conflict:

> They pretend to be friends, but restaurant-people all hate each other. I know, because they all come here, eat sweets and speak the truth to Abdul. Who doesn't want to be known as the best chef in Little India? Whose business couldn't use the publicity?

Leicester might not be a perfect space of communal harmony, but it remains the heart of the community, conflicts notwithstanding. For big events like Holi, it is where people go to celebrate. In representing the Holi celebrations, *Jadoo*, too, does something similar to the flash mob dance in Waterloo Station. As the colours of Holi are unleashed, the camera zooms out and up, taking in the community celebrations from a high-angle shot that reinforces scale. This is no longer a marginal celebration, important only to a small group of ethnic minorities. Through the heterotopia that is Asian Leicester, through the nostalgically driven homemaking process that leads to the construction of communities like Leicester, it has been transformed into a 'counter-site', a place where conventional norms no longer apply.

Similarly to Gurinder Chadha and Shaad Ali, director Amit Gupta also uses montage to introduce his audience to Leicester. Both *Jhoom Barabar Jhoom* and *Jadoo* use iconic Bollywood songs from the sixties and seventies to create the appropriate nostalgia – specifically that song of everlasting friendship from 1975 classic *Sholay*: 'We will never break this friendship, will give up breathing/ but will never give up your company.'

In the original film, the song is just that – a declaration of the power of individual friendship – but in its use in these films, it becomes a proud articulation of the importance of a diasporic subjectivity, and the importance of positive affective connections with places such as Southall and Leicester, a recognition of the importance these places have in the ways in which the diasporic communities think of themselves, the way in which diasporic Asians live their lives.

'NO PLACE LIKE IT': THE SOUTH ASIAN GROCERY SHOP

Perhaps the most iconic and the most recognizable version of such diasporic heterotopias is the Asian grocery shop. Most diasporic Asians – whether in Pollokshields in Glasgow, Tower Hamlets in London, Lavapiés in Madrid or

Devon Street in Chicago – will be familiar with a version of this from their own lives. I go to my local Asian shop regularly, and as it is for countless others, it is an important part of my diasporic subjectivity. Like many other diasporic Asians, I go there for products that are either not available or prohibitively expensive in a 'normal' supermarket. There is great comfort to be found in the bags of onions, jars of pickles, packets of *paneer* and tins of *gulaab jamun*. The shop I go to is not that different from many, many other examples of this species from around the world. As you enter, you have fridges with milk, yoghurt, *paneer* and sweets to your immediate right. Fresh vegetables and dried goods such as biscuits, crisps, and snacks are to your left. Straight ahead is the halal butcher's counter, where you can buy chicken, lamb, or beef in any quantity – on the bone or boneless. Usually one places one's meat order before shopping so the butcher gets to work on it while you pick up the other things you need. By the time you have finished, so has he, and your meat is in a bag ready for you to take to the checkout counter. Around the back, in a separate room that is not noticeable from the outside, is perhaps the heart of the shop – the shelves of spices. Packets of ground and whole spices, in quantities that range from a 100-gram packet for domestic use to a 5-kilogram packet for professional caterers and restaurateurs. It is difficult to say for certain that you can smell each one – the aroma of spices does not normally transcend sealed plastic bags, but you could almost swear that you could smell each individual spice. In front of the spices are the freezers – frozen fish and prawns, second to none in their ability to delight the heart of an expatriate Bengali like myself. Next to the seafood, you can find frozen kebabs, *parathas* and vegetables. Along the far wall, jars of *ghee*, pickles, ginger and garlic paste nestle among other more mainstream but incongruously out-of-place offerings like tomato puree, Worcestershire sauce, and Heinz tomato ketchup. In one corner, you can buy huge bags of flour, or rice, or *daal* of every kind. Dotted around throughout the shop are brand names that are achingly familiar to diasporic south Asians of most generations - Limca Lemon and Lime Drink. Thums-Up Cola. Parachute Coconut Oil. Dabur Chyawanprash Ayurvedic health supplement, Patak's Curry Paste, Tilda Basmati Rice. In another corner. there is a display that is particularly important to me, Nestle Maggi Noodles – perhaps the product most able to transport me back to my childhood and a time when this unappetising and unhealthy product was the most delicious snack one could possibly imagine. There are nooks and corners everywhere, in this shop that is much bigger than it looks from the outside. There is a whole other level downstairs, where you can buy Indian clothes. If you come at certain specific times of the year, there will be products that might not be available all year round. Come in the summer, for example, and the area by the till will be full to bursting with boxes of mangoes, specially imported from India or Pakistan. Come during the month of Ramadan, and these will be replaced with boxes of dates, to cater to the customers who will use these to break their daily fast. When it comes to paying, the member of staff serving you might, depending on whether they recognize you, speak to you in Urdu, or Punjabi. Depending on their generational identity, this may well be Scottish accented. Like the incongruous cartons of Tropicana orange juice, or Heinz Salad Cream, the Scottish accent can sometimes be slightly disconcerting. In a space that is for me marked by an overwhelming nostalgia, the shop can have a timeless feel that comes from its connection to the past home. As Banerjee Divakaruni has written of her shop in *The Mistress of Spices*: 'The store has been here only for a year. But already many look at it and think it was always. I can understand why.'[19] The overwhelming nostalgia evoked by the shop can make its temporality seem necessarily distorted.

Lest you accept too easily the apparent 'pastness' of the experience, however, the presence of the Heinz Salad Cream, or the noticeable Scottish accent to the Urdu spoken by the young member of staff is always there, symbolizing the diasporic present, always there to remind you of the fact that the heterotopia of nostalgia is always, and of necessity, a dislocated space. As Catherine Belsey has written in a different context, 'the present is all too present'.[20] Belsey is discussing the attempt at recovering the past in a living museum, but her point that access to the past can only ever be limited applies equally well to the abilities of nostalgia to recover one's history. Nostalgia can certainly not offer an immediate, unmediated access to the past, but, in a manner not dissimilar to Belsey's conception of cultural history, it can allow an imaginative rereading and remaking:

> I want to define a distinct practice, which I shall call history at the level of the signifier. This is a form of cultural history which involves neither translation nor experience, but depends on reading. Moreover, it is a material practice – as material in its own way as social history, to which it can be related.[21]

My case study of the south Asian grocery shop is very different from Belsey's in many ways, but it does share a similarity in that they both record 'meanings and values'.[22] The south Asian grocery shop is not an object of cultural history in the way that Belsey conceptualizes it, but it is a place to which the past adheres; the way it is constructed and used, the importance it has to people's lives shows the ways in which people use the past in the present, the way in which things that were back-there-and-then continue to persist in the here and now.

The reader will hopefully forgive the self-indulgence of this detailed description of one particular Scottish Asian grocery shop. There is a point to this lengthy account, however. As I have outlined above, part of the heterotopic nature of these spaces lies in their specificity. Even Chitra Banerjee Divakaruni, in her magical-realist portrayal of a south Asian grocery store in

Oakland, California, remembers to locate it specifically, to emplace it, in Foucault's words:

> Turn the crooked corner of Esperanza where the Oakland buses hiss to a stop and you'll see it. Perfect-fitted between the narrow barred doors of Rosa's Weekly Hotel, still blackened from a year-ago fire, and Lee Ying's sewing Machine and Vacuum Cleaner Repair with the glass cracked between the *R* and the *e*. Grease-smudged window. Looped letters that say SPICE BAZAAR faded into a dried-mud brown.[23]

Like the smell of turmeric, the sensations that the diasporic south Asian shop evokes is all too familiar:

> When you open the bin that sits by the entrance to the store you smell it right away, though it will take a little while for your brain to register that subtle scent, faintly bitter like your skin and almost as familiar.[24]

Whether it is an invention of an author like Banerjee Divakaruni, whether it is depicted through the lens of filmmakers like Gurinder Chadha or Amit Gupta, or whether it is one of the many shops that diasporic south Asians visit every day, these spaces evoke a nostalgic desire for the past and the home that was more securely located then:

> And in the corners accumulated among dustballs, exhaled by those who have entered here, the desires. Of all things in my store, they are the most ancient. For even here in this new land America, this city which prides itself on being no older than a heartbeat, it is the same things we want, again and again.[25]

It is the articulation of these desires, and the promise that they might to some extent be fulfilled, that makes the British Asian shop so special. In Tilo's words, 'there is no other place in the world quite like this'.[26]

If this too sounds as self-indulgent as my description of my own local shop, it is of course meant to be. There is a specific self-indulgence inherent in nostalgic makings and remakings of home. But this self-indulgence is also always political, as Banerjee Divakaruni acknowledges in her writing:

> Even for those who know nothing of the inner room with its sacred, secret shelves, the store is an excursion into the land of might-have-been. A self-indulgence dangerous for a brown people who come from elsewhere, to whom real Americans might say *Why?*[27]

This American demand to justify one's presence challenges the value placed on the space of the Indian shop. It refuses to recognize the importance of this transnational, multiply dislocated institution. It does not understand why this place should matter so much to many:

> Around me, buckets of *bajra* flour, squat casks of rapeseed oil, reassuringly-solid. Sacks of sparking sea salt to keep me company. The spices whispering their secrets, sighing their pleasure.
> I too sigh my pleasure.[28]

What this American demand does recognize and implicitly reinforce, though, is the belief that the south Asian grocery shop does not belong here; it is out of place. The refusal to recognize the importance the diasporic Asian shop has is also a refusal to recognize the legitimacy of the diasporic communities themselves. The shop does not belong in the here and now of Europe, America or Australia. The American demand to explain the need for the spice shop is also a white demand that the non-white immigrants explain their existence, justify the space they occupy as a diasporic subject. The deviance, the alterity that makes these heterotopias of nostalgia what they are is also fundamentally political. To the extent that Southall or Leicester can be reimagined as part of India, it represents a refusal to assimilate to and with hegemonic notions of a British nationhood. In their difference, these places represent the otherness that cannot easily be appropriated and the danger that this unassimilability poses to a fantasy of a homogenous (white) nationhood. As Marco Cenzatti has put it,

> Modern heterotopias, then, are 'other spaces' on the one hand because they are made other by the top-down making of places of exclusion; on the other hand, they are made other by the deviant groups that live in and appropriate those places.[29]

Heterotopia's otherness then, is always contingent on the hegemonic demand to conform, and a demonization of the deviant's refusal to conform. On 17 October 2011, journalist Anthony Bond, writing in the online edition of the British tabloid *Daily Mail*, did an 'exposé' of 'illegal immigrants' who were unlawfully occupying space in Southall:

> It looks like something which could be seen in the hit film *Slumdog Millionaire*.
>
> But these shocking images – which show garden sheds and garages transformed into dodgy homes for immigrants – are not from the slums of Mumbai. Incredibly, they are from a west London suburb.[30]

Bond's incendiary reporting in the *Daily Mail* (which includes a completely gratuitous pairing of a photograph of the Punjabi sign in Southall railway station with a photograph of Rubina Ali, one of the actors of *Slumdog Millionaire*, standing in the ruins of what were once her slums in Mumbai) is predicated on what he sees as an illegitimate use of space. Southall's very existence is a threat to Bond and the *Daily Mail*'s sense of what Britishness should look like. This threat is constituted of Southall's apparent refusal to accept the demand that everyone in Britain adhere to this sense of nationhood. Its alterity remains its threat because its alterity represents the futility of the demand to assimilate.

It is this demand that makes these places of nostalgia heterotopic. Before Foucault used the word to talk about human beings and their use of space, it existed (and indeed is still used) as a medical term to describe a specific kind of anatomical anomaly:

> Heterotopia is originally a medical term referring to a particular tissue that develops at another place than is usual. The tissue is not diseased or particularly dangerous but merely placed elsewhere, a dislocation.[31]

Writing about heterotopias, Heidi Sohn has claimed that Foucault's use of the word differs significantly from its medical origins:

> While medical heterotopias have no known causes, no secondary effects, and do not affect the normal functioning of the overall organism in which they appear, Foucault's heterotopias have an essentially disturbing function: they are meant to overturn established orders, to subvert language and signification, to contrast sameness, and to reflect the inverse of reverse side of society.[32]

Notwithstanding Sohn's argument, however, there are certainly enough medical uses of the term to indicate a trauma or at least a pathology. Heterotopic ossification, for example, refers to 'the development of bone in abnormal areas, usually in soft tissues' which can lead to multiple problems:

> When heterotopic ossification occurs around the hip, there is usually swelling of the leg (most pronounced around the hip area). There may be redness, heat in the leg, and the patient may have a low grade fever. The physician will then have to differentiate between other problems which can cause leg swelling, particularly thrombophlebitis, deep venous thrombosis, cellulitis, joint sepsis, hematoma, fracture and trauma.[33]

It is not clear if Foucault knew about the medical use of the word, but this sense of occupying the wrong or unusual place is something that is central to Foucault's conception of heterotopia, and it is of central importance to the ways in which heterotopias of diasporic nostalgia can be identified, analysed and understood. Like the displaced tissues in the human body, the bodies occupying these heterotopic places are similarly dislocated. The immigrant being constructed through the *Daily Mail* is, like the heterotopic tissue, occupying a space that is not intended for her and, through her illegitimate presence, is challenging the normal. Both the diasporic subject and the anomalous tissue can be seen to 'render organisms – and by analogy also certain architectural constructs and cities – as either healthy, sick or anomalous.'[34]

There is a direct line of connection between this existence as resistance on the one hand, and the spices, *jalebis*, *samosas*, Bollywood cinema and all the other accoutrements of home which attract south Asians to this space in the first place. The nostalgia evoked by these sensory experiences makes Southall, Leicester or Lavapiés what they are, and it is this nostalgic connection to these places that lend them their potential for heterotopic resistance.

SPACE INVADERS

In 2011, I moved to Tower Hamlets in East London. In nearly fifteen years of being a diasporic subject, I had never lived in an area that could be identified as 'Asian', in the way the areas around Commercial Road and Whitechapel Road could be. This was within a stone's throw of Brick Lane, London's Banglatown. Less than five minutes from my house was the East London Mosque, serving Great Britain's largest Muslim community. I cannot claim to be part of this community in any meaningful way, and I have certainly little expertise or authority to speak about it, or on behalf of its people, but what I do vividly remember is the sense of joyous dislocation I felt at realizing that I would henceforth be able to do my weekly grocery shopping without having to speak in English. Across the street from my flat was Watney Street Market – I well remember my surprised delight when, on my first walk around the neighbourhood after moving in, I came across a truck parked outside an Indian vegetable shop. It was full of jackfruit, a fruit widely available through much of south Asia, and, not incidentally, the national fruit of Bangladesh. The fruit's distinctive aroma was no less capable of evoking memories, experiences and sensations than Proust's much celebrated madeleine. This same delight would repeat itself over and over again, as I would discover more things that reminded me of home, things that I did not expect to be able to buy in London – vegetables like *ucche* (bitter gourd) or *potol* (pointed gourd), varieties of Bengali fishes that even I had never heard of before, as well as domestic products such as *jhanta* (an indigenous broom), *gamcha* (an indigenous towel) and a *mora* (an indigenous stool). This is not to say that these products were not then, or are not now, available in other parts of Britain, or indeed more generally among diasporic south Asian communities of other countries. It is to say, however, that my shock, and my delight, says something about my own connection to my invented homeland, and more generally, about the homemaking impulse that nostalgia often leads to among diasporic populations. There is also a more serious point implied in my own involuntary surprise – a recognition that this was London, England, and that these sorts of objects are not supposed to be found here. This, for me, explains the importance of these heterotopias. Through their existence, they help to change what London, or indeed, Great Britain, might mean. Their continued existence in the face of increased state-endorsed assimilationist policies in Britain, continental Europe, Australia and North America speaks to the possibility of a quiet, mundane, quotidian resistance – a refusal to assimilate, a rejection of narratives and meanings being foisted from above.

These diasporic heterotopias remind me of the question posed by Nirmal Puwar in her pioneering account *Space Invaders: Race, Gender and Bodies Out of Place*:

> What happens when those embodied differently come to occupy spaces rarely occupied by them? This question could be asked of all spaces. There is a two-way relationship between spaces and bodies, which locates the coexistence of 'different' bodies in specific spaces as 'space invaders': first, over time specific bodies are associated with specific spaces (these could be institutional positions, organisations, neighbourhoods, cities, nations) and, secondly, spaces become marked as territories belonging to particular bodies.[35]

While Puwar is concerned with the consequences of human beings who are embodied differently occupying positions of privilege and power, and is therefore looking at cases very different from the kind of heterotopias I have been examining in this chapter, I think her notion of the destabilizing potential of invading space is still relevant. The diasporic subject is 'matter out of place' and therefore 'problematizes the liberal assertion that bodies do not matter and that positions are constituted in neutered, neutral, colourless terms'.[36] As Anthony Bond's reporting in the *Daily Mail* demonstrates, it is the racial otherness of the inhabitants of Southall that is centrally connected to their undesirability, in the eyes of the authorities. The very existence of Southall is a surprise; it 'induces a "double take"', in Puwar's words. It is this discordant tone set by the nostalgic homemaking that Southall represents that persists as a challenge, a resistance to an ethnocentric, white-nationalist perception of what Britain looks like, and what it should value.

It should be pointed out that this potential for resistance may, and indeed, frequently does coexist with its own, internal, deeply problematic and oppressive relations of power. Indeed, there is something of a tradition of cultural representation depicting these heterotopias as places of oppression. Monica Ali's *Brick Lane* (2003); Ayub Khan-Din's 1996 play *East Is East* and its 1999 film adaptation, directed by Damien O'Donnell; Salvador Calvo's 2007 film *Masala*; and Fernando Coloma's *El próximo oriente* from 2006 are all texts that fit this pattern. It is undeniably the case that the heterotopic places I have been discussing in this chapter can and do reveal lines of gender, race, religion, caste and class oppression, exploitation and exclusion. I am certainly not romanticizing these places as simplistically counter-hegemonic or progressive in any sense.

Rather, following Sudesh Mishra's analysis of the 'tazia' religious performances among indentured labourers on Fiji, I argue that some of the 'radical potentiality' that he identifies there may also be applicable to the very different case of these diasporic heterotopias. While the tazia performances take place in communities that are marked by much sharper and more unequal power lines than those between the heterotopia and the mainstream in the cases I am discussing here, there is perhaps something of the same carnivalesque that Mishra identifies in his argument. Like the tazia, perhaps these heterotopias can be seen to:

> represent a temporary actualization of a yet-to-be-realized social arrangement; it signal[s] a coming community that [bear]s no exact relation to subcontinental practices nor to the alienating regimes of . . . [the present].[37]

The fear mongering and marginalization that these heterotopias are subject to suggests that their existence represents a potential challenge to orthodoxy. This challenge may remain unfulfilled; it may well be compromised by deeply problematic, anti-egalitarian politics of many kinds, but the potential still remains for using the diasporic heterotopias to imagine a different future, marked by different, alternative connections between bodies and space, between memories, emotions, sensations and material objects.

Balli Kaur Jaswal's Southall-based novel *Erotic Stories for Punjabi Widows* both identifies and undermines this tradition of representing south Asian spaces as oppressive by initially presenting Southall as an uncomplicated site of patriarchal oppression before cleverly identifying examples of female agency within the fabric of this diasporic heterotopia. The story centres on Nikki, a Westernized British Sikh who takes a part-time job teaching creative writing to a group of Punjabi widows in Southall Gurdwara. As a politically engaged young woman, she starts the job with a desire to help to liberate these women through encouraging them to take up writing. In her mind, Nikki associates the women she is teaching with her widowed mother and her sister who is trying to get an arranged marriage – all, for her, equally symbols of a regressive traditionalism, against which she can pose herself as the progressive, liberal saviour. What she discovers, however, is that her students are treating the classroom space as a heterotopia-within-a-heterotopia – the all-female space can quickly become a space of confession and sharing, as the women start to write erotic fantasy stories, finally finding an outlet for their sexuality that their conservative, patriarchal upbringing had always denied them. Like all communities, then, power moves through Southall in every direction, and for the undeniable examples of violent patriarchy, there are also spaces of resistance where these women can exert their own agency – beyond the control of not just male authority within Southall, but also white-male authority within the rest of Britain. Moreover, there are multiple examples of these women actively deploying their own nostalgia to articulate their most private, deepest sexual fantasies. Thus, Manjeet's first story features a woman called Sunita and her sexual fantasies while lying on the roof of her home in the Punjab:

> Sunita climbed onto the roof of her house and stared up into the sky. Somewhere out there was a husband for her. Not a boy. A man. She rested flat on her back. This was a bold thing to do. Anybody looking out of their window could see this single girl lying in the dark, daring the world to join her. A breeze sighed through the fields, lifting and dropping the hem of Sunita's cotton tunic like a winking eye.[38]

In Manjeet's writing, her nostalgia attempts to erase the distance between a rooftop of a house in a Punjabi village and a terraced house in Southall, while at the same time realigning the memories to allow space to express her own transgressive desire. To say this is not to efface the brutal layers of patriarchal power that she has lived through all her life, but it is to say that a nostalgic reconstruction of one's home does not have to be defined solely in terms of said patriarchy. It is to say that the nostalgia that enables the making of Southall, the nostalgia that creates another version of the Punjab in London, has the potential to include many kinds memories and experiences – from the deeply traditional to the shatteringly transgressive.

FOOD AND MUSIC – EXAMPLES OF CRITICAL DIASPORIC HETEROTOPIAS

While in many cases this counter-hegemonic potential remains unactualized, sometimes it can be seen explicitly in action. As an example, I want to turn to the work of two musicians – British Pakistani actor and singer Riz MC (perhaps better known as the actor Riz Ahmed) and Indian American singer and writer Heems. Together they constitute the group Swet Shop Boys. Following an EP in 2014, *Swet Shop*, they released their debut album *Cashmere* in 2016. Their music is unabashedly political – taking as its subject matter the racism of border control ('T5' and 'No Fly List'), governmental surveillance ('Phone Tap') and Islam and masculinity ('Zayn Malik'). The specific song and accompanying video I want to focus on here, however, is 'Aaja' featuring Pakistani singer, musician, and writer, Ali Sethi. While this video gained significant traction in the music media, its significance was not always properly appreciated. Thus, Ben Kaye, writing for the site *Consequence of Sound* describes it as 'essentially a Bollywood romance, so it's fitting that they went with an Indian aesthetic for the track's visuals'.[39] Tom Breihan in *Stereogum* does no better when he rather patronizingly describes the song as 'a simple and sweet love story about two kids in Coney Island'.[40] Writing in

Spin, Emma May comes closer to the mark by recognizing the importance of the 'first and second-generation immigrant upbringing' on Swet Shop Boys' music, but she too limits her description of the song itself to the 'the developing romance of two young Brooklynites'.[41]

On the contrary, it is my contention that the song, and its accompanying video, is much more interesting, much more critical, and much more politically engaged than these critics give it credit for. I further argue that a large part of the political significance of the song comes from its recognition of the importance of diasporic nostalgia and the heterotopias it helps to create.

The video is set in the Flushing, Queens, and Coney Island areas of New York and charts the efforts of a young south Asian teenager to attract the attention of a young south Asian woman wearing a hijab. He is not visibly identified as Indian or Hindu, but the two areas chosen for filming are clearly symbolic – Flushing, Queens, was one of the first areas in North America to be called 'Little India' and has one of its first traditional Hindu temples. Coney Island, on the other hand, is known as Little Pakistan, and the video prominently features street signs and shop signs in Urdu as well as English. Our male protagonist has been given the job of putting up posters advertising a concert by the Swet Shop Boys in the guise of the group The Sufi Sensation. Contrary to the reviews of the song cited above, the music and video owes little to Bollywood and much more to the distinctively south Asian Islamic tradition of Qawwali music. As the Swet Shop Boys put it in a press release to accompany the song:

> 'In large part, "Cashmere" was an album that eschewed Bollywood samples to look hundreds of years further back to Qawwali,' explain Swet Shop Boys in a press release. 'Qawwali is a Sufi devotional music popular in both Pakistan and India, fusing together Persian, Arabic, Turkish and Indian musical traditions. The lyrics often blur the line between spiritual and hedonistic, and thus Qawwali performances are typically spaces where one could mix sacred and profane sentiments with a gender and age-mixed audience. While we shot the video in August, our mission is even more important today: to respond to fear and divisiveness with defiant love.'[42]

The video then features three distinct, but interrelated heterotopias: Coney Island; Flushing; and the specific music concert, performed by the Swet Shop Boys, at which our couple will finally get together. In the process, the video takes us across a whole list of specific south Asian spaces – the grocery shop where the female protagonist works, the kind of mobile phone and electronics shops that help diasporic communities keep in touch with family back home, halal butchers, restaurants, and kebab shops. The camera follows the boy around the spice shelves of the shop where she works, as he tries to invite her to the music concert. The song and the video were designed to help 'bridg[e] the gap between our Indian and Pakistani communities the same way Qawwali has'.⁴³ To highlight this political point, there is a close-up shot featuring bank notes of both countries.

In attempting to bridge the gap, of course, the Swet Shop Boys are also undermining the racist homogenizing of diasporic south Asians, while simultaneously reaffirming the role nostalgia has in helping these communities connect with and construct a sense of home through food, music and communication. In a particularly important moment, the male protagonist uses one of the posters advertising the music concert to cover up a Trump campaign poster. Given the importance of a white-supremacist nostalgia in the eventual success of the Trump campaign, it is difficult not to read this act as the proud articulation of the desirability of a critical, heterogeneous, and counter-hegemonic nostalgia over the reactionary politics espoused by Trump.

Perhaps the most important and the most poignant political allusion in the video as a whole, however, is to Qandeel Baloch, a Pakistani model, actress, women's rights activist and social media celebrity. Baloch came to fame initially on the reality TV show *Pakistan Idol* but then through YouTube for her controversial videos, comments, articles and songs protesting against patriarchal restrictions on women in Pakistan and for the right of Pakistani women to live their lives on their own terms. In July 2016, Baloch was drugged and strangled by her own brother, in a so-called honour killing. Her murder led to widespread condemnation around the world, and vigils were held for her in Pakistan and abroad. The Swet Shop Boys dedicated the song to her memory, and she is given the last words, as they sample from one of her own videos a line that matches the message of the song: 'Seriously? I mean, he's so charming. Seriously I would love to be with him. I would love to be with him.'

Nostalgic heterotopias can thus be used to critique reactionary and reprehensible politics both in the here and now of diasporic life, and back home. Far from nostalgia leading to an exclusive, homogenized, hierarchical view of the world, the nostalgia that the Swet Shop Boys evoke and celebrate is unashamedly heterogeneous – including, on the one hand, lines like 'You're sweet like baklava' while matching it with references to 'Polish girl', 'Mario, Luigi' and 'Adobe Photoshop'.⁴⁴ The nostalgic diasporic subject is not necessarily simplistically and uncritically looking backwards – rather they are able to fuse their nostalgic affective connections to places, memories and experiences together to create and celebrate a riotously heterogeneous, defiantly political, uncompromisingly critical view of the world that is always also forward looking, progressive. It would be a huge misunderstanding of the significance of the music of the Swet Shop Boys to try to separate out the representation of the heterotopias from their critical political message. One is always connected to the other, and it is only from being rooted in a diasporic heterotopia, the message of the song seems to be, that one can be critical in this manner.

A similar political message can be seen in Riz MC's solo work as well. As an example, I am going to look at the video for his song 'Englistan', part of the 2016 mix-tape of the same name. The video opens with a long panning shot of multiple anti-immigrant, xenophobic and racist headlines from the British tabloid media. The scene changes to show Riz MC dressed in a t-shirt that is made up from the England football and the Pakistani cricket colours. Riz is shown walking through streets of contemporary England; places of worship such as mosques, synagogues, temples and gurdwaras; as well as restaurants, kebab shops, halal butchers and south Asian grocery stores. The cacophony of images of an apparent harmonious multiculturalism – 'This is England / The bridge we living in / A kicharee simmering' – contrasts with a deeply critical mediation on race relations in Britain: 'Politeness mixed with violence', 'a free trial later detention first', 'Pigs hit kids so/Bricks hit windows and the High Street burns'.[45] There is a deliberate discordance between the sense of community created through the visuals, and the lack of community suggested through the lyrics – a discordance that allows Riz MC to cleverly highlight the importance of heterotopias, places in which people who are embodied differently can belong, while simultaneously resisting the mainstream appropriation of these heterotopic places into anything so anodyne as an official narrative of multiculturalism. This ambivalence allows him to claim on the one hand that Britain 'is where I live and why my heart beats' while also describing it as 'a mean and pleasant land'. Riz MC's walk through the streets of Britain, his interaction with 'everyday' Britons – from taxi drivers to Hare Krishna devotees, from kebab-shop owners to football-playing children – performs a similar role to the backing dancers who follow Amitabh Bachchan's movements in Waterloo Station. In both these cases, the bodies occupying these places are used to change what they might mean and how they might be regulated. Riz MC and Amitabh Bachchan, as well as the other less famous subjects in these videos, can be seen as analogous to Puwar's notion of space invaders:

> Being both insiders and outsiders, they occupy a tenuous location. Not being the somatic norm, they don't have an undisputed right to occupy this space.... Their arrival brings into clear relief what has been able to pass as the invisible, unmarked and undeclared somatic norm. These new bodies highlight the constitutive boundaries of who can pass as the universal human.[46]

If Riz MC and the Swet Shop Boys provide one example of a counter-hegemonic heterotopia, then the British Indian restaurant Dishoom provides another example of a very different kind. The first Dishoom restaurant opened on St Martin's Lane in London in July 2010. Since then, they have opened at another three locations in London and one in Edinburgh. For two years running, in 2015 and 2016, Dishoom was named the UK's best place in the Yelp Top 100 Eateries list.[47] The most obvious affect in the food and ambience of any Dishoom restaurant is nostalgia. This is a nostalgia for a very specific aspect of Indian culinary history – the Bombay Irani Café. As the blurb for the restaurant puts it:

> The old Irani Cafés of Bombay have almost all disappeared. Their faded elegance welcomed all: rich businessmen, sweaty taxi-wallas and courting couples. Fans turned slowly. Bentwood chairs were reflected in stained mirrors, next to sepia family portraits. Students had breakfast. Families dined. Lawyers read briefs. Writers found their characters.
>
> Opened early last century by Zoroastrian immigrants from Iran, there were almost four hundred cafés at their peak in the 1960s. Now, fewer than thirty remain. Their loss is much mourned by Bombayites.[48]

This nostalgia can be seen in the restaurants' menu, with dishes like 'Kejriwal' – two fried eggs on chilli cheese toast, a favourite of Bombay's Wilingdon Club – 'Pau Bhaji, Chowpatty Beach style' and 'Chicken Berry Britannia'. The nostalgia can be seen in the restaurants' décor as well – from the rotating fans above, to the fake taps next to the toilets that jokingly replicate the indigenous south Asian hygiene practice, to the dark brown wooden partitions which remind one of government office buildings in Nehruvian India. It is easy to be dismissive of these gestures which are, after all, ultimately nothing more than an attempt to increase sales. As Jay Rayner wrote in *The Guardian*:

> It is . . . a hunk of corporate image management, a fully realised 'concept' which could be flat-packed and distributed to every brand-heavy high street in the land. Check out the black and white tiled floors and marble tabletops, the grey banquettes and slabs of oak panelling. Most of all, check out the framed vintage Bollywood-style adverts, which look as though they were bought by the yard.[49]

This suspicion is not limited to food critics like Rayner, either. Writing in *The Guardian*, Stuart Jeffries identified Dishoom with what he saw as a wave of colonial nostalgia taking over Britain:

> Dishoom is catching a wave of colonial nostalgia as Britons time-travel to the era when the people of this rain-soaked dot in the dismal north Atlantic raped, traded, pillaged and murdered their way to running the biggest empire the world has ever seen. And today's bankable nostalgia, if that's what it is, focuses on the jewel in the crown, India.[50]

Jeffries provides, as an example of Dishoom's pandering to colonial nostalgia, the sign in the Kings Cross location, 'No foreign clothes':

What does 'foreign' mean in a London restaurant that simulates the food and decor of Bombay cafes in the early years of the 20th century? Are saris unacceptable? Should I have checked my pith helmet? Are dashikis out or in?

While he quotes Alex, his waiter's explanation that this sign refers to Gandhi's *swadeshi* movement's boycott of foreign-made goods, as a strategy to make India less lucrative for the British, Jeffries does not think that this truth complicates his diagnosis of colonial nostalgia. He ignores two other signs that make it to the same list: 'No Simon Commission' and 'No Rowlatt Act', referring respectively to a deeply unpopular British commission designed to explore constitutional reform in colonized India, and to an even more unpopular act extending the British government's emergency powers in India, leading to the massacre in Jallianwallah Bagh, Amritsar.

The explicitly political nature of these signs suggests, I think, that there might be something more complex, and, dare I say it, more interesting going on in the nostalgia that Dishoom evokes. In some ways not unlike the politics of the Swet Shop Boys and Riz MC, Dishoom is constructing a diasporic heterotopia that retains the power to be critical, subtly undermining hegemonic notions both in the diaspora and 'back home'.

For example, one of the aspects of the restaurants' distinctive 'look' that Rayner and Jeffries do not mention is the use of Hindi-language signs. There are numerous jokes in Hindi throughout Dishoom restaurants. A door in the Edinburgh location has a sign in English saying 'Private: Staff Only', but in Hindi it says 'Ghosts live here'. By the window of the same restaurant, it says, again in Hindi, 'Draw the curtains before getting drunk.' Outside the Kings Cross restaurant, it says, 'Don't cause nuisance' and 'Don't be drunk and disorderly'. On the large glass windows in Kings Cross, it says, alluding to a famous song from the 1956 film *CID*, 'Be alert, be careful, this is a glass my love.' There has clearly been a lot of thought put into these signs, and it is not immediately obvious what the resulting payback might be. After all, the proportion of Dishoom's clientele who will be able to read Hindi and therefore appreciate these jokes must be so small that, in a strict commercial sense, it is hardly worth the trouble.

Instead, I read these signs as analogous to the fictive linguistic community of the Bollywood diasporic cinema that I analyse in Chapter 5. They represent an unspoken, unspeakable desire for the removal of linguistic hierarchies and the fantasy that when the diaspora enters the heart of the old Empire, it might do so as an equal. As the first blog post from Dishoom's website puts it:

> And before you know it, you're sitting on a bentwood chair at a marble table, looking at sepia portraits of your family, sipping chai and eating a Bombay omelette. In the middle of London. . . . Passers-by are peering through the

windows wondering what has just turned up and made itself comfortable on St. Martin's Lane in that gap between Jamie's Italian and Stringfellows.⁵¹

It is undeniably true that Dishoom is a commercial establishment and is therefore, on one level, complicit in all the systemic oppressive forces that capitalism constitutes. Even so, I do think the restaurants can also be read as attempts to explore the consequences of a diaspora that has not just invaded the spaces of Empire, to paraphrase Nirmal Puwar, but also has made itself at home within it. The entry of Dishoom into the old metropolitan capital cityscape can thus be thought of as an inverse invasion, a reminder that the previously colonized are not just here, but that they have turned up and made themselves comfortable.

This critical potential within tongue-in-cheek humour can be seen in Dishoom's advertising as well. To mark Valentine's Day 2011, they released a video on YouTube revealing what they claimed was 'the real story of Valentine's Day'.⁵² The video claims that the belief that 'Valentine's Day traces its origins to an early Christian martyr, St Valentine' is 'a worthy illusion'. The truth is that it originated in 'the medieval times in the state of Gujarat', where it started as 'Velan-times Day', to mark the actions of a rebellious wife who, tired of her husband's incessant demands, hit him with a rolling-pin, or a 'velan'. In the process, 'the humble rolling-pin . . . had become an instrument for the emancipation of women.' This, the video insists, is what the annual ritual of Valentine's Day is really about.

On one level, this joke can be seen to gently satirize the perceived south Asian tendency to claim cultural supremacy over other people, a tendency made famous through the *Goodness Gracious Me* sketches featuring the father who claims that everyone from Superman to Prince Charles, Jesus Christ and Da Vinci were all Indian. More interesting, however, is the undeniable political connotations of attempting to trace Valentine's Day back not just to India, but specifically to Gujarat, in so many ways the home of the Hindu Right in India. For some years now, the Hindu Right have attacked the celebration of Valentine's Day as an unacceptably decadent, immoral Western invasion. In 2014, *The Hindu* reported that far-right activists of the Bajrang Dal and Vishwa Hindu Parishad (VHP) had thrown 'rotten tomatoes at couples celebrating Valentine's Day on the banks of Sabarmati River in Ahmedabad'⁵³ in Gujarat. Jwalit Mehta, city president of the Bajrang Dal, was quoted in the report as saying that the 'VHP and Bajrang Dal are against obscenity in the name of westernization. Valentine's Day is one such obscene celebration.' This form of moral censoring is not limited to Gujarat, either. In 2012, firebrand Hindu-nationalist leader from Bombay, Bal Thackeray, was quoted as saying:

> This shameless festival has been celebrated by our young people. . . . But it is totally contrary to Indian culture. We should focus on good work, good thoughts, love and harmony in our society, and not let such Western culture spoil us.[54]

Since then, as the Hindu Right has become more and more powerful throughout much of India, these attacks have grown in both prominence and ferocity – leading to multiple reports of forced marriages and forced conversion for couples who publicly celebrate Valentine's Day in any form.

I have no idea if the owners of Dishoom had this context in mind when they produced the video, but it is difficult not to read it in these terms. If I am correct in thinking about the restaurant space, and the discourse surrounding it as examples of a diasporic heterotopia, however, then the nostalgia for the Bombay Irani Café culture, and 'their willingness to serve anybody who wanted to eat or drink there without paying attention to their age, occupation or faith',[55] can be read as opening up spaces, from which cultural exclusivity, whether in London or in India, can be critiqued equally. In and through this critique, then, Dishoom is able to construct an alternative history of British Indian connections. As an example, they released an album of 'Bombay London Grooves' called *Slip-Disc*, presented as another way 'to bridge the gap between London and Bombay in the 1960s'. The cover image of the album shows a fashionable south Asian couple walking the streets of the London of the swinging sixties, with a Red Routemaster bus in the background. Their stride is confident as they hold hands and stare unhesitatingly into the distance. A white man to the side looks at them – such a sight presumably still a novelty for all the progressiveness of 1960s London. The restaurant, its music and its surrounding discourse help to recover the memories of a different sort of connection between Bombay and London – one not based on memories of war or the Raj or even of independence, but instead one based on a similar 'desire for change and cultural revolution'. It is this same desire that I read in the food and décor of the restaurants today, and it is this desire, for all of its complicity with capitalism and commodity fetishism, that can still represent a challenge to both a white-British nostalgia for a more homogenous British nation, and a Hindu-Right nostalgia for a mono-religious Indian nation. Like the Swet Shop Boys who can use their music, a cross between rap and Qawwali, to criticize both Donald Trump and Qandeel Baloch's murderers, the nostalgia that Dishoom creates is similarly powerful in realigning the imperial dynamic that has dominated British Indian relations for so many centuries.

NOTES

1. Kamal Ahmed, "Welcome Back, TSB, as Bank Splits from Lloyds", *The Telegraph*, 7 September 2013. Accessed on 14 August 2017, available at: http://www.telegraph.co.uk/finance/newsbysector/banksandfinance/10293493/Welcome-back-TSB-as-bank-splits-from-Lloyds.html
2. harjapbhangal, "Lloyds Bank Southall Branch Re-Opening after the Split from TSB . . . but in True Punjabi Style", 30 September 2013. Accessed on 14 August 2017, available at: https://www.youtube.com/watch?v=d_0MtWMwZ_U&t=30s
3. Mark Steel, "Southall", *Mark Steel's in Town Series 5* (BBC, Radio 4, 29 January 2014)
4. Henri Lefebvre, *The Production of Space* (Oxford: Blackwell Publishing, 2002), 170
5. Michel Foucault, *Aesthetics, Method, and Epistemology*, 178
6. Michel Foucault, "Of Other Spaces", *Diacritics* 16, Spring 1986, 24
7. Michel Foucault, *Aesthetics, Method, and Epistemology*, 181
8. Brennan Ortiz, "NYC's Micro Neighborhoods: Little India in Jackson Heights, Queens", *Untapped Cities*, 3 April 2014. Accessed on 14 August 2017, available at: http://untappedcities.com/2014/03/04/nycs-micro-neighborhoods-little-india-in-jackson-heights-queens/
9. Stephen McClarence, "Diwali in Leicester: An Indian Adventure on British Soil", *The Telegraph*, 2 November 2015. Accessed on 14 August 2017, available at: http://www.telegraph.co.uk/travel/destinations/europe/united-kingdom/england/leicestershire/articles/Diwali-in-Leicester-An-Indian-adventure-on-British-soil/
10. Balli Kaur Jaswal, *Erotic Stories for Punjabi Widows* (London: HarperCollins, 2017), 41-42
11. Michel Foucault, *Aesthetics, Method, and Epistemology*, 177
12. Gaston Bachelard, *The Poetics of Space*, 6
13. Rajinder Dudrah, *Bollywood Travels: Culture, Diaspora, and Border Crossings in Popular Hindi Cinema* (Oxford and New York: Routledge, 2012), 30
14. Rajinder Dudrah, *Bollywood Travels*, 36
15. Michel Foucault, *The Order of Things: An Archaeology of the Human Sciences* (London and New York: Routledge, 2002), xix
16. Marc Augé, *Non-Places: Introduction to an Anthropology of Supermodernity* (London and New York: Verso, 1995), 82
17. Marc Augé, *Non-Places*, 81
18. Jhumpa Lahiri, *The Namesake* (Boston, MA, and New York: Mariner Books, 2004), 127
19. Chitra Banerjee Divakaruni, *The Mistress of Spices* (London: Black Swan, 1997), 4
20. Catherine Belsey, "Reading Cultural History" in Tamsin Spargo (ed.) *Reading the Past: Literature and History* (London: Palgrave, 2000), 106
21. Catherine Belsey, "Reading Cultural History", 106
22. Catherine Belsey, "Reading Cultural History", 107
23. Chitra Banerjee Divakaruni, *The Mistress of Spices*, 4
24. Chitra Banerjee Divakaruni, *The Mistress of Spices*, 13
25. Chitra Banerjee Divakaruni, *The Mistress of Spices*, 4
26. Chitra Banerjee Divakaruni, *The Mistress of Spices*, 3
27. Chitra Banerjee Divakaruni, *The Mistress of Spices*, 5
28. Chitra Banerjee Divakaruni, *The Mistress of Spices*, 60
29. Marco Cenzatti, "Heterotopias of Difference" in Michiel Dehaene and Lieven De Cauter (eds) *Heterotopia and the City: Public Space in a Postcivil Society* (London and New York: Routledge, 2008), 77
30. Anthony Bond, "Welcome to the Slums of Southall", *Mail Online*, 17 October 2011. Accessed on 15 August 2017, available at: http://www.dailymail.co.uk/news/article-2049676/Welcome-Slums-Southall-How-unscrupulous-landlords-illegally-built-squalid-homes-immigrants.html
31. Sigurd F. Lax, "Heterotopia from a Biological and Medical Point of View" in Roland Ritter and Bernd Knaller-Vlay (eds.) *Other Spaces. The Affair of the Heterotopia* (Graz, Austria: Haus der Architektur, 1998), 114

32. Heidi Sohn, "Heterotopia: Anamnesis of a Medical Term" in Michiel Dehaene and Lieven De Cauter (eds) *Heterotopia and the City*, 44
33. C.T. Huang, "Heterotopic Ossification", *Spinal Cord Injury Infosheet 12*, March 2009. Accessed on 15 August 2017, available at: http://images.main.uab.edu/spinalcord/SCI%20Infosheets%20in%20PDF/Heterotopic%20Ossification.pdf
34. Heidi Sohn, "Heterotopia: Anamnesis of a Medical Term", 43
35. Nirmal Puwar, *Space Invaders: Race, Gender and Bodies Out of Place* (Oxford and New York: Berg, 2004), 141
36. Nirmal Puwar, *Space Invaders*, 144
37. Sudesh Mishra, "Tazia Fiji!: The Place of Potentiality" in Susan Koshy and R. Radhakrishnan (eds) *Transnational South Asians: The Making of a Neo-Diaspora* (New Delhi: Oxford University Press, 2008), 88
38. Balli Kaur Jaswal, *Erotic Stories for Punjabi Widows*, 77
39. Ben Kaye, "A Bit of Bollywood Romance for the Ali Sethi-Featuring Track", *Consequence of Sound*, 2 March 2017. Accessed on 15 August 2017, available at: https://consequenceofsound.net/2017/03/swet-shop-boys-perform-a-classic-indian-concert-in-aaja-video-watch/
40. Tom Breihan, "Swet Shop Boys – 'Aaja' Video", *Stereogum*, 2 March 2017. Accessed on 15 August 2017, available at:http://www.stereogum.com/1927712/swet-shop-boys-aaja-video/video
41. Emma May, "Video: Swet Shop Boys – 'Aaja'", *Spin*, 2 March 2017. Accessed on 15 August 2017, available at:http://www.spin.com/2017/03/video-swet-shop-boys-aaja/
42. El Hunt, "Swet Shop Boys Have a New Video for 'Aaja (Ft. Ali Sethi)'", *DIY*, 2 March 2017. Accessed on 15 August 2017, available at: http://diymag.com/2017/03/02/swet-shop-boys-video-aaja-ali-sethi
43. El Hunt, "Swet Shop Boys Have a New Video for 'Aaja (Ft. Ali Sethi)'"
44. Swet Shop Boys, "Aaja", *Cashmere* (Customs, 2016)
45. Riz MC, "Englistan", *Englistan* (Riz MC, 2016)
46. Nirmal Puwar, *Space Invaders*, 8
47. Leah Hislop, "Indian Restaurant Dishoom Voted Britain's Favourite Eatery (Again)", *The Telegraph*, 10 February 2016. Accessed on 15 August 2017, available at: http://www.telegraph.co.uk/food-and-drink/restaurants/indian-restaurant-dishoom-voted-britains-favourite-eatery-again/
48. http://www.dishoom.com. Accessed on 15 August 2017
49. Jay Rayner, "Restaurant Review: Dishoom", *The Guardian*, 15 August 2010. Accessed on 14 August 2017, available at: https://www.theguardian.com/lifeandstyle/2010/aug/15/restaurant-review-jay-rayner-dishoom-indian-london
50. Stuart Jeffries, "The Best Exotic Nostalgia Boom: Why Colonial Style Is Back", *The Guardian*, 19 March 2015. Accessed on 15 August 2017, available at: https://www.theguardian.com/culture/2015/mar/19/the-best-exotic-nostalgia-boom-why-colonial-style-is-back
51. http://www.dishoom.com. Accessed on 15 August 2017
52. Dishoom Covent Garden, "Velantimes Day – The real story of Valentine's Day from Dishoom", 12 April 2011. Accessed on 15 August 2017 https://www.youtube.com/watch?v=Yh6u7KU0uJA
53. "Valentine's Day: Bajrang Dal, VHP Activists Throw Rotten Tomatoes on Couples," *The Hindu*, 14 February 2014. Accessed on 23 October 2017, available at: http://www.thehindu.com/news/national/other-states/valentines-day-bajrang-dal-vhp-activists-throw-rotten-tomatoes-on-couples/article5689272.ece
54. Palash Ghosh, "India's War on Valentine's Day", *International Business Times*, 26 January 2012. Accessed on 15 August 2017, available at: http://www.ibtimes.com/indias-war-valentines-day-213852
55. Alice Burns, "The History of the Indian Chain Restaurant Dishoom" in *The Culture Club*, 9 February 2017. Accessed on 15 August 2017, available at: https://theculturetrip.com/europe/united-kingdom/england/london/articles/dishoom-a-history/

Chapter Five

Salaam, London

Bollywood, Wish Fulfilment, and the Fictive Geographies of the Diaspora

Ever since Amrish Puri appeared on screens worldwide as Chawdhary Baldev Singh, feeding pigeons in London's Trafalgar Square and dreaming about life in his village in Punjab, it has become almost a commonplace for film scholars to identify Bollywood representations of diaspora as vehicles for a nostalgia that seeks to return, if only imaginatively, to a lost and irrecoverable homeland that never really existed anyway. Nostalgia, according to this argument, is little more than an attempt to recover and reinforce problematic narratives of conservative nationalism. For those who may need reminding, Baldev Singh was the father of Simran (played by Kajol), whose romance with Raj (Shah Rukh Khan) became one of the most iconic Bollywood stories ever, with the release in 1995 of Aditya Chopra's record-breaking blockbuster, *Dilwale Dulhaniya Le Jayenge* (*DDLJ*).

Even before audiences witnessed Baldev Singh's nostalgia, however, scholars had been linking the global south Asian diaspora's interest in Bollywood and their apparent nostalgia for the lost home. Writing in 1985, Beatrix Pfleiderer and Luther Lutze were arguing:

> For the first-generation immigrants who remain nostalgic for the home country, these films, with their familiar sights and sounds, provide an emotional satisfaction, irrespective of the quality of the picture, which few others can rival.[1]

Writing about *DDLJ* and its follow-up Shah Rukh Khan/Amrish Puri–starred diasporic film *Pardes*, Patricia Uberoi argued that they represented a 'caricature of the nostalgic NRI (Non-Resident Indian) and his long-distance patriotism'.² More recently, Ingrid Therwath is one of a number of scholars who have made connections with the representation of diaspora on screen with the increased financial success and political conservatism of the global south Asian, chiefly Hindu, diaspora. As Therwath argues, the NRIs in these films represent:

> a kind of über Indian able to assert his ethnic and national identity in a globalized world: successful, capitalist, male, family-oriented, technology-savvy and a devout Hindu all at once.³

Therwath uses statistical data to demonstrate NRI support for the successive BJP (Bharatiya Janata Party) governments (perhaps culminating in Narendra Modi's rally in Madison Square Garden in September 2014) to make a case for the neo-liberal, conservative Hindu, and national-chauvinist identity that is apparently reinforced by the Bollywood version of the NRI. Therwath has argued that the NRI hero, embodied ultimately by Shah Rukh Khan, constructs a model for Indian masculinity:

> Hence it is not surprising that the Non Resident Indian (NRI), who is imagined to be necessarily rich and westernized but who is also known to contribute financially to the Sangh Parivar, became a role model for a fast growing middle class facing the challenges of globalization and its own anguish or feeling of guilt due to a possible acculturation. Unsurprisingly, the popularity of themes related to the diaspora and the nationalist ethnic and cultural discourse aimed at people of Indian origin living abroad reached a peak during the period corresponding to the BJP-led governments (1998–2004). The 1990s and early 2000s could in fact be considered the Golden Age of the NRI, heralded as the emblem of the emerging middle class and the new material aspirations of an India in the midst of economic liberalization.⁴

Building on this relationship between Hindu nationalism in indigenous and diasporic Indian politics, Adrian Athique has argued that:

> the Bollywood archetype is defined by the high-budget saccharine upper middle-class melodrama which represents a tongue-in-cheek blockbuster repackaging of the *masala* movie of old within an affluent, nostalgic and highly exclusive view of Indian culture and society.⁵

Even when scholars like Jigna Desai have questioned this reading of mainstream, blockbuster Bollywood movies as necessarily reinforcing a simplistic, homogenous, and hegemonic narrative of Hindu nationalism, her reading clearly indicates an unquestioned slippage between the affect of nostalgia on the one hand, and an ethnically absolutist, politically conservative, neo-liberal nationalism on the other. Thus, she argues:

However, while most analyses of the consumption of Indian cinema assume simple nostalgia as the primary impetus for viewing films, this essay suggests that this narrow and essentialist explanation has too long been used to describe heterogenous, contradictory, and complex viewing practices.[6]

In this argument, Desai is clearly setting up a binary between narrow simplistic essentialism and nostalgia on the one hand and heterogeneity, contradiction and complexity on the other. Elsewhere in her writing, she reveals this equation of nostalgia and simplistic conservatism even more fully:

Nostalgia has been a significant trope in narratives of nationalism that hearken back to the days when the nation was whole and stable, unhampered by alienation, difference, and change.[7]

Behind this reading of the representation of the successful NRI on screen as an example of 'simple' nostalgia, there seem to me to be a number of assumptions that are usually left unquestioned. Firstly, there is an assumption that there exists a relationship of equivalence between the representation of capitalist success on screen and the material success that some sections of the south Asian diaspora have experienced. In other words, critics seem to think that the intention on the part of the filmmakers is for the various south Asian communities to identify with the portrayal of the financially successful NRI on screen – insofar as he represents their success in a realist manner. This relationship of equivalence extends to the political leanings of some sections of the diaspora, with their interest in and identification with Bollywood representations of diaspora. In other words, the argument is that the conservatism of some sections of the diaspora must be apparent through their portrayal on screen. Finally, and most unquestioned of all, remains the assumption that the nostalgia expressed in and through the film must always be for the lost homeland, and must always, and of necessity, exist in a relationship of equivalence with the mode of nationalism espoused by the Hindu Right which large sections of the diaspora actively supports. In short, there remains, in the words of Patricia Uberoi, a belief that 'forms of popular and mass culture can open up dimensions of humane experience that are otherwise relatively inaccessible to sociological scrutiny.'[8] Or as Jigna Desai has argued: 'South Asian diasporic identificatory processes are centrally configured and contested through the cinematic apparatus.'[9] Rajinder Dudrah, on the other hand, provides a more convincing theory of the role played by Bollywood in the diasporic world when he argues, of the 2007 film *Jhoom Barabar Jhoom (JBJ)*, that:

it very much uses and plays on popular Hindi cinema's forays into everyday love stories, fantasy, the song and dance spectacle, and a tongue-in-cheek nod to earlier Hindi cinema through pastiche and parody in the contemporary moment, all with attempted sincerity.[10]

While Dudrah's analysis is much more convincing, he does not make the link between this knowing, self-referential reading of Bollywood and the nostalgia that the diasporic communities experience and put to work.

In this chapter, I attempt to do so by offering a counter-reading of Bollywood representations of the Indian diaspora. I concentrate on Bollywood representations of diaspora that date from the 1990s' liberalization of the Indian economy and all of the social, economic and cultural effects that followed that crucial moment in Indian history. Thus, I look at a wide range of films, from the earliest of these 'new' depictions of the successful NRI in films such as *Dilwale Dulhaniya Le Jayenge* (1995) and *Pardes* (1997), to the blockbusters of the early 2000s such as *Kabhi Khushi Kabhie Gham* (2001) and *Kal Ho Naa Ho* (2003), to more recent films such as *London, Paris, New York* (2012) and *Total Siyapaa* (2014). While these films are quite different in many ways, I argue that there are commonalities in the way they mobilize nostalgia to reimagine the relationship between the home back there, and the home that has been re-created in the diaspora. This nostalgic re-creation allows the diaspora to feel at home and to project a knowingly fictionalized view of diasporic success in order to claim their right to belong, and to shield themselves from the racism that continues to alienate them from the mainstream.

It is of course true that these films, while depicting diasporic worlds, are made predominantly for an indigenous audience in India, and it is probably safe to say that the needs and desires of this audience must be recognized as a large factor in the way Bollywood has conceptualized its diasporic subjects. It is nevertheless undeniable that Bollywood representations of diaspora have proven to be hugely influential in the ways in which these diasporic communities conceive of themselves, in ways perhaps never intended by the films' producers, or indeed shared by the films' audience in south Asia.

BOLLYWOOD AND NOSTALGIA FOR THE FUTURE

While all of these films display clear tropes of nostalgia, there is, as far as I am aware, only one instance of the actual English word *nostalgic* being used. This appears in the opening scene of Anu Menon's 2012 directorial debut, *London, Paris, New York*. The film opens with new filmmaker Nikhil Chopra being interviewed at the New York premier of his first film. The interviewer asks him to talk about his first visit to the city. He replies:

> I have a strange relationship with this city. I was supposed to have come here a few years ago, but I couldn't come. Now that finally, I am here, I'm actually a little nostalgic about the place.

Nikhil is clearly not using his nostalgia to re-create a lost home back in India, but rather to attempt an imaginative reconstruction of a place that could have been his home, had he made the trip and reconnected with the woman of his dreams as he was meant to. Far from nostalgia being an affect that reclaims a simple, idealized and romanticized past, nostalgia actually works to destabilize the boundaries between the 'here' and the 'there', as well as the boundary between the 'now' and the 'then'. Existing both spatially and temporally, nostalgia blurs not just the boundaries between the 'over there' and the 'right here', but also the past and the future, in the process creating a new fictive space that is all of these at once. Instead of holding onto a simple, uncomplicated and idealized past, nostalgia actually becomes about collapsing the past and the present into a new world where the home is in the here and the now, and where the diaspora need not feel homesick for a lost home, nor alienated in an unfamiliar and unfriendly present.

The title song of Nikhil Advani's 2003 film *Kal Ho Naa Ho* (*KHNH*) provides a useful example of what I mean. The refrain of the song, which on screen is sung by the most iconic star Bollywood has produced in the last thirty years, Shah Rukh Khan, goes: 'Every moment here, live life to the fullest, / This ambience we have today, may or may not be tomorrow.' The visual image of Shah Rukh Khan as Aman, singing and dancing in a stereotypically Bollywood fashion in front of the Brooklyn Bridge, clearly harks back to the glory days of Bollywood when exotic locations were used for little more than set dressing. In this sequence, as in many of the other films I discuss, the self-referentiality of these films is used to direct nostalgia towards Bollywood's own history. However, in this case, the words would at first sight seem to completely undermine any nostalgic sense of the permanence of home. Rather, the song evokes a sense of *carpe diem* that undercuts the lingering presence of the 'there' and the 'then' in the 'here' and the 'now'. And it is not as if this is the only instance of a *carpe diem* sentiment visible in films that are nostalgically driven accounts of the diaspora, either. The title song in Siddharth Anand's 2005 film *Salaam, Namaste* features Nick and Ambar (Saif Ali Khan and Preity Zinta respectively) dancing on a beach near Melbourne, Australia. The lyrics of the refrain here are: 'One day, one moment, one love / Here today, but will fly off tomorrow.' A similar trope is also noticeable in the first song of Kabir Khan's 2009 film *New York*. Omar is a young student from Delhi, newly arrived at New York State University. Here he becomes friends with two second-generation Indian Americans – Maya and Sam. As Omar nostalgically looks back to the heady days of student life, when he started to make America his home, the song accompanying this montage follows the same pattern: 'Hey friends, let's live this moment to the fullest. / It seems now, our time is about to come.'

In all these examples, then, the nostalgia is directed not simply at a stable past that is a referent for the home country, but at a complex mixture of past, present and future, as well as a complex halfway point between the home that was over there, and the home that is being built here. Thus, Aman in *KHNH* is singing in front of Brooklyn Bridge; Nick and Ambar in *Salaam, Namaste* are singing on a beach in Melbourne; while Omar, Sam and Maya in *New York* are playing American football. Prior to the game, Sam's entry into the film was made through a race that echoes the famous Trinity Great Court race in *Chariots of Fire*. Sam challenges another student (white, blond, American) to a race against the bell tolling twelve. Of course, Sam wins and gets to hoist the American flag over the university buildings. The juxtaposition of the American flag with the south Asian male body points to the complexity of the nostalgia that works in and through these films. The characters and, perhaps by extension, the audience are encouraged to feel nostalgic, paradoxically, for a moment characterized by this *carpe diem* where temporal and spatial borders can be collapsed into a new space that could be called *yahaan* – the 'here' that Shah Rukh Khan is singing in. This *yahaan* is at once 'here' and 'now', though of course it is not supposed to be read as the here/now of New York, but rather as an imaginary, fictive geography where the present of New York and the past of India can occupy the same space and time. Nostalgia, in short, works in these films as wish fulfilment, through which a global diaspora can feel connected and at home in an imaginary, fictional, heterogeneous and at least potentially radical space. Creating this new space by fusing the home and the abroad is an exercise in wish fulfilment in that it allows the diaspora to exercise control over the spaces in the home and in the world that they fear they don't quite belong in.

NOSTALGIA BEYOND BORDERS

The *yahaan* is structured around in-between, liminal spaces – airports, railway stations, journeys across and between cities. As I will discuss below, many of these films culminate in a journey across the city as (usually) the man goes after the woman, in order to be reunited in the happy-ever-after ending. In and through this journey, however, the world is mapped and remapped in interesting and different ways, as spaces of control that are often experienced by the diaspora as oppressive (airport security control or immigration checks) are appropriated into fictive spaces of liberation, in and through which the diaspora can claim ownership of the spaces they find themselves in. As spatial and temporal borders collapse, a new, imaginary geography of the *yahaan* is created which becomes the diaspora's true home.

This collapse of borders can be seen cinematically through the juxtaposition of scenes set in India and in the 'West'. Famously, in the opening scenes of *DDLJ*, Baldev Singh is transported through the magic of song from Trafalgar Square to what scholars like Patricia Uberoi and Rajinder Dudrah have both written about as 'golden mustard fields, icon of the Punjab'.[11] The song evokes an appropriately nostalgic sense of the fantasy of homecoming, and has generally been criticized for its conservative approach to diaspora-indigenous relations. The cinematic device of cutting in the middle of a song-and-dance routine, in order to imaginatively go back home, is, however, a device that has been used many times since. This device can be seen in *JBJ*, which, as Dudrah argues, is a very different film. In Dudrah's words, *JBJ* 'plays with the idea of the homeland as a figurative relationship that we only witness, largely in and through song and dance sequences.'[12] An obvious example is the song 'Bol na halke', which oscillates between Waterloo Station and an unnamed station in India in a way that is very reminiscent of the opening scenes of *DDLJ*. Through what is perhaps the most characteristic feature of Bollywood cinema – song and dance – the audience is thus transported into an imaginary version of homeland, which they can use to nostalgically reconstruct whatever *home* may mean for them.

It is interesting how critics have received these non-diegetic cuts in the middle of songs in very different ways. Patricia Uberoi has identified them as evidence of the films' nostalgically driven endorsement of conservative nationalism. She argues that through these cuts, 'the chief protagonists are constantly reminded of the moral responsibility of being 'Indian' and that 'these reminders constitute major sign-posts and crisis-points in the unfolding of the film narrative'.[13] Writing about the latter example, however, Dudrah identifies it as part of the 'aesthetics of a postmodern Bollywood', which marks 'the referent of a global commercial Hindi cinema'. Dudrah does point out that these cinematic gestures 'are not in any way exclusive to the post-1990s',[14] though, in his focus on one film, he is perhaps unable to make the connections that link these very different films.

One way of doing so, I would argue, is to place a critical emphasis on the fictiveness of this space – the inherent fictiveness of the golden mustard seeds in *DDLJ* or the railway station in *JBJ*. If, in other words, we place our emphasis on the cinematic cuts that link the two landscapes within the here/now of the *yahaan*, the resulting reading opens up a space that is at once more complex, more interesting, and possibly more radical than scholars have been prepared to admit. This imaginary middle ground, or third space, is what the nostalgia of these films is directed towards, and it is a space where many of the normal rules do not apply.

An interesting example is provided by Lajjo Kapur (Sushma Seth) in *KHNH*. Lajjo is presented as a devout Hindu woman, whose animosity towards her widowed daughter-in-law is presented as deriving from her dislike of her daughter-in-law's Christian faith and the association she makes between that faith and her son's death. Lajjo and her friends do their best to recreate a deeply problematic narrative of India in New York. Her dream is that 'New York should become part of Punjab' – though the narrative of the film does seem to undermine the conservatism that marks her observance of her faith, her twin insistence on Indian food and Indian television, and her consequent tirades against her daughter-in-law and grandchildren for not being Indian enough. When Aman (Shah Rukh Khan) arrives at this island of India in an American sea that is New York, Lajjo and her friends are immediately nervous because they have heard that Indian men try to seduce Indian American women in order to get a 'card'. They are, however, confused as to the nature of this card – whether is a 'ration card', which is a form of identity that allows people to access government subsidized food in India, or a 'green card', which allows the holder to become a permanent resident of the United States. In the here/now that is the *yahaan*, the material hierarchy that divides these two documents is being erased in a way that mirrors the non-diegetic cinematic cuts I describe above. By appropriating space of the 'here' and the 'there', and by re-inscribing the rules that govern movement between these spaces, the *yahaan* is able to effectively challenge hegemonic notions of nation-states and the forces that regulate movement between them.

This appropriation of space can often be seen through what is effectively an exercise in cartographic control. I have already referred to the opening scene of *DDLJ*, where Baldev Singh sits in Trafalgar Square feeding the pigeons. Having done so, he walks to work following a route that makes no geographic sense whatsoever – in sequence, he walks along the Embankment towards the Houses of Parliament, then along the South Bank across the river from Big Ben, then north to south along Westminster Bridge, then along the Mall in front of Buckingham Palace, then in front of Tower Bridge, and finally to his shop, in the very 'Indian' neighbourhood of Southall. Throughout most of this walk, London is almost completely empty, and Baldev Singh cuts a lonely figure walking through the old imperial capital. What he is doing on this walk is, of course, claiming ownership of the city in a way that is not dissimilar to the imperial strategy of claiming ownership of the old colonies through the technologies of cartography. The fictiveness of this geography, and the obviously imaginary emptiness of London, is clear evidence that this representation is not meant to be a realistic depiction of diasporic life in the 'West'. Through this walk, rather, Baldev Singh is being allowed to appropriate the geography of London, with all its familiar landmarks, as part of the *yahaan*. Once London is part of this *yahaan*, it belongs to Baldev Singh and, by extension, to diasporic Asians as much as it does to the indigenous British.

The introductory montage to Vipul Shah's 2007 film *Namastey London* replaces a particular character's viewpoint with a depersonalized, aerial view over all the same landmarks. Shots of Buckingham Palace, the Houses of Parliament, Trafalgar Square and the London Eye are interspersed with shots of 'Asian' spaces such as Southall and Brick Lane. In contrast to the montage in *DDLJ*, London here is busy: populated by pedestrians who help to mark London as a multicultural, multi-faith and multi-racial city, as the camera follows people who are visibly Hindu, Muslim, Sikh, as well as non–south Asians. Once again, south Asians are allowed to take ownership of the city, as the camera focuses on a woman of south Asian origin giving directions to a tourist. This montage of London is paired with a song that is clearly designed to evoke a sense of nostalgic belonging: 'Wherever I am, in whatever way, / Your memories are always with me.'

Like Nikhil's nostalgic attachment to New York in *London, Paris, New York*, the nostalgia evoked here seems to be for the fictive *yahaan* that London has become part of.

Similar strategies are noticeable near the end of both Siddharth Anand's *Salaam, Namaste* and Nikhil Advani's 2011 film *Patiala House*. In the former, Nick, a chef, and Ambar, a medical student and part-time radio DJ, get together and then break up. Nick manages to use Ambar's radio station to track her down across the city of Melbourne. He asks the people of the city to phone him if they see her, and shop owners, taxi drivers, bus passengers and pedestrians are all seen to help him, as he, following their instructions, tracks her down to Fisherman's Wharf. Punjabi-speaking taxi drivers and pedestrians with an Australian accent are equally likely to be listeners of Ambar's non-Anglophone programme, demonstrating that an Asian radio station clearly has enough listeners to completely take over the city. I examine in more detail the role played by Asian broadcasting in the next chapter, but for the moment, it is enough to recognize that whether it is New York, London or Melbourne, they can all be appropriated into the *yahaan* and be owned by the diasporic south Asian.

The climax of Nikhil Advani's *Patiala House* sees Parghat Singh Kahlon (Akshay Kumar) secretly playing cricket for England against Australia, contrary to his father Gurtej's (Rishi Kapoor) express instructions. Watching the match on television, Gurtej sees how his son has fulfilled his own prediction – that one day the angry shouts of hatred would be subsumed by the roars of applause. Gurtej and his entire family rush to Lord's cricket grounds in his black and yellow, very Indian, Hindustan Motors Ambassador taxi. Stopped on the way for speeding, the police change their mind when Gurtej explains where they are heading. The same British police who had arrested and humiliated Gurtej for fighting back against racism at the start of the film now provide his Ambassador taxi an escort so they can get to Lord's on time. Parghat bowls the last over and wins the match for England. Patiala House of the film's title is no longer just the building that Gurtej built and now houses his entire family. Patiala House, named for a district in Punjab, now encompasses the entirety of London, where the quintessentially English features – Tower Bridge, red double-decker buses, the flag of St George, all become markers of Indian success in Britain.

The Ambassador's journey across London, Nick's journey across Melbourne, or Baldev's journey across London in *DDLJ* are all so obviously, deliberately fictional that they can only be the wish fulfilment of a diasporic population which is using the cinematic experience to imagine a different reality, where a thirty-five-year-old Indian shopkeeper could make it straight to the English cricket team, where the cricket commentary at Lord's could be in Hindi, and where the Metropolitan police could escort an Ambassador taxi from Southall so that an Indian man could watch his Indian son win a famous victory for England. This different reality, where normal rules do not apply, where an Asian radio station can bring together an entire city, allowing an Indian man to gain control over the city through his movement – this is what constitutes the *yahaan*.

Viewed from this angle, it becomes clear that the financial success represented in these films need not be read as representative of actual financial success as experienced by some sections of the diaspora. There is nothing in these films that implies any such identification on the part of the audience. In a film like *JBJ*, this representation is clearly knowingly fictional – as Rikki Thukral's (Avishek Bachchan) imaginary fiancée, Anaida (Lara Dutta), becomes the manager of Hotel Ritz in Paris, and Rikki, a small-time broker and shady businessman, can be in the hotel lobby the day Princess Diana died, while Alvira's (Preity Zinta) imaginary fiancé, Steve (Bobby Deol), is a lawyer who is driven around in a chauffeur-driven limousine, and whose home is actually Somerset House in London. However, what is interesting is how similar these tropes are to the apparently more conventional Bollywood diasporic films. Thus, in *Kabhi Khushi Kabhie Gham* (*KKKG*), the Raichand family home is Waddesden Manor, and Rahul, (played by Shah Rukh Khan himself) is shown to be arriving in a helicopter. His entrance is not, in fact, dissimilar to his famous trip to his university graduation ceremony in *DDLJ*, in which he drove a white Lamborghini. In *Namastey London*, on Jazz's (Katrina Kaif) first date with Charlie Brown (Clive Standen), he takes her in his Ferrari to Buckingham Palace, where she gets to meet Prince Charles. Surely all this could only ever happen in the *yahaan*. It is, in short, difficult to maintain the position that these tropes were ever designed to be, or indeed, should be read as representative of NRI success in the 'West'.

In other words, I disagree with Vijay Mishra when he argues:

> The ideology in question then is not one that examines social ruptures . . . but one that reworks a number of diasporic fantasies. When these fantasies are reconfigured by the homeland as the 'real' of diasporic lives, they have the curious role of actually becoming 'truths' to which the diaspora aspires.[15]

Through his sociological study of cinema, Rajinder Dudrah has critiqued this argument by pointing out how 'Mishra is . . . unable to suggest or demonstrate more detailed readings or complex uses of Bollywood film cultures by its diasporic audiences'.[16] To be fair to Mishra, the work I am citing predates many of the films that I am examining here, and these films may well represent a change to the traditions of diasporic film that Bollywood has produced over the years. Either way, however, the self-aware fictionality of the representations of diasporic communities suggests to me that what is happening is more interesting and perhaps more important than either simplistic realism, or aspirational in any real sense.

BOLLYWOOD, NOSTALGIA AND DIASPORIC DREAMING

Based on these films, I find it much more convincing to argue that the financial success that is portrayed in the *yahaan* is not meant to be realist or aspirational, but rather, the *yahaan* serves as a space in which diasporic dreams of belonging, of not having to justify one's presence, can in fact be fulfilled. Watching Shah Rukh Khan drive a Lamborghini or get off a helicopter, then, serves the same purpose as the scene in *DDLJ* in which Raj and Simran get on a train in Kings Cross Station, and seconds later find themselves in Switzerland. This is, in other words, make-believe – a world constructed in terms of the politics of the apparently impossible, but which can then be used to imaginatively counter the real alienation often experienced by the diaspora. Like many of the nostalgically constructed homelands that I am examining in this book, the *yahaan* is, of course, imaginary and romanticized, but that is not to say that it does not do important work in the psychic life of the diaspora.

A perfect example is the climax of Vipul Shah's 2009 film *London Dreams*. The film centres around two childhood friends, Arjun and Mannu (played by Ajay Devgan and Salman Khan respectively). They leave Punjab in order to follow their musical dreams, and, in London, they set up a band with two expat Pakistanis and a second-generation British Indian. This band, appropriately called London Dreams, embarks on a European tour, culminating in a sell-out performance at Wembley. The notion of a fledgling British Indo-Pak music band being able to sell out Wembley Arena is a marker of diasporic success, yes, but it is of the same order as Shah Rukh Khan driving a Lamborghini, or commuting home in a helicopter – it is meant to be neither a realistic portrayal of diasporic capitalist success nor a neo-liberal marker of aspiration. In other words, London Dreams selling out Wembley Arena is not equivalent to Indian Prime Minister and Hindu nationalist leader Narendra Modi selling out Madison Square Garden in September 2014.

One reason why these two scenarios, one fantastical and the other all too real, should be seen as different in their performance is that the nostalgically constructed *yahaan* in which London Dreams plays Wembley is not a homogenous space. The *yahaan* is able to transcend borders, nostalgically linking people and places that would not necessarily be possible in the homelands. The band London Dreams, for example, is half Indian and half Pakistani. *Jhoom Barabar Jhoom* (*JBJ*), *Total Siyapaa*, and *PK* all feature cross-border India-Pakistan romances which, while not unknown to Bollywood films set within the subcontinent, are much more common in the *yahaan* of the diasporic cinema. In *JTHJ*, Samar, as a busker in London, shares his room with Zain from Lahore; in *JBJ*, Rikki Thukral's best friend is Huffy Bhai from Pakistan – on meeting Alvira from Lahore, Rikki claims: 'Oh you're a Pakistani. Same to same'. The eponymous radio station in *Salaam, Namaste*, recognizes the heterogeneity of the diaspora – combining as it does the Islamic and Hindu forms of greeting in one phrase. Of course, it is possible to argue that this heterogeneity is but another example of the hegemonic secularism of the Indian state, which conceals beneath it a rampant and virulent Islamophobia. This argument is not without merit, but must be placed against the rapid lurch to the right that the Indian state has undergone in the months after Narendra Modi's election as Prime Minister. As the Madison Square Garden rally arguably demonstrates, the BJP government, along with its other Hindu nationalist allies, is attempting to reinforce, and benefit from, a latent Islamophobia in the diasporic Hindu communities. Set in this context, the spectacle of a fictional Indo-Pak music group, selling out Wembley arena through a fictionalized depiction of cross-border solidarity, cannot be seen as simplistically hegemonic.

DIASPORIC NOSTALGIA, INDIA, PAKISTAN AND THE MALE MUSLIM BODY

The proliferation of cross-border romantic relationships as well as friendships in these films complicates the relationship between nostalgia and nationalism. The *yahaan* comprises so many spaces, across so many nations, that it is difficult to sustain the idea that it can ever really be used to reinforce narrow and essentialist nationalism, or that Hindu-supremacist politics can ever be simply mapped onto the politics of these films.

These depictions of Indo-Pak friendship, and even romance, are thus always tinged with the awareness of the political dimension, as Rikki and Alvira in *JBJ* demonstrate when their bickering in Waterloo Station also turns to cross-border troubles in the homelands. Jaggu (Anushka Sharma) and Sarfaraz (Sushant Singh Rajput) in Rajkumar Hirani's 2014 film *PK* initially meet in Bruges, but then, due to a misunderstanding, end up separated. They both return home – Jaggu to Delhi and Sarfaraz to Lahore. Their reunion can only happen over the phone via the Pakistan embassy in Bruges. The diasporic space of the *yahaan* is thus essential in order to overcome the practical political problems associated with Indo-Pak border crossings. While not directly linked to the diaspora, it is noticeable that the anti-superstition, anti-religion message of *PK*, which underpins the cross-border romance initiated in the diaspora, is also a thinly veiled attack at the saffronization of public life that Narendra Modi's government has reinforced. The cross-border romances might be occurring in the fictive space of the *yahaan*, but the politics they represent is just as firmly based in the contemporary reality of the geopolitics of the subcontinent.

In *Total Siyapaa*, for example, it is not just the two leads, Aman (Ali Zafar) and Asha (Yami Gautam), who manage to transcend their national differences, but also their friends and family, who are shown to unite against an idiotic but racist policeman who spots terror plots everywhere. The drunken policeman attempts to divide the Indians and Pakistanis in order to decide which group are the more dangerous as terrorists – instead they get together to beat up the policeman and effect their escape. The politics of the south Asian partition of 1947, and the politics of the post-9/11 war on terror are thus cinematically linked, with the *yahaan* once again figuring as wish fulfilment as the division of partition is undone, in order to fight the effects of post-9/11 racism. The film is only too aware of the global politics of this family-based romantic comedy. One of Aman and Asha's arguments ends up in a shouting match about ISI and RAW, the Pakistani and Indian intelligence agencies respectively. It is no coincidence that the names of the two leads – Aman and Asha – mean peace and hope, and derive from Arabic and Sanskrit respectively. The nostalgically constructed *yahaan* then is at once the multicultural London of the present (where official, securitized racism is rewritten as ineffective), a united, pre-partition subcontinent, and an imagined future where the countries of the subcontinent could exist in peace. Whatever else they may do, the politics of these films certainly do not simplistically mirror Narendra Modi's brand of Hindu nationalism.

Wish fulfilment as a way to counter post-9/11 racism can also be seen at work in *Jab Tak Hai Jaan* (*JTHJ*). Shah Rukh Khan plays Major Samar Anand of the bomb disposal squad of the Indian Army. Even though he is suffering from retrograde amnesia following a traffic accident, he is able to defuse a bomb placed on a train in London, thus undermining the comically inefficient British police. In the process, the south Asian male body, so commonly coded as the dangerous other in the War on Terror, is being nostalgically re-inscribed as the saviour. The *yahaan* of the diasporic cinema is a world in which the south Asian community belongs because it is up to the south Asian community to save the day. Similar tropes are noticeable in Kabir Khan's 2009 thriller *New York*, which is set in the context of the post-

9/11 war on terror. Irrfan Khan plays Roshan, an Indian Muslim FBI agent who has been given the responsibility to track down a south Asian Islamic-terror sleeper cell headed by Samir (John Abraham). In order to get his man, Roshan initially frames and then recruits Omar (Neil Nitin Mukesh), another Indian Muslim, and an old friend of Samir and his wife, Maya. As in the case of Samar Anand, the south Asian (in this case Muslim) body is being appropriated in the counterterrorism struggle. As Roshan puts it, 'This hostility towards Muslims that you sense in this corner of the world, or in any other country, it is only a Muslim who can transform that hostility into respect. Maybe you and I are here today to do just that.' What marks Roshan out much more than his faith, however, is his Indianness. His FBI interrogation of Omar takes place mostly in Hindi, and in spite of periodic intrusions from white Americans, the narrative of the film is able to hold up Indian masculinity, not as a source of terror, but as the solution to it. These films reflect a deeply nostalgic desire for a world in which the white 'West' values rather than vilifies brown Indian male bodies. In the heterogeneous space that is the *yahaan*, these bodies are not othered but re-inscribed as essential for the survival of both the home back there and the home in the here and now.

The heterogeneity of the *yahaan* is not limited to Indo-Pakistani relationships either. In *KHNH*, Aman's arrival in New York is accompanied by an extended song and dance sequence which creates not just an Asian public space but a deeply multi-ethnic one. The song samples Roy Orbison's 1964 hit 'Pretty Woman', as well as incorporating hip-hop, rap, bhangra, and gospel, among many others. Standing in front of a giant star-spangled banner, Aman leads a multi-ethnic backing dance troupe, which eventually take over the whole street. As with the case of Sam hoisting the American flag over his university in *New York*, the shot of Aman dancing in front of the flag here precludes any simple nostalgic attachment to India, let alone to the Indian nation-state. Nostalgia, according to this reading, is less a patriotic endorsement of any kind of triumphalist nationalism and more an imaginary that refers to a carnivalesque, unstable, and ambiguous space that resists easy simplification.

To say this is not to say that there is nothing politically problematic about this *yahaan* or to undermine the very real criticism of the troubling gendered and racial politics that these films have and continue to reinforce. Vijay Mishra is correct when he argues that

> the global in this case is not to be read as a critical internationalism that transcends difference and creates a decidedly 'hybrid' diasporic self overnight.[17]

As an example of a politically problematic use of nostalgia, one could turn to the sequence in *KHNH*, in which Aman (played by Shah Rukh Khan) helps the Kapoor family to resurrect their restaurant. When Jennifer's restaurant is about to be closed down because of debts, Aman comes to the rescue. 'We have a power which we need to use, and that power is called, India!' – with this bold declaration, Aman leads everyone else in a song-and-dance routine that dramatizes their efforts to refurbish the restaurant. The song used is 'Chale Chalo' from the 2001 anti-colonial cricket-themed blockbuster, *Lagaan*. In the original film, set in colonial India, the villagers challenge the British to a game of cricket, with the annual tax burden as the wager. This song accompanies a training montage, as the cricket equipment is transformed into the weapons of an anti-colonial war. Two years later, *KHNH* uses the song in a knowingly self-referential manner to turn the refurbishment of the restaurant into a similarly counter-colonial struggle. The cricket bats are replaced with brooms, hammers and cooking equipment, as the whole Indian community comes together to rescue the Kapoor family. The name Café New York is changed to Café New Delhi as the American flag is replaced by the Indian flag. Of course, the restaurant is reopened to great success, and a deeply nostalgic sense of the power of the homeland (not coincidentally articulated through food) saves the day. The problem, however, is that throughout this sequence, the Indian restaurant is not pitted against the old colonial enemy (Britain) or its twenty-first-century descendant (America) but, instead, the neighbouring, competing Chinese restaurant. What should have been a rallying call for counter-imperialist activism becomes, in this scene, a deeply problematic narrative of racial superiority of India over China. Similarly, as has been argued many times, the use of nostalgia to reinforce patriarchy in many of these films, and certainly most of the earlier films – *DDLJ*, *Pardes*, *KKKG*, and so on – is deeply problematic. My point is not to hold up the *yahaan* as a utopian space of counter-hegemony, nor to reject it as simplistically homogenous and conservative. Rather, to borrow from Vijay Mishra's analysis of *DDLJ*:

> Even as *DDLJ* advances a rather reactionary ideology vis-à-vis the diaspora, there are moments of controlled transgressions . . . moments of disruption . . . that introduces a disharmony, an ambiguity, into the social.[18]

This 'imaginative realism', to use Mishra's phrase, that constructs and structures the *yahaan* thus cannot, I argue, be simplistically aligned with the conservative nationalism that many sections of the diaspora uphold. In other words, the *yahaan* may often display conservative traits in terms of gender and racial politics, but it is not inevitable that it will do so. The *yahaan* for me is rather what Sudesh Mishra has, in another context, called a 'heterotopian socius', which is characterized by a radical potentiality that may never be actualized, but is important because it 'dramatized the potential for an alternative social arrangement . . . [which] was fluid, unbounded, and transnational'.[19] It is this radical potentiality of the *yahaan* which these films enact that I am interested in.

The *yahaan* is a fictive linguistic community where everybody always speaks fluent Hindi. In every single one of the films that I have been looking at, the second-generation diaspora is always fluent in Hindi. Most of the time, this linguistic fluency is not even addressed explicitly but is rather taken for granted. Sometimes, as in *DDLJ* and *KKKG*, the ability to speak Hindi is inscribed as evidence of their attachment to traditional values. Famously, Baldev Singh in *DDLJ* exclaims with pride: 'I've kept India even in the heart of London'. More often, however, this ability to speak Hindi is matched with a distinctively diasporic ability to adjust, through the creation of a hybridized culture. When Omar first meets Maya in *New York*, she explains her knowledge of Hindi thus: 'I speak Hindi. I even watch Hindi films. I don't like them but I have to. My mother, you know. She would dump my Dad for Shah Rukh Khan in a heartbeat.' Later she introduces the equally fluent Sam thus: 'He doesn't have too many Indian friends . . . he is just so American in his ways. He's been living here since he was four years old. His father is a professor, an expert in Indian culture, that's why his Hindi is so fluent. Otherwise he would have been totally American.' However, neither Maya nor Sam is held up as the kind of traditional second-generation Asians as Simran and her sister Rajeshwari are in *DDLJ*. The nostalgia here is not so much for a morally superior Indian homeland and its values, but rather for a diaspora which is able to feel connected to the 'West' through its ability to adapt, and to the homelands through its linguistic knowledge. Even in the much more conservative *DDLJ*, what is celebrated through the narrative is not just Baldev's attachment to and belief in the superiority of Indian cultural values, but his daughters' ability to adjust and change register between 'Indian' and 'British' as they successfully navigate life as diasporic Indians in London. If anything, the film is able to gently mock the patriarchal authority that Baldev embodies, by demonstrating how easily and quickly his family can switch their behaviour when they hear him approach.

From taxi drivers to waiters to shopkeepers – everybody in this *yahaan* can speak and understand Hindi whether or not they are actually Indian. In Shakun Batra's 2012 film *Ek Main Aur Ekk Tu*, both Rahul and Riana (played by Imran Khan and Kareena Kapoor respectively) visit therapists in Las Vegas, both of whom speak fluent Hindi, even though they are not evidently south Asian. In *JTHJ*, Samar is in London as a young man, working variously as a cleaner, a waiter, handyman and busker. Everyone he meets understands Hindi, and he is able to charm everyone. A decade later, when he returns to London, he can still recognize and be recognized by all his old busking friends and his old colleagues. The transitory world of ad hoc, hourly paid employment, a world that is only too familiar to large sections of the diaspora, is thus nostalgically co-opted into the *yahaan* where no one questions one's right to belong, and the attachments one makes can become permanent.

It is of course true that the films need to depict the British or American characters speaking Hindi to cater to its large indigenous, non-English-speaking audience. Nevertheless, this motif of repeatedly depicting the Euro-American present in which the diasporic subject exists as a fictive linguistic community also has the effect of allowing the diaspora to dream of such a possibility. The nostalgia of these films allows the creation of a fictive linguistic community, which in turn allows the diaspora to imagine a world where they are not linguistically alienated from their surroundings.

There is another aspect to this reading of the close connections between the diaspora and the homelands, and that is through the audience's awareness of the biography of actors like Katrina Kaif. Kaif, who stars in *JTHJ*, *New York* and *Namastey London*, was born to a British Indian father and a white British mother, and had a peripatetic childhood, which mirrors the global rootless nature of large sections of the diaspora. Kaif is one of a number of stars (Sunny Leone and Nargis Fakhri being some of the others) who have made the transition from the diaspora to success in the indigenous world of the Bollywood film industry. Kaif's own story thus aids the wish fulfilment on the part of the diasporic audience, as they can imagine a borderless world that matches her own public persona.

Perhaps the most obvious, and yet least noted argument against the idea that the diasporic representation simplistically privileges a conservative, Hindu nationalism is that the figure most closely associated with this trope is himself Muslim, Shah Rukh Khan. It is true that in most of these films, he plays a Hindu Indian – Raj in *DDLJ*, Rahul in *KKKG*, Aman in *KHNH*, Samar in *JTHJ* – but that does not take away the audience's awareness of his identity as a Muslim. This is important for several reasons. Firstly, Shah Rukh Khan has featured in the news multiple times for being detained by airport security in the United States – stories in which his religious identity was obviously of key importance. In 2009, it was reported[20] that he had been detained and questioned for over an hour at Newark Liberty International Airport in New Jersey, while in 2012, he was detained for more than ninety minutes at White Plains Airport near New York. Newspaper accounts of both incidents blamed them on the fact that 'his name came up on a computer alert list.' He has also become embroiled in controversy when an article he wrote in *Outlook* magazine in India on being Muslim and Indian was picked up and unfavourably commented on on both sides of the Indo-Pakistan border. Writing about the frequent attacks he has undergone as perhaps the most high-profile Muslim figure in India:

> I sometimes become the inadvertent object of political leaders who choose to make me a symbol of all that they think is wrong and unpatriotic about Mus-

lims in India. There have been occasions when I have been accused of bearing allegiance to our neighboring nation rather than my own country – this even though I am an Indian whose father fought for the freedom of India. Rallies have been held where leaders have exhorted me to leave my home and return to what they refer to as my 'original homeland'.[21]

The controversy that followed this article[22] gained widespread coverage in the subcontinent and beyond – all of which means that for most of the audience, indigenous and diasporic, Shah Rukh Khan's religious identity is part of his public persona, and therefore, part of the trope of the diasporic Indian he portrays on screen.

If Katrina Kaif's own biography becomes part of the diasporic characters she plays, then the same is true of Shah Rukh Khan, and nowhere more so than in his portrayal of Rizvan Khan in Karan Johar's 2010 film *My Name Is Khan*. Shah Rukh plays a man with Asperger's syndrome whose life in the United States changes completely as a result of 9/11. In the article I cite above, Shah Rukh refers to this film as part of his response to his numerous unpleasant experiences at the hands of airport security officers:

> I became so sick of being mistaken for some crazed terrorist who coincidentally carries the same last name as mine that I made a film, subtly titled *My Name is Khan* (and I am not a terrorist) to prove a point. Ironically, I was interrogated at the airport for hours about my last name when I was going to present the film in America for the first time.[23]

Rizvan journeys across America in a manner similar to Forrest Gump in the 1994 film of the same name, directed by Robert Zemeckis, in order to meet the President. Rizvan's refrain 'My name is Khan and I am not a terrorist' is used by the filmmakers to challenge the ignorance, prejudice and hypocrisy that is manifested in the form of Islamophobia both on the part of white racists and prejudiced Hindu Indians alike. The ease with which Rizvan is able to respond to racism reflects the nostalgic yearnings of the diaspora, who, through the *yahaan*, can imagine a real world where it would be equally easy to tackle the after-effects of 9/11.

To say this is not to suggest that either *MNIK* or the other films that deal with the effects of 9/11 on South Asians are underestimating the force of official racism that has underpinned the war on terror. Rizvan goes through terrible torture, while Omar's detention under the Patriot Act in *New York* is certainly not sugar coated, either. These films make it clear that the stakes are very high. Terms such as 'enemy combatant' and 'extraordinary rendition' are given their full meaning. Even in the much more light-hearted *Total Siyapaa*, where the British police are cartoonish in their ignorance and incompetence, the humiliating effects on Aman are made painfully evident.

Rather, what *MNIK* allows its audience is a glimpse into the possibilities that may lie within this nostalgically constructed, heterogenous *yahaan* – a space of cross-community solidarity. Attending a memorial service for soldiers killed in Iraq and Afghanistan, in a Black Church in Wilhemina, Georgia, Rizvan finds solace for his grief at the loss of his son Sam, through a joint rendition of 'We Shall Overcome' – the Hindi version of which he used to sing with his wife Mandira. This song with its illustrious history in the civil rights movement in America, as well as Indian adaptations in Hindi, Bengali and Malayalam, with another parallel history of left-wing and counter-hegemonic resistance, becomes in this *yahaan* an anthem of solidarity – both for the struggles of Muslims after 9/11 and the socioeconomic struggles of African Americans. These struggles become even more difficult and dangerous when Wilhemina is struck by Hurricane Molly, clearly meant to represent Hurricane Katrina. The nostalgic narrative of the film does require the co-opting (once again) of the male Muslim body on the 'good' side in the War on Terror, but this is done partly through a denunciation of Bush-era policies – both in foreign relations and the wars in Iraq and Afghanistan, and in domestic affairs, through the administration's lack of response to Hurricane Katrina. Rizvan is able to not just expose official racism against Muslims, and provide them with the inspiration to fight back, but is also able to step in and make up for the Government's inaction in response to the hurricane. 'Indian man moves America', reads a TV news headline, while, a journalist says:

> Just recently this man was arrested and tortured for being an enemy combatant of this country. Wonder what the government officials would call this Muslim enemy combatant today. . . . If the authorities want to find the true enemy combatant of this country, then they would find it in the grief and debris of Wilhemina.

Rizvan Khan's body is both tortured by US counterterrorist security forces, as well as Islamist terrorists, who attack him in retaliation for his perceived treason. The male, south Asian, Muslim body is nostalgically rewritten as heroic, but this heroism comes at a cost.

The climax of the film represents affirmation, as Rizvan is allowed to meet President-elect Obama, who recognizes his efforts and his identity: 'Your name is Khan, and you are not a terrorist.' The optimism depicted at the end of the film reflects the optimism that accompanied Obama's election in 2008 – but it is also an optimism that is generated from the nostalgia for the future. As Mandira says, addressing the memory of her dead son:

> Our Khan has managed to achieve with his love and humanity, what my hatred could never achieve. My anger threw us apart, but today his love has brought us together in a way where we remember you with renewed hope. Now I will

never let him go anywhere, Sam. I will keep this love with me, for me, for you, forever.

In humanizing Rizvan Khan thus, the filmmakers are of course re-inscribing the Muslim male as the symbol of nostalgic hope, a nostalgia for a secular, harmonious but heterogenous future, represented on screen through Rizvan and Mandira's interfaith relationship. They are shown peacefully occupying the same room, busy with their different religious rituals – Mandira does her Hindu *puja*, while Rizvan does his Islamic *namaaz*. It is of course no coincidence that this interfaith relationship is played on screen by a Hindu woman (Kajol) and a Muslim man (Shah Rukh Khan). They do not just represent a functional Hindu-Muslim couple on screen, but as the two actors who, more than anybody, represent the archetypal romantic couple in diasporic Bollywood cinema, they also represent the fact that, with the only possible exception of the Indian cricket team, Bollywood has been the most important public bastion of Indian secularism. Few other Muslim public figures inspire as much popular adulation as Bollywood stars, either in south Asia or among the global south Asia diaspora. In a world where cross-community relationships can still cause controversy, the universal acceptance of Shah Rukh–Kajol as the iconic couple who always win against all odds to live happily ever after, adds to the heterogeneous potential of the *yahaan*, the potential that allows these films to end on a note of renewed hope.

DIASPORIC NOSTALGIA AND THE SELF-REFERENTIALITY OF BOLLYWOOD

The reason why the public persona of these actors plays such a crucial role is that one of the main characteristics of the *yahaan* is that it remains deeply self-referential. I have already alluded to particular moments of self-referentiality – the echo of *Lagaan* in *KHNH*, for example, or Maya's knowing reference to Shah Rukh Khan in *New York*. These are just a couple of isolated examples of a trend that cuts across many of these films. The role played by the audience's knowledge of the actors and their public persona is brought to the fore in *JBJ*. Perhaps the only actor with an even bigger profile than Shah Rukh Khan, Amitabh Bachchan, stars in this film as Bulla Man, a 'gypsyesque nomad',[24] in Rajinder Dudrah's words. He dips in and out of the narrative, always with his guitar, leading a group of non-Indian dancers in everyday clothes in a song-and-dance routine in the main concourse of Waterloo Station. Even apart from this deliberate parody of Bollywood musical routines, the film is suffused with a knowing awareness of Bachchan's megastar status. The lead male role is played by his son Avishek Bachchan, whose entry is marked by a knowing nod and smile as he greets his real-life father with a light-hearted, 'What's up?' Later on, when Alvira mentions Madame

Tussaud's as the place where she apparently first met her fiancé, Rikki (played by Bachchan junior), responds with another knowing nod and wink: 'Of course I've been. They have so many models of our people. Gandhiji, Nehruji, Indiraji, Ashji, Amitji, – our own Bachchan.' The watching audience is fully aware that Rikki, played by Avishek Bachchan, has just referred not only to his real-life father, but also to his real-life wife in Aishwarya Rai. When Bollywood represents such an important medium of connection between the diaspora and the homeland, such knowing references play an important role in helping to structure the *yahaan* that these films are constructing.

The public persona of Amitabh Bachchan is also used self-referentially in *PK*. As a student in Bruges, Jaggu is desperate to go to a poetry reading where Amitabh would be reading from his father's, the late poet Harivansh Rai Bachchan's, works. When Bruges comes to be appropriated into the *yahaan*, it becomes entirely possible that the event would be sold out, and that a ticket-tout, fluent in Hindi, would be available to sell tickets at an exorbitant rate. What the figure of Amitabh allows, though, is for Jaggu and Sarfaraz to meet, initiating a cross-border, Indo-Pak romance that will be resolved through the narrative of the film.

Often, the diasporic nostalgia is directed specifically at other landmark Bollywood moments. In *Total Siyapaa*, Asha's young niece Anjali is obsessed with Raj and Simran from *DDLJ*. Our introduction to this diasporic Indian family is through their television screen, as Anjali is watching the famous scene from *DDLJ* as Simran runs to get on the moving train to be united with Raj. Anjali's nostalgia for this most iconic example of Bollywood diasporic cinema is designed to evoke a similar nostalgia on the part of the audience. A similar trope is noticeable in Tarun Mansukhani's 2008 film *Dostana*. Set entirely in Miami, diasporic nostalgia is evoked through Neha's (Priyanka Chopra) love of the movie *Kuch Kuch Hota Hai* – like *DDLJ*, another Shah Rukh-Kajol vehicle. In a famous scene in the original film, Rahul (Shah Rukh Khan) beckons Anjali (Kajol) for a dance in the rain. When she points out that there is no music, he mimics the movements of playing a piano. Immediately, the opening bars of the theme song can be heard, and they start dancing. In *Dostana*, this scene is repeated when Kunal (John Abraham) invites Neha on a picnic. He has prepared an open-air cinema which starts playing her favourite film. At the appropriate moment, he beckons to her for a dance. Playing along knowingly, she complains that there is no music. This time, he shows her an iPod on which he has cued up the relevant song. The shots are choreographed so that we can see both Rahul's movements on the screen (in the past), and Kunal's matching movements in the present. As soon as they start dancing, it starts to rain. At first, Neha is confused, and Kunal moves sideways to reveal a child with a garden sprinkler. The post-liberalization access to the West and its technology (iPod and garden sprinklers) is contrasted with the nostalgia for an earlier brand of Bollywood cinema – with the self-aware references indulging in and undercutting the sentimentalized nostalgia in the same moment. This self-referentiality is built into the names of these films, which often borrow from famous songs of previous films. In the case of Karan Johar's Dharma Productions, which is responsible for many of the films I am looking at here, the musical refrain from *Kuch Kuch Hota Hai*, which signalled the famous dance between Rahul and Anjali and which was echoed in *Dostana*, has become the signature theme tune accompanying the logo of the production house. It appears at the beginning of every Karan Johar film, and thus serves as a reminder to the audience that what follows is make believe. The audience's sense of nostalgia for earlier Bollywood films is being appropriated here but not directed towards any particular specific place, and certainly not used to reinforce any particular brand of nationalism. Through multiple, intertwined references and knowing intertextuality, these films construct the imaginary *yahaan* as a filmscape, a world which joyously celebrates its own fictiveness and luxuriates in the possibility that this fictiveness entails.

The here/now of the *yahaan*, then, is neither the 'West' nor an imagined, idealized version of India, nor even an uncritical transnational fusing of the two. It is, in fact, a nostalgically constructed new space, a filmscape, where normal rules don't apply, and hegemonic hierarchies of power may be subverted. It is not necessarily always a space of progressive politics, and it can certainly be appropriated to reinforce problematic gendered, ethnic, nationalist and class politics. It does, however, also contain within it the radical potential of a different *yahaan*, through allowing the audience to imagine another here/now, a fantastical home which one day may indeed exist in the here and now.

NOTES

1. Beatrix Pfleiderer and Lothar Lutze (eds), *The Hindi Film: Agent and Re-Agent of Cultural Change* (New Delhi: Manohar, 1985), 6
2. Patricia Uberoi, "The Diaspora Comes Home: Disciplining Desire in DDLJ", *Contributions to Indian Sociology* 32, November 1998, 328
3. Ingrid Therwath, "'Shining Indians': Diaspora and Exemplarity in Bollywood", *South Asia Multidisciplinary Academic Journal* 4, 2010. Accessed 9 August 2017, available at: http://samaj.revues.org/3000
4. Ingrid Therwath, "Shining Indians"
5. Adrian Athique, "Diasporic Audiences and Non-Resident Media: The Case of Indian Films", *Participations: Journal of Audience and Reception Studies* 8.2, November 2011, 4
6. Jigna Desai, "'Ever Since You've Discovered the Video, I've Had No Peace': Diasporic Spectators Talk Back to Bollywood Masala" in Rajinder Dudrah and Jigna Desai (eds) *The Bollywood Reader* (Maidenhead and New York: Open University Press, 2008), 229
7. Jigna Desai, *Beyond Bollywood: The Cultural Politics of South Asian Diasporic Film* (New York and London: Routledge, 2004), 233
8. Patricia Uberoi, "The Diaspora Comes Home", 306

9. Jigna Desai, *Beyond Bollywood*, 35
10. Rajinder Dudrah, *Bollywood Travels: Culture, Diaspora, and Border Crossings in Popular Hindi Cinema* (Oxford and New York: Routledge, 2012), 28
11. Patricia Uberoi, "The Diaspora Comes Home", 316
12. Rajinder Dudrah, *Bollywood Travels*, 29
13. Patricia Uberoi, "The Diaspora Comes Home", 316
14. Rajinder Dudrah, *Bollywood Travels*, 35
15. Vijay Mishra, *Bollywood Cinema: Temples of Desire* (New York and London: Routledge, 2002), 250
16. Rajinder Dudrah, *Bollywood: Sociology Goes to the Movies* (New Delhi: Sage, 2006), 40
17. Vijay Mishra, *Bollywood Cinema*, 237–38
18. Vijay Mishra, *Bollywood Cinema*, 256–57
19. Sudesh Mishra, "Tazia Fiji!: The Place of Potentiality" in Susan Koshy and R. Radhakrishnan (eds) *Transnational South Asians: The Making of a Neo-Diaspora* (New Delhi: Oxford University Press, 2008), 77
20. http://www.telegraph.co.uk/news/celebritynews/6040296/Bollywood-star-Shah-Rukh-Khan-detained-at-US-airport.html (Accessed 9 August 2017)
21. Shah Rukh Khan, "Inside My Khanate", *Outlook*, 7 January 2013. Accessed on 10 August 2017, available at: https://www.outlookindia.com/magazine/story/inside-my-khanate/283674
22. See, for example, Rahul Bedi, "Shah Rukh Khan Article Spars War of Words Between India and Pakistan", *The Telegraph*, 30 January 2013. Accessed on 10 August 2017, available at: http://www.telegraph.co.uk/news/worldnews/asia/india/9836191/Shah-Rukh-Khan-article-sparks-war-of-words-between-India-and-Pakistan.html
23. Shah Rukh Khan, "Inside My Khanate"
24. Rajinder Dudrah, *Bollywood Travels*, 29

Chapter Six

Making Yourself at Home

Homemaking and Diasporic Asian Broadcasting

On 3 June 2000, Asian Dub Foundation released 'New Way New Life' – their sixth single, and the first from their fourth album *Community Music*. The video, directed by Babak Sarrafan, opens in the living room of a British Asian family. On top of the television and the mantelpiece there are family photographs and a video cassette with a photograph of Bollywood icon Lata Mangeshkar on the cover. The camera zooms out to reveal a multigenerational family, sitting in front of the television, as one person holds a microphone to record what is being broadcast.

The reference is to *Nai Zindagi Naya Jeevan* – a programme broadcast on BBC One on Sunday mornings from 1968 to 1982 aimed at the Hindi- and Urdu-speaking people of Britain. This was the third iteration of a programme that had run under various names from 1965 and would lead, ultimately, to the formation of the BBC Asian Network. ADF's lyrics pay tribute to the comforting and sustaining role that early British Asian broadcasting played for its British Asian audience:

> Every Sunday morning in front of the TV
> Recording with a microphone *Naya Zindagi*
> Pioneer Gurdas Maan
> Nusrat Fateh Ali Khan
> Kept our parents alive
> Gave them the will to survive
> Working inna de factories
> Sometimes sweeping de floor
> Unsung heroines and heroes
> They open de door[1]

The video shows band members performing their song on the streets of London – in neighbourhoods that are coded as Asian, such as Southall and Tower Hamlets. The video is a montage featuring restaurants, market stalls, music shops and Asian grocery shops, as well as residential streets. The community that is invoked in the album title *Community Music* is seen in action, as London's streets are taken over by a multi-religious, multi-ethnic, multigenerational body of people dancing to the tunes of Asian Dub Foundation.

On 28 May 2016, British Asian rapper Raxstar featured in a two-minute video advert, produced by Augusto Sola at 101, directed by Josh Cole, and aimed at 'defin[ing] a new identity for Asian Network that represented the collective identity of the generation it wanted to attract.'[2] Called '100% British 100% Asian', this film, according to its producers, came from the realization that:

> Young British Asians' identity crisis came from the pressure to decide. Were they British or Asian? The realisation hit us. They should not have to. Their playlists weren't divided into 'Asian' and 'British', and neither were their lives. The answer was to create a cultural space that connected with both sides of their identity.

The video has many similarities with the one for 'New Way New Life'. Raxstar walks along some of the same streets that ADF performed on, such as Watney Street Market. Both videos represent the heterogeneity of the British Asian communities – shopkeepers, boxers, people practicing dancing, playing football, doing Tai Chi, as well as families in more domestic settings such as living rooms, bedrooms, and at the dining room table. Like the ADF video, this too depicts a multi-religious, multi-ethnic, and multigenerational community of British Asians. On the video, Raxstar does a spoken-word piece that highlights this diversity:

> I could be a doctor, poet, or chart-topping producer. I am everything the past has made me and I am the future. I'm the son of my parents who put their children first. The language they were most fluent in was hard work. Steering clear of every box anyone can put me in. . . . We could start a revolution – first, let's have a cup of tea. I am more than just the beard or the nation's favourite dish. There's four million different ways to understand what British Asian is. I am culture and tradition mixed with fish and chips and visions of five rivers – it's a modern day collision. That's just how we live it. . . . We are everything the past has made us and we are the future. We've found a place to call our own, not one city not one town. You know what British Asian looks like. This is how it sounds.[3]

Raxstar's walk through the same streets that featured in the ADF video sixteen years previously can be seen as enacting their claim that partly as a consequence of Asian broadcasting:

> now we're walking down de street
> Wid a brand new pride
> A spring inna de step
> Wid our heads held high
> Young asian brothers an sisters
> Moving forward, side by side[4]

I connect these two videos not just because of their visual similarities. I argue that, put together, they depict the journey of British Asian broadcasting – from its beginnings in Britain with the BBC Immigrants' Programmes Unit (IPU) to contemporary Asian broadcasting – both within the BBC through the BBC Asian Network, and through independent and commercial broadcasters such as Sunrise Radio and the Zee TV network. In the process, these videos, and the stages of diasporic Asian broadcasting that they represent, mark the transition that Asian Dub Foundation spoke of in 2000: 'They came a long time ago / But now it seems we've arrived'.

In this chapter, I am interested in the role of Asian broadcasting in completing the journey from coming to arriving. This evolution has, at its heart, the building of a community, the process through which people can make a home for themselves. A crucial aspect of this homemaking was diasporic Asian broadcasting, and the contested history of Asian broadcasting can be used to chart a history of the diasporic Asian communities and the way they fought to establish themselves. One of the ways of telling this history is to look at the ways in which nostalgia features in this contest for meanings – between those who help to produce Asian broadcasting, and those who consume it. The difference between coming and arriving lies, I believe, in finding a place to call one's own in being able to make a home for oneself through articulating the complex, contradictory nostalgic attachments to the place one left behind and the place one chose to live in. In this chapter, I look for signs of nostalgia in the archival records that tell the story of the origins of BBC Asian broadcasting, connect these early signs with the role played by nostalgia in the BBC Asian Network today and, finally, conclude with an examination of nostalgia in two fictional representations of diasporic Asian broadcasting.

NOSTALGIA AND THE HISTORY OF BBC ASIAN BROADCASTING

In his history of multiculturalism in the 'Golden Age' of British television, Gavin Schaffer makes a compelling case for the view that through the 1960s and 1970s, debates about race and representation 'were very much about "making" in the most conscious sense of the term',[5] and what was being made was, in the words of the title of Schaffer's book, *The Vision of a Nation*:

> Television production in the 1960s and 1970s, taken as a whole, attempted to create specific visions of multiculturalism, immigration and race relations and ... these had an enduring impact across and beyond the British broadcast media ... television's presentation of multiculturalism, immigration and race relations has played a significant role in shaping the way these issues came to be understood in Britain.[6]

Schaffer does a very good job of demonstrating how the BBC consciously and deliberately used their Asian broadcasting in order to create a different narrative of race relations in Britain. Borrowing from his work, and returning to the archives that he examines, I will focus on how the British Asian communities – both the audience and those individuals who had the chance to influence BBC policy – were engaged in a parallel process of homemaking. In upholding the importance of a nostalgic attachment to distinctively British Asian experiences and values, this represents a challenge to the BBC integrationist policy and goes a long way towards explaining how, in spite of a widespread institutional desire to do so, the BBC never managed to abandon their Asian broadcasting.

The origins of Asian programming on the BBC can be traced to a letter written in February 1965 by the then Postmaster General, Tony Benn, to the Director General of the BBC, Hugh Greene. Benn forwarded to Greene a copy of an article in *The Guardian* written by Taya Zinkin. Zinkin attacked the failure of the British government to help immigrants from South Asia integrate, which, Benn said 'opens up a most interesting possibility which you will no doubt wish to examine'.[7] The letter and the copy of the article are held at the BBC Written Archives Centre in Reading, and the following passage from the article has been highlighted, presumably by Benn himself:

> The BBC finds time once a fortnight for a television programme for the deaf and dumb; it should find time, at least once a week for a programme in Hindustani (understood by both Indians and Pakistanis). The effect on the women, of seeing women like themselves telling them how to adapt to life in Britain would be very great indeed.[8]

This governmental suggestion would lead to two conferences to discuss the possibility of specifically targeted programming to cater to the Afro-Caribbean and the south Asian populations of Britain respectively. Based on the discussion at these conferences, the BBC set up the IPU in 1965, whose mission, in the words of the first Immigrant Programmes Organisor, David

Gretton, was to help immigrants 'to understand the language, the people, the institutions and the physical resources of life in English towns'.[9] Along with the IPU, the BBC also set up an Immigrants' Programmes Advisory Committee (IPAC) chaired by Philip Mason, the first director of the Institute of Race Relations, and including diplomatic representatives of India and Pakistan, along with various immigrant community leaders, experts, academics and local politicians.

At 9 a.m., on 10 October 1965, the IPU launched its first programme – *Apna Hi Ghar Samajhiye* or *Make Yourself at Home*. Broadcast on Radio and on BBC One on Sunday mornings, this programme would continue until November 1968, when it was replaced with a magazine programme called *Nai Zindagi Naya Jeevan* (*New Life*), which would, almost forty years later, inspire the Asian Dub Foundation song with which I started this chapter. Eventually, *Nai Zindagi* would make way in turn for *Asian Magazine* in 1982, which was targeted more specifically at younger British Asians. *Asian Magazine* would continue until 1987 – representing in total a twenty-two-year phenomenon of the Sunday morning Asian programme on BBC One. Asian programming would continue, however, through various local and regional television and radio stations, culminating today in the BBC Asian Network, which is available on DAB Digital Radio, on the BBC Radio App and online.

While the institutional forces and interests that led to the introduction of Asian programming on the BBC were many and varied, it would be true to say that as far as the BBC was concerned, the central rationale of their Asian programming was the perceived need to promote integration. Thus, the invitation letter to the initial conference declares that the BBC was 'considering ways in which it could help to meet the needs and special interests of immigrants to this country'.[10] In 1969, four years after the launch of Asian programming, this desire for integration was still clearly paramount. For example, one member of the Advisory Committee suggested that the programme 'should show faults of the [immigrant] community . . . which caused lack of understanding between the communities'.[11]

By 1973, however, there were some members of the Advisory Committee who were questioning the BBC's approach. A Mr I. Aziz complained that the BBC were unable to recognize that 'after a process of self-education and resettlement . . . [immigrants] could and should become citizens of this country and be treated as such in programme terms'.[12] The BBC were, however, still, doubtful. Responding to Mr Aziz at this meeting, John Grist (Controller of the English Regions) argued that 'it would be wrong to assume that because people had been in this country for some years, they understood everything about it'.[13]

In 1974, the IPU changed its name to the Asian Programmes Unit and the IPAC changed its name to the Asian Programmes Advisory Committee, but the central belief in the necessity of helping British Asians to integrate into life in Britain remained unchanged. Thus, when in November 1975, the BBC submitted a Memorandum on Broadcasting and Racial Minorities to the Annan Committee on the Future of Broadcasting, this was the reason given for the decision to have programming for south Asian immigrants:

> The religions, culture and languages of the subcontinent are entirely different from those of Britain and it was felt that there was a vital need to break down the resultant feelings of alienation among Asians.[14]

Evidence of this belief can be found in internal BBC documents as well. In February 1972, Patrick Beech (Controller of the Midlands Region) underlined his belief in the rationale for Asian programming:

> The unit was originally set up to help these immigrants to settle into this country. For five years our main effort was directed toward the simplest form of teaching of the English language.[15]

This integrationist approach had a number of consequences – not least of which was the BBC's tendency to view the British Asian community as a homogenous whole, defined largely through their shared immigrant experience. Writing in 1965, Gretton stated that 'Our object was to treat immigrants from India and Pakistan as one community, not two' and that 'most of the mail [received] reveals the essential unity in this country of the two communities.'[16]

This combination of belief in the homogeneity of the British Asian community, and the desire to help this community integrate into life in Britain led to what was known as the 'main stream' policy, which served to downplay any programming content that might reinforce British Asian distinctiveness. Thus, in 1967, Patrick Beech reported back from a meeting of the Immigrants Programmes Advisory Committee where the members had asked for the programming to reflect religious customs of the British Asian communities. Beech's response reveals the institution's suspicion of anything that could be characterized as multicultural divisiveness: 'I realise that this might introduce a small but very important crack in the 'main stream' policy, and one that is not tolerable.'[17]

It would not be too simplistic to say that the BBC felt their job was to help make the British Asian communities become British, and that anything that distracted from this process or helped to remind the British Asian communities of their difference was to be avoided. In other words, the BBC viewed their own Asian broadcasting as a way to undermine any positive nostalgic attachment the incoming British Asian communities might have for the homes they left behind. David Gretton makes this point in his report from April 1966:

> Not all those who watch our programmes are prepared to relax their ties with the home country. . . . These demands are mutually irreconcilable, and in totality they conflict with our original brief, which is summed up in the phrase 'make yourself at home'.[18]

The deliberate effect of the mainstream policy, then, was to undermine any nostalgic connection these new British Asians might have for the home they left behind, and to encourage a rejection of the identities, memories and values associated with said home in favour of a total embracing of the British way of life.

At a General Advisory Council meeting on 19 February 1977, the BBC responded to a request for 'more programmes explaining the cultural and religious backgrounds of immigrant families' with the declaration that 'BBC feels that integration is better achieved by normal programme treatment than by exceptional action.'[19]

The BBC's integrationist approach was highlighted by the title of the very first major programme of the IPU – *Make Yourself at Home*, as Gretton points out above. At an IPAC meeting on 12 February 1969, the two diplomatic members, Abdul Qayyum from the Pakistani High Commission and K. Darashah of the Indian High Commission, both spoke about the success of the BBC's integrationist philosophy:

> Mr Darashah and other members felt that the programme had already helped many people to settle down in this country. . . . When encouraging them to accept this land as their home we were working towards the purposeful objective of enabling them to settle down.[20]

However, anxieties about the success or otherwise of integrationist policies persisted and led, according to one of the presenters of the show, Saleem Shahed, to the decision to change the name from *Apna Hi Ghar Samajhiye* to *Nai Zindagi Naya Jeevan*:

> We changed the name from *Make Yourself at Home* to *New Life* because we were receiving thousands of letters from the viewers . . . and they were getting the message wrong. It appears, you know, because they used to write to us that we feel as if we are still back home in Mirpur, or in Jalandhar or Sylhet, so that wasn't the message we wanted to convey. So we thought that they were getting the wrong message. We wanted to make them aware – that they are in a new country, it is a different system here. Different society. They should feel at home in this country, not there.[21]

The reason why this anxiety about the failure of integration is relevant to my discussion here is that this failure was repeatedly linked to the audience's nostalgia for the home they left behind. Reporting on an IPAC meeting on 24 October 1967, Patrick Beech cited 'one very sensible member' who, spoke up well about the danger of making integration more difficult if there were too many programmes re-inforcing nostalgia and tending to perpetrate an insulated community within the community.[22]

Five years later, Beech was making the same point himself in a note dated 21 February 1972:

> I think they [BBC Asian programmes] increasingly appeal to the nostalgic strings in the audience, emphasizing the difference between their culture and that surrounding them. I believe it could be held to be divisive rather than tending to unify.[23]

This suspicion of nostalgia and desire for integration in Britain resulted in the BBC being suspicious of the emotional ties to the subcontinent that their British Asian audience might have been experiencing. The subcontinent, when it appears in the archives of the BBC in connection with its early Asian programming, appears as a problem – a source of conflict, or a space of cultural backwardness.

This can be seen in the way in which the BBC dealt with the repercussions of the original decision to include representatives from the Indian, Pakistani and (after 1971) Bangladeshi High Commissions on the Advisory Committee as ex officio members. In January 1979, David Webster, Director, Public Affairs, argued that 'the presence of these representatives has a divisive influence' and that 'on balance it would at this stage be advantageous to begin in a diplomatic manner the phasing out of these ex-officio members'.[24] There seems to have been a general agreement, as early as 1974, that 'on the basis that these programmes are designed to help Asian immigrants integrate with the host community such representation is illogical'.[25] There are numerous examples from 1974 to suggest that this measure was considered then, but not implemented until 1978 because of possible political ramifications arising from alienating the British Asian communities. When the decision was eventually made in April 1979, it was to prove unpopular, not least because it seems to have been made without even informing the Advisory Committee.

One cannot help but read the desire of the BBC to remove these representatives from the Advisory Committee as connected to the institutional suspicion of subcontinental influences and, in the words of Gavin Schaffer, evidence that 'the perceived cultural superiority of Britishness, or more specifically white Britishness, as well as the English language was ever-present in the background.'[26]

Indeed, the vision of the Advisory Committee that one gets from the BBC Written Archive is that of a group of spoilt children whom the BBC felt they must try to mollify in order to have their own way. Patrick Beech wrote in October 1968 that 'it takes some time to educate them in the facts of life',[27] while John Grist discussed the 'tedious problems created by the multiplicity of languages and the irascibility of that particular type of humanity'.[28] The BBC had worried in 1965 that the Indo-Pakistan war would force them to start the advisory committee with an ad hoc group comprising 'one or two of the more enlightened and responsible of the immigrant community leaders'.[29] A week later, however, and the Board of Management were surprised 'that the Indian and Pakistani communities in Britain were behaving responsibly towards one another.'[30]

Perhaps because the BBC preferred to see its British Asian audience as a homogenous body, the principle source of conflict seems to be its inherent heterogeneity. Almost every reference to the Advisory Committee is couched in terms of a problem that needs to be contained, and the problem is almost always that of divisiveness. Conflict and division was, according to the BBC, located specifically in the heterogeneity of the British Asian communities, which conflicted with the BBC's desire to see their target audience as a homogenous, completely integrated group whose distinctiveness was a problem to be contained, rather than an asset to be celebrated. Unlike the contemporary commonsensical correlation between nostalgia and homogeneity, the BBC's institutional suspicion of diasporic nostalgia seems to have stemmed from the understanding that this most powerful affect might promote a divisive multiculturalism.

In an unsigned report dated 30 June 1965, and clearly part of the BBC's original research into the immigrant communities, the author divides 'The Asians' into three groups – 'the Sikhs' who are 'most likely to integrate' and whose 'religion is Hindu' (*sic*); the Pakistanis, 'few of . . . [whom] speak English'; and the Indians who 'apparently have a tendency to internal divisions'.[31] Institutional knowledge would improve over the years, but the perception of the British Asian community as unhelpfully divided would not go away. In October 1967, for example, Beech reported on a particular cause for disagreement in the Advisory Committee meeting:

> Discussions at the meeting on October 24th were as diffuse as ever, and are typified by the request of the representative of the High Commissioner of Pakistan that we should cease our practice of beginning and ending our programmes with the words 'Good Morning . . . good-bye'. To use English, he suggested, was insulting to the immigrant community. However, when we asked for an alternative, it transpired that you use one form of greeting in Pakistan and another in India and the usual interminable wrangle began. After ten minutes to avoid communal bloodshed it was agreed to revert to English![32]

In fact, one of the key areas of disagreement between the BBC and the Advisory Committee was always the choice of language. From the beginning, the BBC had decided to broadcast in what it defined as 'basic Hindustani' – 'a mixture of simple Hindi and simple Urdu' that it believed would be comprehensible to most people from the subcontinent.[33] However, from the earliest days, the minutes of the Advisory Committee are marked by their consistent attempts to persuade the BBC to broadcast programmes in other Asian languages, and the BBC's equally persistent insistence on the impossibility of this due to limitations on time and resources. Of particular note was the repeated demand on the part of the Advisory Committee to broadcast programmes in Bengali. In November 1965, Mr Muneer and Dr Prem argued that 'the Bengali-speaking members of the community would welcome the inclusion of Bengali songs in the programme.'[34] In October 1972, the representative of the Bangladeshi High Commission, Mr Choudhury noted that 'it was thought there was not enough time given to Bengali speaking people'. In April 1976, a Mrs Banu had requested 'more programme content in Bengali';[35] by 1978, she had resigned from the committee because she 'felt that her arguments for the importance of the Bengali language and the use of Bangladeshi artists in programmes had not succeeded'.[36]

In spite of this consistent pressure over many years, the BBC was largely successful in resisting because of their belief that catering to differing languages would contravene their 'main stream' policy. In October 1973, Gerry Hynes had argued that branching out into other languages would be 'potentially divisive', while the previous year, Philip Mason had justified sticking to Hindi/Urdu on the grounds that it 'was still regarded as the most widely understood language in the sub-continent'.[37]

The BBC's antipathy to considering other languages carried on, however, and when, in February 1974, the Advisory Committee expressed a desire to change the name of the unit to Asian Programmes Unit, the then Director General Charles Curran agreed only on the condition that 'the change of title is not seen . . . as an argument in favour of broadcasting nationally in this country in additional languages'.[38]

Even so, as late as 1979, Phil Sidey, Head of the Network Production Centre, was writing that 'English can be the only lingua franca but I would not care to be the person who has to convince the sub-continent (or even the Asian Advisory Committee) that this is so'. Tellingly, his reason for this was that the use of Asian languages meant that 'the programme can be positively divisive despite its best endeavours', because 'the quarrels of the sub-continent are transferred to Britain'.[39]

This difference in approach between the BBC and its Asian audience, and its Advisory Committee matters, can be mapped out in terms of diametrically opposite approaches to nostalgia. The BBC's position, as I have already pointed out, was characterized by a mistrust of nostalgia, and this mistrust manifested itself in the rejection of anything that might compromise their integrationist policies. This rejection meant that the BBC were fundamentally unable to understand why their Asian programming was of such crucial importance to their audience. This explains why throughout the first two decades of Asian programming, they consistently saw it as a temporary feature, which would cease to have a function once the British Asian community was perfectly integrated. Thus, in its report to the Annan Committee, the BBC foresaw 'a time when the ... Asian Programmes Unit can be said to have completed its task, and its programmes disappear from the BBC schedules.'[40] Even two years previously, the BBC was seriously considering abandoning the APU. In February 1972, Gerry Hynes wrote that 'a sound argument could be made for' the case that 'the original purpose of the Unit has ... now been served' because 'the welfare element of programming is less necessary' and 'the separate treatment of Asian immigrants could today arguably be said to be working against integration.'[41]

On the other hand, John Grist was of the opinion that the BBC should 'stick with the status quo' because 'we might create an almighty stink if we bailed out of the Immigrants programme at present.'[42] The BBC seem to have increasingly felt that the original decision to start Asian programming had been a mistake, and this resulted in the BBC being saddled with a problem of their own making. The logic of the BBC executives is perfectly understandable. It is because they saw the only purpose of the APU to be encouraging integration; as soon as integration was felt to be a success, the APU was thought to have outlived its usefulness.

The problem, however, as Gavin Schaffer has argued, is that there was no necessary connection between the interests and desires of mainstream broadcasters like the BBC in commissioning programmes directed at British Asians and the ways in which the audience consumed these programmes in their own lives. As a result, Asian programming was always going to be a contest between the BBC who felt the programming to be redundant because they felt that integration had been mostly achieved, and the target audience, represented in part by the Asian Advisory Committee, who were attracted to the APU's programmes because they provided them access to a world that they had left behind. The nostalgia that the BBC considered to be backward looking, and a hurdle to successful integration, was considered by large sections of the audience to be a fundamental part of their identity. In his first report on the IPU in 1965, David Gretton recognized 'an immense hunger' for 'sheer musical entertainment'.[43] He goes on to say: 'I was not required in my original brief to become a department of Indian light entertainment, but clearly this must be and shall be attempted.' By the time of his second report the following year, however, he is already suspicious of this attachment to Indian music:

> I am rather disconcerted at the number of letters which indicate that the gramophone record element in our radio programme is valued for tape recording purposes. I have even seen a handbill for an Indian cinema inviting the cus-

tomers to bring their tape recorders to the show and record the big song numbers. Under English copyright law, this is downright piracy.[44]

It is perhaps not surprising that a BBC producer should be horrified by such illicit recordings of his programmes, but it does also indicate a lack of awareness of the significance the music had for British Asians. In Schaffer's words,

> there is little evidence that the programme's audiences were engaging with the output at all in the way envisaged. . . . Alongside the simple pleasure of seeing Asian people speaking an Asian language on television, it was doubtless the Asian music, which was mostly absent from the British broadcast media, which impelled viewers to turn on and tune in.[45]

Schaffer is quite correct about the disjunction between the purpose of Asian broadcasting, as conceptualized by the BBC, and the role it had within the British Asian community. He notes how a 'viewer recalled that in the later age of video recorders, his family would record the music content of Asian programmes and "string them together into one music video"'. Schaffer's interviewee and Gretton's anonymous copyright infringer remind me of the opening to Asian Dub Foundation's video for 'New Way New Life'. It is arguable, however, that Schaffer underestimates the huge importance cultural representation had on community building – the ADF video suggests, I think, that watching Asian faces on television was not a 'simple pleasure', but rather, it is the articulation of a nostalgic attachment to one's home and sense of belonging. This fierce pride in one's sense of identity would, in time, become part of what allows current and future generations of British Asians to walk 'down de street / Wid a brand new pride'.[46]

It is particularly crucial, I think, that in the video, it is clearly a young person holding a toy microphone in front of the television – the nostalgia that ADF are depicting is clearly being painted as multigenerational. In the context of the BBC's attitude towards nostalgia, this is important because the BBC equally clearly considered nostalgia for the life left behind as solely the preserve of the first-generation immigrant. This was clear from the closing monologue, delivered by host Rashid Ashraf, that ended the last ever episode of *Asian Magazine* and marked the end, after twenty-one years, of the Sunday morning Asian slot on BBC One:

> So now the time has come to take your leave. For 21 years, every Sunday morning through the small screen of the television, we would open a small window, to show you glimpses of that life, the one you have left behind. In this country, whether people of my age agree with it or not, the memories we have in our hearts of the old days, the impressions – those images are now covered with twenty one years' worth of dust. And those images are now stale. So our children, those who have been born here, how can they feel part of these

memories? It's an old saying – new homes have to be built, and old houses pulled down to make way.[47]

The attempt (one of many before and since) to bring to a close Asian broadcasting on the BBC was clearly being justified on the grounds that it is only the first-generation immigrant who experiences nostalgia for the home that was left behind, and that the second-generation immigrant, born in this country, is free from that pull, and therefore free to build their life here unencumbered by the past. The irony, of course, is that not only have the second generation not been immune to a nostalgia of their own, but the decades of British Asian broadcasting have since inspired nostalgia of its own, as can be seen from the current incarnation of BBC Asian broadcasting, the Asian Network.

GOING 'OLD SKOOL': NOSTALGIA AND THE BBC ASIAN NETWORK

The year 2007 marked the fiftieth anniversary of Asian broadcasting on the BBC. To mark this occasion, Sarfraz Mansoor presented the Radio 4 documentary *Make Yourself at Home* on 25 August 2007 as part of the *Archive Hour*, and Sonia Deol presented the two-part documentary *Asian Network Presents: 50 Years of Asian Programming* on the Asian Network. While Deol and Mansoor take different approaches to the BBC's legacy – Mansoor is much more critical of the narrative of progress than is Deol, for example – both programmes highlight the role of the BBC Asian broadcasting in helping to build a British Asian identity, and to help sustain it from alienation and racism over the years. In the process, and in a very similar manner to ADF, both Mansoor and Deol are helping to construct a nostalgia that is not just distinctively British Asian, but one that has as its object British Asian life. Deol asks her audience to imagine a very different world:

> In a world where we can now access anything from anywhere, anytime we want, imagine a time when the only way to connect with the motherland you'd recently left behind was via airmail and thirty minutes of TV programming on a Sunday morning.[48]

Over two hours, Deol then plays clips from various programmes, and narrates the history of British Asian broadcasting from the early days of the IPU, through *Nai Zindagi*, through nineties and noughties British Asian programming such as *Network East*, *Bollywood or Bust*, and *Desi DNA* to the contemporary BBC Asian Network. In the process, Deol demonstrates 'just how far Asian culture can extend to the mainstream'.

Sarfraz Mansoor places the first broadcast of *Apna Hi Ghar Samjhiye* in the context of cultural landmarks of 1960s Britain – the Rolling Stones had just topped the charts with 'Satisfaction', and the Beatles were about to release 'Love Me Do'. He compares the new, hardly heard-of programme on Sunday mornings with contemporary giants of BBC Television – William Hartnell in *Doctor Who* and Jack Warner in *Dixon of Dock Green*. This is more than just historic contextualization – Mansoor's purpose is very like Deol's:

> To understand its [the programme's] significance is to chart the story of British Asians over the past forty years. It is a compelling and controversial journey that begins with them on the periphery and ends with them knocking down the doors of mainstream culture.[49]

This nostalgic writing of history has many consequences, not least of which is the subversion of the BBC's original mainstream policy. Going from a view of the mainstream, which implied the erasure of all difference, the BBC Asian Network today can thus be seen now to have appropriated the mainstream and turned it on its head. In the words of ADF,

> We could never have known
> Dat in de future
> Our role models would be home grown[50]

This nostalgia that is being coded as sustaining and comforting is thus also counter-hegemonic. It has the explicit effect of subverting and rewriting hierarchies placed on cultural norms and values, implicitly challenging the widely held BBC view that not catering to their Western audience would be a waste of time. Instead, the audience's nostalgia, as evoked by the BBC's Asian broadcasting, can help to rewrite who one's national audience is, what they look like, and how far their interests need to be taken into account. In other words, it would not be hyperbolic to say that the trajectory of the BBC's Asian broadcasting, and the persistence of many forms of British Asian nostalgia as a factor in determining its content and reception, together help to redefine not just what it means to be British Asian, but also what it means to be British.

In the more than five decades since the advent of Asian broadcasting on the BBC, it has become not just a vehicle for British Asian nostalgia, but also an object of it. Gavin Schaffer, in closing his analysis of the archival history of the origins of BBC's Asian broadcasting, notes that the programmes 'are now almost or entirely forgotten, occasionally revisited in a spirit of nostalgia or as a marker of how far we have come'.[51] Perhaps because he immediately follows this with a statement about the use these programmes have for the historian, it is difficult not to read a note of dismissiveness in Schaffer's reference to nostalgia. As I have shown in this chapter, however, nostalgia was always one of the prime driving forces that determined how British Asian broadcasting started, was produced and was received by its audience.

The effect of this nostalgia can still be seen in the BBC Asian Network's output today as it tries to cater to multiple generations of British Asians, each with its own nostalgia, which is often mutually contradictory. Thus, Nosheen Iqbal, writing in *The Guardian*, sums up the 'tricky territory' that the BBC Asian Network has to cover, producing and broadcasting content that would cater to 'nostalgic fondness for AR Rahman [and] also extend to a taste for Punjabi R&B mash-ups.'[52] In the process, however, the network and its programming demonstrates nostalgia to be a much more complex, multivalent force than it is often given credit for.

Perhaps the programme where nostalgia is most frequently on display is the 'Old Skool Hour', a regular segment on Noreen Khan's weekly show which takes place Mondays to Fridays, from 1.30 to 5 p.m.; during this segment she dedicates an hour to playing what the show describes as 'old skool tracks' – which seems to encompass any music from the fifties to the nineties. Noreen Khan plays film music from India and Pakistan, as well as other genres of music – bhangra, ghazal, Qawwali, as well as usually one non-*desi* track. In her own words, 'I'm not sure which other show on the planet would go from Stevie Wonder straight to Pankaj Udhas'.[53] The guiding principle, at least of this segment, seems to be the following message:

> That's what happens . . . we associate our memories with certain tunes. And that's what all comes flooding back during Old School Hour. That's why we love it so much.[54]

In constructing an avowedly multivalent, multi-ethnic audiotopia through the music, Khan's show as a whole, and 'The Old Skool Hour' specifically mobilizes nostalgia in a way not dissimilar to Gayatri Gopinath's analysis of British Asian bands like Cornershop, Asian Dub Foundation and Fun'da'mental:

> Nostalgia in their music functions not to reify the nation . . . rather [it] destabilizes notions of 'Britishness' espoused by New Right ideology, while also calling into question the status of South Asia as the locus of an originary, redemptive cultural identity.[55]

In its past incarnations, the BBC's Asian programmes would only recognize the first-generation nostalgia that Rashid Ashraf alluded to in his farewell at the end of the last episode of *Asian Magazine*. The BBC Asian Network today, however, engages with and deploys the multiple levels of nostalgia that different generations of British Asians experience – embodying, in Gopinath's words, 'the affective ties of diaspora [which] can be mobilized for competing and contradictory interests simultaneously'[56] Thus, Harpz Kaur, sitting in for Noreen Khan, defended her cross-generational connection to the 'old skool' music she was playing in this particular segment:

> A lot of you out there are probably wondering 'Harpz? On Old Skool Hour? How does that work out? Does she even know what she's talking about?' Let me tell you – My mamma taught me well, all right? My mamma is an old school Bollywood lover. If you're tuning in, I want to say hello. And I am going to play some of your favourite tracks over the next hour.[57]

Later on, in the same show, Harpz Kaur makes her familial connection to old school tracks even more explicit, as she discusses the importance of the song 'Maar Chhadapa' – a song from 1988 by British bhangra group Heera:

> I have this one memory that's going to stay with me for the rest of my life and I just thought I would share it with you all. So you know my baby video right? Everyone has got their baby videos. Unfortunately now if you are my age you can't really play them anymore because they are on VHS tapes. . . . But when I did used to watch it back. My *taya* back in the day, he used to do all the filming, he was obsessed with the camera – he used to film me when I was dancing at the age of 1, 2 . . . up to around 3. And every time you play this video, when you watch it, all you can hear is Heera over the top of it, like, Heera tracks. 'Maar Chhadapa' is one of the ones that stand out for me the most. Because when I think baby memories, I just think of my videos and from beginning to end it is just Heera playing.[58]

Harpz Kaur's anecdote highlights the potential that diasporic nostalgia has, in Gopinath's words, to disrupt 'the way in which diaspora is traditionally conceived as always and forever being oriented toward a phantasmatic lost homeland.'[59] The nostalgia is, here, for a distinctively British Asian life – one which is able to incorporate influences from Britain and the homelands, and in the process, create a new syncretic culture, which can become an object of a nostalgia all of its own. Rather like the VHS tapes that the home videos were recorded on, the anecdote speaks of childhood memories that are now of the past – presumably rendered inaccessible through bereavement or relocation or the simple act of growing up.

A further example can be seen from the way in which Noreen Khan speaks of one of the most iconic songs of Bollywood rom-coms from the nineties – 'Pehla Nasha' from *Joh Jeeta Wohi Sikander* from 1992. She discusses[60] how many listeners had this famously romantic song as their first dance at a wedding (emphatically not a *desi* custom), as well as how it reminds her of *desi* wedding videos which reproduce the faces of the bride and the groom multiple times on the same screen. The song itself thus becomes a palimpsest which can hold multiple contradictory meanings at once. It can evoke nostalgia for a pre-liberalized 1990s India, along with the indigenous commodities I write about in other chapters, as well as a second- or even third-generation British Asian life, where memories of the homeland are inevitably mediated across generational and geographical divides. Like the now out-dated technology of the VHS, the songs and the videos which feature the music can evoke a fond attachment to the days gone by. This sentimental attachment to music helps to continue to impose meanings which then help to create a new, imaginary geography, or an audiotopia, in Josh Kun's words:

> sonic spaces of affective utopian longings where several sites normally deemed incompatible are brought together not only in the space of a particular piece of music itself, but in the production of social space and mapping of geographical space that music makes possible.[61]

In other words, the journey from Stevie Wonder to Pankaj Udhas, via Heera and 'Pehla Nasha' helps to create an imaginary musical home that is then the object of nostalgia. This home is not connected to national borders; rather it encompasses what ADF have described as a 'community of sound' characterized by its impossible-to-define heterogeneity. Indeed, the 'community of sound' makes its appearance on Noreen Khan's show – through the constant listener messages that are read out, but also through the segment where listener requests are played. This segment is called 'The Khandaan Takeover' – *khandaan* being a Hindi/Urdu word for *family* that would perhaps be best translated as dynasty. If it is a dynasty, it is a transnational, multi-ethnic, multilingual and multigenerational one. In Noreen Khan's words, her 'Khandaan is spread around the whole world'.[62] Frequent messages from North America, the Middle East and Australia, as well as south and south-east Asia show this to be perfectly true. This is the community that ADF and Raxstar depict in their videos – a community which can represent a new, imaginative geography connecting India and Pakistan and London and North England, and America and Canada through creative new links that are not easily contained by any national or central authority. The construction of the *khandaan* is thus an act of mapping through music, reminiscent of Kun's description of the role music played in his own life:

> Music can offer maps in this way, and when I was younger the maps I heard were not just maps of the song's cultural and historic genesis, but the map of my own life, a musical 'You are Here' that positioned me within the larger social world.[63]

Through listening to and engaging with the BBC Asian Network, the *khandaan* brings itself into existence – the listeners join together through the performance of listening, becoming a community of music.

I don't want to romanticize this transnational population as necessarily representing a challenge to global hegemony. Indeed, the choice of the word *khandaan*, however ironically meant, reveals the truth that it is perfectly possible that this 'community of sound' is no more immune to 'dangers of positing certain notions of genealogy and patrilineality as the underlying logic of diaspora'[64] than any nationally bound population. This caveat notwithstanding, I would still argue that the diffuse nostalgia represented by this heterogeneous group can be seen to represent a potential challenge to both national and global hegemony. In articulating the right to conceptualize their relationship with the country that they left behind, and the country that they made a home for themselves out of, south Asian diasporic communities are deploying this heterogeneous nostalgia in various, imaginative ways. This imagined, alternative reality may or may not develop into a significant counter-hegemonic challenge, but even in this most basic form, Noreen Khan, Harpz Kaur and the BBC Asian Network demonstrate that diasporic nostalgia is able to make the case 'that the culture of diasporic immigrants is central to British national identity' and thus is able to articulate a demand that 'South Asian cultural forms be recognised by mainstream culture in ways that do not quite so easily resolve into mere absorption or appropriation'.[65]

NOSTALGIA AND DIASPORIC ASIAN BROADCASTING: *PSYCHORAAG* AND *SALAAM NAMASTE*

On the face of it, *Salaam Namaste* and *Psychoraag* have little in common. The former is an as-mainstream-as-they-come romantic comedy blockbuster from the Yash Raj Films production house. Directed by first-time director Siddharth Anand, and starring Saif Ali Khan and Preity Zinta, it was the first Bollywood film to be filmed entirely in Australia and became one of the biggest hits of the year in 2005. The latter is a deliberately edgy novel written by Scottish Asian writer Suhayl Saadi – it was published in 2004, and was, according to Alan Bissett, 'the first novel to chronicle the life of Glasgow's Asian community'.[66]

Salaam Namaste tells the story of Nick and Ambar, two Indians living in Australia, the first a chef and the second a medical student and part-time radio presenter. The film follows a year of their life, as they are initially involved in an argument over Nick's appearance on Ambar's show, then meet, get together, and split up after they discover Ambar is pregnant. The climax of the film sees Nick trace Ambar through the streets of Melbourne in order to apologize and get back together. He goes on air to ask the listeners for their assistance; they phone in when they see her, which allows Nick to travel across Melbourne, eventually catching up with her, and thus proceeding to the inevitable happy conclusion.

Psychoraag tells the story of Zaf, as he presents the last ever night-time show on Radio Chaandni, a Glasgow-based Asian radio station. As he presents his show, Zaf's mind wanders over his life, his lost loves, his family's origins in Pakistan, and their/his life in contemporary Glasgow. On his last ever show, and the last show ever to be broadcast on Radio Chaandni, Zaf decides to ignore listeners' requests and instead play music that means something to him, that tells him something about who he is and where he comes from. The novel features a playlist, helping the reader to travel with Zaf across time and space, as the heterogeneity of his choice of music reflects his own multiple origins, as well as the diversity of his listening community. As different as these two texts are, then, they do depict the building of a community through music and through Asian broadcasting in surprisingly similar ways.

At the start of *Salaam Namaste*, Nick might have been labouring under the illusion that the only people who listen to Ambar's show on the eponymous radio station were 'a clutch of Indian taxi-drivers', but as the narrative of the film progresses, it becomes clear that the radio station has a much wider, much more diverse audience than Nick assumes. In the final sequence of the film (about which much more later) the film depicts this heterogeneity – not just a Punjabi-speaking taxi driver, but also a south Asian man in a suit speaking English in an Australian accent, and a south Asian woman also speaking English – all of whom help to guide Nick towards Ambar, through listening to the radio station. We also see an Asian man leave his shop and women leaving yoga classes and getting on their bikes to try to track Ambar across the city. The film thus visually depicts the construction of a community – a body of people connected to each other, and being encouraged to perform the same role, through listening to this specific radio station.

The montage in *Salaam Namaste* is reminiscent of Saadi's evocation of the community of listeners. Saadi is much less celebratory than Anand, and the Glasgow that he creates is certainly darker and grittier than Anand's Melbourne, but the process through which the radio station is able to connect its listeners to one another is very similar:

> Someone listens, right enough. Tired ex-gangstas, dyin eyes, hangin around in musty rooms; hot blades, sleekin back their sable hair, dreaming of a fast club lay; young women on the brink who no longer desired to sing with the voices of girls; minicab drivers who, in another *zameen*, had been government ministers; doctors and nurses dancin on the long caffeine shift; lovers with thin walls, slidin up the volume to hide both the sounds of pleasure and their own guilt; members of wacky religious sects, mud-wrestlin with their souls, *madrasah* junkies, avoidin mirrors; off-duty, multiculturally-inclined strippers; on-duty, curry-lovin polis; hookers of all descriptions; mothers whose babies wouldn't go down; city *biviis*, with *kisaan*-heid hubbies, up the night to move down an out; *mitai*-makers – 'Purveyors since Nineteen Seventy-Two' of

sweet, sweet happiness; multi-*balti*--millionaires with twenty-four carat worries; tramps clutchin bags of rancid eggs; migrants from north, south, east an west; those who'd never fitted in; clerks with scores to settle; parkin wardens wearin false moustaches; aficionados of cross-over, the Kings of the Night; kebab-shop runners; and internet-crazed insomniacs.[67]

This diversity is built into the way both fictional radio stations operate. *Salaam Namaste* is named after the two common forms of greeting for Hindus and Muslims in south Asia. Zaf's opening greeting on his show similarly includes Hindus, Muslims and Sikhs –

Salaam alaikum, sat sri akaal, namaste ji good evenin oan this hoat, hoat summer's night! Fae the peaks ae Kirkintilloch tae the dips ae Cambuslang, fae the invisible mines ae Easterhoose tae the mudflats ae Clydebank, welcome, ivirywan, welcome Glasgae, welcome Scoatland, tae *The Junnune Show.*[68]

Zaf makes it clear that his audience is multi-religious, south Asian, and distinctively Glaswegian. The contrast between this and Patrick Beech's fears about 'communal bloodshed' at the thought of greeting the audience in a language other than English is only too apparent. If these fictional radio stations, like the BBC's Asian Programmes Unit can be seen as vehicles for diasporic Asian nostalgia, then the community, the home that this nostalgia is helping to create is emphatically not monolithic or exclusive.

Having said that, it is also clear that, at various times in the novel, Zaf is suspicious of this nostalgia that he himself is evoking, and its efficacy – 'he wis beginning to sound like the host of some crap nostalgia show',[69] but even so he acknowledges its power and explicitly connects it to his (and his parents') nostalgia for the home left behind:

The violins coursed up and down and, in spite of the fact that he had been playin this music, night after night, for almost three months, Zaf still felt his insides go soft every time he heard that bit where Rafi's voice flowed like the Ravi River – before the pollution had come – slow, slow and majestic. And he felt that, if he had leapt into it, he would have known instantly that Sikander, Emperor of the Greeks had been there, in that same place, before him. And mibbee Mohammad Rafi had been there too and mibbee he had been there before even Sikander since surely the voice must've been the first of all musics. Tonight, Zaf had brought in his favourite songs.[70]

This connection between music and nostalgia is, as it were, Zaf's birthright. When his parents eloped and ran away from Lahore, to finally end up in Glasgow, music featured as part of the treasure that they took away with them:

> in a crazy moment, she had stolen one object from her *majaaz-i-khuda's* house and that was the radio. It was hardly a sensible thing to carry across five thousand miles – especially not in the trunk of a small car – and Rashida never knew just why she had decided, on impulse, to lift the thing. But she was carried on the heady swell of a greater madness – it was as though every little action or thought had meaning, even if their meaning remained elusive.[71]

If music signifies, among other things, the past for Zaf and his family, then this vision of the past, of one's own history is juxtaposed with the Glasgow cityscape that seems to have lost its own history:

> There was no trace whatsoever of the old stone or of chanting choirs or of formaldehyde. It was as though the entire past of the building had been erased. And yet, more and more, as the weeks had progressed, Zaf had found himself playing the old songs and so what the listeners had been getting had grown into a mixture of music which spanned some one hundred years. The whole of recording history. Before radio, some of it. Certainly before the community centre.[72]

If Glasgow has lost its sense of the past, then Lahore, it seems, is nothing but. For Zaf and, by extension, for most of his listeners, music serves as the link to the lost cityscape of Lahore. Music is thus used to symbolize the past – either through the memory of the radio that his mother stole from her first husband or through the music that Zaf plays on his show, 'songs of torn hearts or borders that closed and never reopened, of final partins and last glances'.[73] Alienated from the (H)istory of Britain that they could never be a part of, Zaf and his listeners do the next best thing – they create their own, using music to help recreate and reconstruct their own memories, their own histories. In the process, they are inevitably transforming the oppressive hegemonic narrative of the past and replacing it with something more meaningful, more personal. These new memories, new histories, result in a new, imaginative geography that allows the connecting of the home that Zaf's parents left behind with the home they have made for themselves in the present:

> The monsoon was like music, the pull of its rhythm sweeping her westward and north to the land of holy water and dreaming stones and circle crosses. And dead wolves howling amongst the stars.[74]

It is this nostalgia that helps to build the community of listeners, the *Khandaan* of Noreen Khan's show, or the diasporic communities that Zaf and Ambar cater to:

> It is an Asian station, he thought. All the bits, past an future, that daily jostled and sang the state of Asian-ness into being, that reconstructed something that

wasn't real from something that wis . . . Radio Chaandni bellowed out its hymns into the unlistenin darkness of Glasgow.[75]

For all of Zaf's anxieties about whether the 'darkness of Glasgow' is even listening to his music, he is also clear about the redemptive role his music, and Asian broadcasting itself, has had:

> It's *kaafi* dark thenight and it's rainin. But it's no as dark as it wis then. That wis the time before radio stations or at least before Asian radio stations, ye know?[76]

The prejudice and racism that the incoming migrants faced is connected, in Zaf's mind, with the absence of Asian broadcasting in the early days of Asian immigration. Zaf describes the gangs 'who terrorised . . . anyone who wis in any way different' and links that time to the fact that 'in those days, you wouldn't have heard "Ye Kya Hua Kaise Hua?" anywhere along the length of Paisley Road West.'[77]

Music generally, and Asian broadcasting specifically has helped to change the cityscape of the city and, in the process, made it less unfamiliar, less hostile for its Asian population: 'this city is a great auld city. Iviry brick, iviry slice ae stane wis carved in the shape ae equality. Iviry block wis cut wi a soang.'[78]

Music has changed Glasgow – Paisley Road West is now a different place to what it was before the advent of Asian broadcasting. It is no coincidence that this is Zaf's stated aim on his last ever show: "Aye, that's whit we'll do. We'll redraw aw the maps an, whun we come oot ae here in the morning, we willnae recognize the waruld, we willnae know oorsels'.[79]

Nick's journey following Ambar across Melbourne visually creates a different map of the city in much the same way. Just as Paisley Road West is now a different space because Kishore Kumar can now be heard on it, Williamstown, the Route 72 bus and Fisherman's Wharf are now different spaces because they can be connected by an Asian radio station. Nick and Ambar's journey across Melbourne changes the city, as they map and remap it in different ways to create a narrative that is distinctively diasporic Asian.

It is of course true that this remapping in the case of *Salaam Namaste* at least does not represent any kind of a challenge to normativity. The gender politics of a man employing the entire community in order to assist him to trace a woman, chase her down until she consents to marrying him, is deeply problematic to say the least. Nick and Ambar might be creating a distinctive diasporic Asian audiotopia out of the geography of Melbourne, but this new geography of sound is hardly counter-normative. There are no guarantees that the nostalgic soundscapes that diasporic Asian broadcasting help to create will pose any kind of a challenge to status quo.

The point, however, is not that an audiotopia will inevitably be a progressive space but that it *might* be. Depending on the context of the production and reception of music, and the networks of broadcasting, this redrawing of space can also be synonymous with some of the deepest, most fundamentally counter-normative social movements. The landscape that Zaf is constructing using music that is as diverse as Asian Dub Foundation, Mohammad Rafi, and The Stranglers, is simultaneously a revolutionary space:

> Deep London Underground chords, janglin, monsoon guitars, cocaine drums, shouted vocals, the nineties' tale of early seventies' revolution in West Bengal, land of the darling *daryaon*, the god rivers, an angry-man song in purple Jamaican Cockney.[80]

The soundscapes that music and Asian broadcasting help to create are multiple, fragmented and polysemic. The radical potential they contain within them may never end up being actualized, as in the case of *Salaam Namaste*, or they may well prove ineffective at liberating an individual or a community, as could be argued is the case in *Psychoraag*, but the potential is there nonetheless. In Zaf's own words, diasporic Asian broadcasting may well be

> a superficial take on an impossibly deep structure, seven-eights of which wis unpalatable. Too much of all that lovey-dovey stuff depended on there bein some kind of level playin field to start with. It depended on a delusion. But, then, what wis the alternative? Mibbee the dream wis the precursor to the reality.[81]

Both *Salaam Namaste* and *Psychoraag*, then, in their very different ways, speak to the importance of the kind of dreaming that nostalgia allows. They both present Asian broadcasting as being able to use the radio waves and the sounds that they transmit to reconfigure the geography of cities like Melbourne and Glasgow. The radio station in *Salaam Namaste* and Radio Chaandni, help to make the cities more homey for their Asian inhabitants, a hominess which allows the kind of daydreaming that Gaston Bachelard has characterized the home with.[82] Diasporic nostalgia helps the community of readers and listeners to dream up a new home where they can belong. As Zaf puts it, 'the pull of dreams is stronger than the anchor ropes of reality'[83] – and while there are no guarantees that the delusion of the dream will lead to a material change in the real world, there remains the possibility that the critique of the present that is inherent in such nostalgic dreaming will spill over into actual, material change.

NOTES

1. Asian Dub Foundation, "New Way New Life", *Community Music* (Ffrr Records, 2000)

2. http://101london.co.uk/case-studies/bbc-asian-network/ (Accessed on 15 August 2017)

3. BBC Asian Network, "You Know What British Asian Looks Like . . . This Is How It Sounds" 27 May 2016. Accessed on 15 August 2017, available at: https://www.youtube.com/watch?v=DleQPDP8Btg

4. Asian Dub Foundation, "New Way New Life"

5. Gavin Schaffer, *The Vision of a Nation: Making Multiculturalism on British Television, 1960-80* (Basingstoke and New York: Palgrave Macmillan, 2014), 1

6. Gavin Schaffer, *The Vision of a Nation*, 2

7. WAC, File R78/1 816/1 Tony Benn to Hugh Greene, 1 February 1965

8. Tanya Zinkin, "Integrating Britain's Immigrants", *The Guardian*, 18 January 1965

9. WAC, File R44/926/1

10. WAC, File R31/105/3

11. WAC File R78/78/1 "The BBC Immigrants Programmes Advisory Committee Minutes", 12 February 1969

12. WAC File R78/78/1 "The BBC Asian Programmes Advisory Committee Minutes", 16 April 1973

13. WAC File R78/78/1 "The BBC Asian Programmes Advisory Committee Minutes", 16 April 1973

14. WAC File R4/93/1

15. WAC File R78/2,966/1

16. WAC File R34/1303/2

17. WAC File R78/688, Memo from Patrick Beech, Controller, Midlands, 1 May 1967

18. WAC File M2/37/1

19. WAC File R78/1816/1 "General Advisory Council Minutes", 19 February 1977

20. WAC File R78/78/1 "The BBC Immigrants Programmes Advisory Committee Minutes", 12 February 1969

21. *Asian Network Presents*, BBC Asian Network, 29 December 2015. Accessed 15 August 2017, available at: https://learningonscreen.ac.uk/ondemand/index.php/prog/0B1567C9

22. WAC File R6/247/1, Report on Immigrants Advisory Committee by Patrick Beech, 5 October 1967

23. WAC File R78/2, 966/1, Memo on Immigrants Programmes Unit by Patrick Beech, 21 February 1972

24. WAC File R78/3345/1

25. WAC File R78/3345/1, "Asian Programmes Advisory Committee Membership", a note from G.T.M. de M. Morgan, Controller, Information Services, 21 August 1974

26. Gavin Schaffer, *The Vision of a Nation*, 54

27. WAC File R78/2 669/1, "Immigrants Programmes Advisory Committee", a note from Patrick Beech, 31 October 1968

28. WAC File R78/2 966/1, "Immigrants Programme Unit", a note from John Grist, 22 February 1972

29. WAC File R78/2 669/1, Extract from Minutes of Board of Management Meeting, 13 September 1965

30. WAC File R78/2, 669/1, Extract from Minutes of Board of Management Meeting, 20 September 1965

31. WAC File R31/104

32. WAC File R6/247/1, "Immigrants Advisory Committee", a memo from Patrick Beech, Controller, Midlands, 25 October 1967

33. WAC File R31/105/3

34. WAC File R78/78/1 "The BBC Immigrants Programmes Advisory Committee Minutes", 10 November 1965

35. WAC File R78/79/1 "The BBC Immigrants Programmes Advisory Committee Minutes", 14 April 1976

36. WAC File R78/79/1 "The BBC Immigrants Programmes Advisory Committee Minutes", 11 April 1978

37. WAC File R78/78/1

38. WAC File R78/2, 669/1, Letter from Charles Curran to Philip Mason, 15 February 1974

39. WAC File R78/2 966/1, "Asian Unit", a note from Phil Sidey, 14 November 1979
40. WAC File R4/93/1
41. WAC File R78/2966/1, "Future of Immigrants Unit", a memo from Gerry Hynes, 7 February 1972
42. WAC File R78/2 966/1, "Immigrants Programme Unit", a note from John Grist, 22 February 1972
43. WAC File M2/37/1, "The Launching of the Programmes for Immigrants", a report by David Gretton
44. WAC File M2/37/1, "The Launching of the Programmes for Immigrants", April 1966, a report by David Gretton
45. Gavin Schaffer, *The Vision of a Nation*, 47
46. Asian Dub Foundation, "New Way New Life"
47. *Asian Network Presents*, BBC Asian Network, 29 December 2015
48. *Asian Network Presents*, BBC Asian Network, 29 December 2015
49. *The Archive Hour: Make Yourself at Home*, BBC Radio 4, 25 August 2007. Accessed on 15 August 2017, available at: https://learningonscreen.ac.uk/ondemand/index.php/prog/00578E0E
50. Asian Dub Foundation, "New Way New Life"
51. Gavin Schaffer, *The Vision of a Nation*, 54
52. Nosheen Iqbal, "BBC Asian Network: 10 Years Old and Still Going Strong", *The Guardian*, 26 October 2012. Accessed on 15 August 2017, available at: https://www.theguardian.com/tv-and-radio/tvandradioblog/2012/oct/26/bbc-asian-network-10-years-old
53. *Noreen Khan*, BBC Asian Network, 20 April 2017
54. *Noreen Khan*, BBC Asian Network, 12 June 2016
55. Gayatri Gopinath, *Impossible Desires: Queer Diasporas and South Asian Popular Cultures* (Durham, NC, and London: Duke University Press, 2005), 39
56. Gayatri Gopinath, *Impossible Desires*, 32
57. *Noreen Khan*, BBC Asian Network, 12 May 2016
58. *Noreen Khan*, BBC Asian Network, 12 May 2016
59. Gayatri Gopinath, *Impossible Desires*, 32
60. *Noreen Khan*, BBC Asian Network, 14 February 2017
61. Josh Kun, *Audiotopia: Music, Race and America* (Berkeley and London: University of California Press, 2005), 23
62. *Noreen Khan*, BBC Asian Network, 3 March 2017
63. Josh Kun, *Audiotopia*, 3
64. Gayatri Gopinath, *Impossible Desires*, 34
65. Gayatri Gopinath, *Impossible Desires*, 41
66. Alan Bissett, "The 'New Weegies': The Glasgow Novel in the Twenty-first Century" in Berthold Schoene (ed.) *Edinburgh Companion to Contemporary Scottish Literature* (Edinburgh: Edinburgh University Press, 2007), 64
67. Suhayl Saadi, *Psychoraag* (Edinburgh: Black and White Publishing, 2004), 19
68. Suhayl Saadi, *Psychoraag*, 1
69. Suhayl Saadi, *Psychoraag*, 93
70. Suhayl Saadi, *Psychoraag*, 47–48
71. Suhayl Saadi, *Psychoraag*, 120
72. Suhayl Saadi, *Psychoraag*, 5
73. Suhayl Saadi, *Psychoraag*, 74
74. Suhayl Saadi, *Psychoraag*, 123
75. Suhayl Saadi, *Psychoraag*, 22
76. Suhayl Saadi, *Psychoraag*, 50
77. Suhayl Saadi, *Psychoraag*, 103
78. Suhayl Saadi, *Psychoraag*, 348
79. Suhayl Saadi, *Psychoraag*, 208
80. Suhayl Saadi, *Psychoraag*, 3–4
81. Suhayl Saadi, *Psychoraag*, 27
82. Gaston Bachelard, *The Poetics of Space* (Boston: Beacon Press, 1994), 6

83. Suhayl Saadi, *Psychoraag*, 121

Conclusion

Going Back Home: Looking Backwards, Looking Forwards

On 7 October 2015, BBC One screened the finale of the sixth season of its flagship baking show, *The Great British Bake Off*. The series winner was a thirty-year-old woman from Leeds who wore a hijab and was called Nadiya Hussain. She had endeared herself to the nation throughout the series, and her acceptance speech became one of the most talked-about moments on television for some time:

> I'm never going to put boundaries on myself ever again. I'm never going to say, 'I can't do it'. I'm never going to say 'maybe'. I'm never going to say, 'I don't think I can'. I can and I will.[1]

Famously, even Mary Berry, one of the judges on the show, cried at the end and, as Catriona Wightman put it in *Digital Spy*: 'we don't remember ever sobbing quite so much as we did last night.'[2] Seemingly overnight, Nadiya Hussain had become one of the most popular Muslim celebrities in the country, and perhaps predictably, it did not take long for the right-wing media to start attacking her. Rod Liddle in *The Spectator* claimed that she had been

> plucked from a group of typically 'diverse' human beings which the BBC presumably thinks is representative of modern Britain. Or perhaps wishes was. A gay here, a foreigner there, a BME Brit.

He goes on to ask rhetorically:

> And so, because a veiled Muslim woman won a reality TV show, a show which embodies great British virtues such as eating cakes and drinking tea, unlimited immigration is perfectly tickety-boo?³

Since her victory and subsequent fame, she has conspicuously spoken out about the racist abuse she has received on the streets and online,⁴ demonstrating, as does the Liddle article quoted above, that the image of a visibly Muslim woman winning a competition called *The Great British Bake-Off* is destabilizing and threatening to many. The diversity depicted on the show was, according to Liddle. 'addled with left-liberal wishful thinking'. In a particularly revealing moment, when *The Telegraph* covered the story of her speaking out about racism, it described her in language carefully chosen to subtly undermine her British identity – rather than describing her as 'British', or even 'British-Bangladeshi', the readers were told that she merely 'grew up in Britain and has Bangladeshi parents'. For her supporters and detractors alike, it seemed that Nadiya Hussain had become 'a poster girl for being British and being a Muslim'.⁵

It was in this context of Nadiya's newfound fame as a prominent British Bangladeshi Muslim that the BBC commissioned her first solo television show – a two-parter called *The Chronicles of Nadiya*, that aired on BBC One in August 2016. The title is clearly an allusion to *The Chronicles of Narnia* and therefore a nostalgic throwback to a specifically British childhood. In formal terms, *The Chronicles of Nadiya* fits a pattern of taking a diasporic south Asian celebrity and making a film or a television programme about their journey 'back home'. In this sense, it followed other similar programmes like Ravi Patel's *Meet the Patels* (2014), Romesh Ranganathan's *Asian Provocateur* (2015) and Tony Singh's *A Chef Abroad* (2015). Later iterations of this genre include Anita Rani's *My Family, Partition and Me* (2017) and Sanjeev Kohli and Aasmah Mir's *Partition: Legacy of the Line* (2017) as well as many, many others.

There is undoubtedly something problematic about this premium being placed on a diasporic subject's more 'authentic' view of life 'back home'. The idea that a British Bangladeshi chef, or a British Sri Lankan comic is necessarily better placed to shed light on life or food in Bangladesh or Sri Lanka is troubling to say the least, because it implies an essentialist view of race and racial identity that can be connected to many of the conservative race-based uses of reactionary nostalgia with which I opened this book. In depicting the 'other' country through the eyes of someone who, racially at least, is from said country, these programmes are often able to insidiously use the race of their presenter to naturalize the orientalized depictions of the country in the first place. When a turbanned Tony Singh is seen joking about the chaos of India's traffic, or a *hijabi* Nadiya Hussain is seen worrying about the water or the spiders in Bangladesh, their own racial identity, intentionally or not, adds greater force to the 'truth' of the picture that is being presented.

These problems notwithstanding, it is still the case that *The Chronicles of Nadiya* helps to demonstrate how nostalgia can perfectly comfortably coexist with indeterminacy when it comes to the concept of home. Far from nostalgia leading to a sense of an authentic, pure, unambiguous homeland, the home that it helps to construct is often fragmented, heterogeneous and fundamentally unstable.

In the voiceover that introduces the audience to the programme, Nadiya Hussain describes it as 'a journey that takes me home to the people and places I have missed so much', though as it turns out, her connection to Bangladesh is often more tenuous than this introduction would suggest. While she says that her father brought them up to be proud of their 'Bangladeshi roots', and, 'We had to know the full address of our village in Bangladesh, so that if anyone asked, we knew', she is also deeply unsure about how much she knows about her place of origin: 'I think I feel very British, and sometimes I feel like I don't know the Bangladeshi side of me that much.' In a conversation with her children, she clarifies: 'I'm not from Bangladesh, I am from here.' She admits that she has not been to Bangladesh for ten years, and when she first arrives, her thoughts turn to Britain. In a particularly self-conscious moment, she talks to her father about the 'typical British weather', on her journey from the airport to her village. In a pattern that will establish itself throughout the programme, she immediately undercuts this by articulating a distinctive positive relationship to the place and her memories of her previous visits: 'The air is different, takes my breath away.'

Affect is the key word here – her relationship with Bangladesh is an emotional, sensuous one, and her memories of her previous visit are those of specifically sensual experiences – walking barefoot in the mud, feeling 'the wind in the hijab' while on a rickshaw ride, and not surprisingly for a programme that is clearly food based, the experiences of cooking, eating and sharing food.

These moments are reminiscent of the 'small external objects'[6] that Johannes Hofer identified as particularly important for the development of nostalgia. Nostalgia involves the bringing of meaning to these objects and relationships and elevating them in value through the relationships that one has with them. In the process, they come to represent home.

Except, of course, the home that they represent is a deeply unstable entity. Throughout the programme, Hussain constantly uses the word 'home' to refer interchangeably to Britain and Bangladesh. Listening to the call to prayers in her village, she becomes nostalgic about a sound that she remembers from the time she spent in Bangladesh as a child, but a sound that was not a part of her life in Britain: 'That's the call to prayer, that's one of the sounds that I used to miss, because you don't hear it when you're back home, in England. That's quite a nice sound to wake up to.' What is interesting about this is that while she is talking about her nostalgic attachment to something that is entirely characteristic of her life in Bangladesh, she still refers to England as 'home'. This constant uncertainty about which place is actually home is a trope that runs through much of the programme:

> It's odd because when I come here I call back home 'home', and when I am back home, I call Bangladesh 'back home' so it is odd because I feel like a confused person myself because I don't know where home is cos home's here and home's there and I'm always constantly fighting for home to be Britain and there's times when I am back in England where I've had abuse just stood on a platform on the train station, and suddenly I question whether it is home. And then I come here and I feel so out of my depth and I think – well how can this be home then? I do sometimes wonder whether I will ever discover where home really is. . . . But I don't know, I quite enjoy the pull of the two, I quite like being a part of two things.

This same ambiguity exists not just between her feeling of hominess in Britain and in Bangladesh, but also between the Bangladesh of the present and the place she remembers from her childhood. If she oscillates between identifying Britain and Bangladesh as her home, she has a similar position with respect to changes to the village: 'Nothing's changed. Everything's changed actually, there are so many more buildings, but everything feels the same.' Later on, she admits to disappointment at the fact 'that things aren't exactly as I left it' but recognizes that 'of course things change'.

I am not of course criticizing her for this ambiguity – on the contrary, this ambiguity will be extremely familiar to many diasporic subjects when visiting 'home'. What is particularly important for my purposes here is that this ambiguity is in no way incompatible to experiencing and expressing powerful nostalgic connections to people and places. In other words, the fact that the home is unstable does not have to mean it is not comforting. Nadiya Hussain admits that she 'was quite nervous about how I would feel' at the start of her visit, but by the end was 'actually quite nervous about leaving'. Echoing an experience with which many other diasporic subjects will be familiar, she says about her impending departure: 'Getting back into the swing of things, starting to feel like home, and now I have to go.'

The first episode, which is set almost entirely in her village, is bookended by tearful exchanges with members of her family. When she first arrives and sees various members of her family again – amid tears of joy and comments about how much the children have grown, she says: 'I thought I didn't miss them – turns out I do.' These are experiences that every diasporic subject will be familiar with, and certainly for myself, the experience of watching her tearful reunion with her extended family is an emotional one as it reminds me of similar moments in my own life. There is nothing particularly special about the nostalgia that such scenes evoke, but then that is precisely the point. This is a nostalgia for the small-scale, rather than the grand, and that is one of the reasons why the home that is thus constructed is so resistant to any kind of nationalist appropriation. When she is about to leave, her farewells are marked with similar emotions, all speaking to a powerfully nostalgic connection with these extended members of family who have come to represent a kind of home:

> I can't help remembering those who have passed away since my last visit, and thinking of our shared family histories. The camera doesn't see what I see, twenty-five years ago, when my grandma used to pick us up and hold us, the way he [her uncle] used to give us piggy back rides. . . . Sometimes when you live away from all of this, you feel like you are the one who made you. You forget that these are the people who quietly sit and pray for you and think about you.

Nadiya Hussain is embodying Walter Benjamin's point about memories being able to 'generate nearness'.[7] Through a particularly rich use of a diverse set of nostalgic affects, Nadiya Hussain is able to create a different imaginary geography where the Bangladesh of twenty-five years ago, contemporary Bangladesh and contemporary Britain can coexist. In a very real sense then, *The Chronicles of Nadiya* is not so much a journey of discovery to Bangladesh, but an imaginative act of homemaking, through which Nadiya Hussain can weave together a number of different emotions, sense experiences and memories in order to make a home within which she can belong.

'THE RETURN OF THE PRODIGAL': NOSTALGIC RETURNINGS IN *ANIL'S GHOST* AND *THE HUNGRY TIDE*

For most of this book, I have been concerned with discursive and imaginative acts of going back home. In a sense, any act of homemaking is also simultaneously an act of going back home. It is in returning to our roots, whatever and wherever they may be, that we are able to create spaces of belonging. Sometimes, as in the case of Duleep Singh, these returns had to be imaginary ones of necessity; in other cases, such as the use of food and music, the metaphorical return is what is important. In this conclusion, however, I am concerned more directly with actual physical acts of return, such as Nadiya Hussain's return to her family's village in Sylhet. How might journeys back home represent instances of progressive nostalgia and consequently help the process of homemaking that I have been engaged with throughout this book?

Michael Ondaatje's *Anil's Ghost* (2000) and Amitav Ghosh's *The Hungry Tide* (2004) both feature diasporic subjects who make the journey back 'home'. Ondaatje tells the story of Anil, a forensic pathologist who was born and raised in Sri Lanka, before moving first to the United Kingdom, and then to the United States. She returns to her war-torn homeland as part of an investigation under the auspices of the United Nations, in an effort to catalogue and identify the dead of both sides in the brutal civil war. Ghosh charts the journeys of Piya, a cetologist, who was born in Calcutta but moved to Seattle as a child, and at the start of the novel, has returned to West Bengal hunting the Orcaella, the marine mammals of the Sundarbans. Piya and Anil have much in common – they are both first-generation diasporic subjects whose status as expats is almost written onto their bodies. When Kanai first sees Piya, it is her foreignness that stands out:

> It occurred to him suddenly that perhaps, despite her silver nose-stud and the tint of her skin, she was not Indian, except by descent. And the moment the thought occurred to him, he was convinced of it: she was a foreigner; it was stamped in her posture, in the way she stood, balancing on her heels like a flyweight boxer, with her feet planted apart.[8]

In standing out as foreign, both Anil and Piya feel the distance between who they actually are and what they look like. Kanai, on first hearing Piya's name, is clearly struck by 'the unmistakably Bengali sound of her name'[9] and how it contrasts with the looks, mannerisms and language skills of 'the foreign girl'.[10] Sarath is even clearer about his belief that Anil no longer belongs in the way that she once used to, describing her arrival in Sri Lanka as the 'return of the prodigal'.[11]

When Sarath and Anil first start working together, her foreignness is a source of suspicion for him: 'I'd believe your arguments more if you lived here. . . . You can't just slip in, make a discovery and leave.'[12] Indeed, at the start of the novel, Anil takes great comfort in her difference, as her relationship to the land of her birth is ambivalent, to say the least:

> In her years abroad, during her European and North American education, Anil had courted foreignness, was at ease whether on the Bakerloo line or the highways around Santa Fe. . . . But here, on this island, she realized she was moving with only one arm of language among uncertain laws and a fear that was everywhere.[13]

If Anil is, to an extent, defined by her inability to speak Sinhala, Piya stands out for not being able to speak Bengali:

> One of the onlookers began to explain, gesticulating with an upraised arm. But the explanation was in Bengali and it was lost on her. She stopped the man with a raised hand and said, in apology, that she knew no Bengali: *ami Bangla jani na*. He could tell from the awkwardness of her pronunciation that this was literally true: like strangers everywhere, she had learnt just enough of the language to be able to provide due warning of her incomprehension.[14]

For Anil, her foreignness is deliberately courted: 'The island no longer held her by the past ... she had now lived abroad long enough to interpret Sri Lanka with a long-distanced gaze.'[15] For Piya, on the other hand, her foreignness is inherited from her father, who attempted to become the ideal diasporic subject by subsuming his attachment to the home he left behind for the new world he had found himself in:

> Having moved around a lot, my father has all these theories about immigrants and refugees. He believes that Indians – Bengalis in particular – don't travel well, because their eyes are always turned backwards, towards home. When we moved to America, he decided he wasn't going to make that mistake: he was going to try to fit in.[16]

In both cases, Piya and Anil end up becoming outsiders, attached to and identified with perhaps their most obvious marker of privilege – their expertise. It is surely no coincidence that they both make explicit connections between their work and hominess. Anil, the forensic pathologist, associates home with the corpses she works on:

> *Honey, I'm home*, she would say, crouching beside a corpse to ascertain the hour of death. The phrase came out caustic or tender, depending on her mood.[17]

Like Anil, Piya also associates her work with a similar sense of hominess: 'for me, home is where the Orcaella are'.[18] It is also no coincidence that both Piya and Anil have picked fields of expertise that require them to travel – Anil has worked in war zones in Guatemala and in the Congo before returning to Sri Lanka, places where her foreignness was even more pronounced. For all her class and education privilege, this foreignness that she cultivated comes at a price:

> The grand logos on letterheads and European office doors meant nothing where there was crisis. If and when you were asked by a government to leave, you left. You took nothing with you.... At the airport, while they searched her clothing, she'd sat almost naked on a stool.[19]

Piya is even more direct about the fact that, for all her attachment to her work, it has also led to a precarious homelessness:

> I have no home, no money and no prospects. My friends are thousands of kilometres away and I get to see them maybe once a year, if I'm lucky. On top of that is the knowledge that what I'm doing is more or less futile.[20]

Homelessness and the desire to reconnect and rebuild lies at the centre of both novels, and not just in the case of the protagonists, Anil and Piya, either.

Both Ondaatje and Ghosh present worlds where people have been rendered homeless – either literally, as in the refugees of Marichjhapi, or figuratively, as in the case of the Sri Lankans like Sanath whose nation has been taken away from them through the violence of civil war. Both novels can be read as meditations on the necessity of making a home for oneself, finding a space within which one can belong. In the context of war and partition, corrupt and uncaring governments and structural inequalities of various kinds, the insistence on such acts of homemaking assumes great political significance. When the contemporary world denies you a home, employing an affective connection with the past to create a home for yourself necessarily involves assuming a critical, counter-hegemonic subjectivity.

Even the most anti-nostalgic characters – people like Anil and Piya's father – who seem to be actively resisting any notion of belonging, are not immune to the poignant pangs of nostalgia. Even though Anil's application to work in Sri Lanka 'had originally been half-hearted', when she finally arrives, 'Suddenly Anil was glad to be back, the buried senses from childhood alive in her.'[21] Anil might have spent most of her adult life running away from notions of belonging, but her memories of her childhood in Sri Lanka are nevertheless suffused with nostalgia:

> Anil recalled the nineteenth-century air of the city she had left behind. The prawn sellers holding out their wares to passing traffic on Duplication Road, the houses in Colombo Seven painted that meticulous flat white. This was where the old money and the politically powerful lived. 'Heaven . . . Colombo Seven . . . ' her father would sing, to the tune of 'Cheek to Cheek' as he let Anil thread his cuff links into his shirtsleeves while he dressed for dinner. There was always this whispering pact between them. And she knew that no matter what time he returned home from dances or other engagements or emergency operations, he would drive her to her dawn swimming practice the next morning, through the empty streets towards the Otters Club. On the drive home they would pause at a stall for a bowl of milk and sugar hoppers, each wrapped in a shiny page from an English magazine.[22]

Anil's nostalgic attachment to the 'eternal prawn sellers'[23] is mirrored by Piya's father's lingering attachment to symbols of the home he had otherwise seemingly rejected:

> Now, suddenly she recalled where it was that she had seen a towel like this before: it was tied to the doorknob of her father's wardrobe, in the eleventh-floor apartment of her childhood. Through the years of her adolescence, the fabric had grown old and tattered and she would have thrown it away but for her father's protests. He was, in general, the least sentimental of men, especially where it concerned 'home'. Where others sought to preserve their memories of the 'old country', he had always tried to expunge them. His feet were in the present, he had liked to say, by which he meant they were planted firmly on

the rungs of his company's career ladder. But when she had asked whether she could throw away that rotting bit of old cloth, he had responded almost with shock. It had been with him for many years, he said, it was almost a part of his body, like his hair or his nail clippings; his luck was woven into it; he could not think of parting with it, of throwing away this –. What was it he had called it? She had known the word once, but time had erased it from her memory.[24]

The word that Piya has forgotten is *gamcha*, referring to an indigenous cotton bathing towel, that can also be used as a garment. In Chapter 4, I talk about my own disorientation at discovering that I could buy an 'authentic' *gamcha* in East London – a disorientation that has at its root a similar association between this piece of fabric and a home that is located several thousand miles away. Both Piya's father and I took the otherwise meaningless object that is the *gamcha* and ascribed notions of home into it. Nilima is performing the same action when she connects home with 'wherever I can brew a pot of good tea'.[25] while for Gamini, like for Anil, his work performs the same function:

He realized Emergency Services had become for him, even in its mad state, a cocoon, as his parents' house had been. Everything that was of value to him took place there. He slept in the wards, he bought his meals from the street vendor just outside the hospital.[26]

All of these and more represent the 'small external objects' of Hofer's argument, and it is through the affect of nostalgia that these objects, otherwise valueless, come to have resonances of home and belonging.

A RADICAL HERMENEUTICS OF NOSTALGIA

Insofar as these acts of homemaking involve the reading of meaning onto places, people and objects, nostalgia can be seen to be an exercise in hermeneutics. In calling for nostalgia to be recognized as one of the primary motivating factors in a series of complex processes of homemaking, I am essentially calling for the recognition of a different model of interpretation, one that sees the act of meaning-making as analogous to the act of homemaking. Reading, in this way, whether it is reading meaning onto places or objects, or reading particular narratives onto the past, can be thought of as a search for somewhere to belong, and within certain contexts, this search can carry within it immense counter-hegemonic and liberatory potential.

In a way, this is not really new. On the contrary, what I am suggesting could be seen to be taking nostalgia back to its roots. Both Johannes Hofer and Robert Hamilton were, I believe, engaging in a similar exercise in hermeneutics when they read 'nostalgia' onto the homesick little girl, or Edwards, the Welsh soldier. Or, and as Alex Davis has observed, in coining the term 'nostalgia', Hofer was engaging in an act of nostalgia himself: 'the function of the neologism was to furnish a home for the new concept.'[27] It is this self-reflexivity which makes nostalgia such a potentially fruitful model for a new model of hermeneutics.

A hermeneutics of nostalgia,[28] then, would recognize and value the need to belong and the critical potential that such a need might have when faced with an alienating and unjust present. A hermeneutics of nostalgia would value the 'small external objects' that nostalgia thrives on and recognize that, contrary to Svetlana Boym, a nostalgia that seeks to restore a lost home does not necessarily have to be directed at a monumentalized past. When Boym argues that restorative nostalgia 'does not think of itself as nostalgia, but rather as truth and tradition',[29] I think she too easily equates an individual or a collective need to belong somewhere, with a Modernist grand-narrative of history that claims objective truth.

Instead of Boym's notion of 'restorative nostalgia', I would prefer to think about Eve Kosofsky Sedgwick's model of 'reparative reading':

> To read from a reparative position is to surrender the knowing, anxious paranoid determination that no horror, however apparently unthinkable, shall ever come to the reader as new; to a reparatively positioned reader, it can seem realistic and necessary to experience surprise. Because there can be terrible surprises, however, there can also be good ones. Hope, often a fracturing, even a traumatic thing to experience, is among the energies by which the reparatively positioned reader tries to organise the fragments and part-objects she encounters or creates. Because the reader has room to realize that the future may be different from the present, it is also possible for her to entertain such profoundly painful, profoundly relieving, ethically crucial possibilities as that the past, in turn, could have happened differently from the way it actually did.[30]

The falsification that Boym identifies as part of a Modernist, illusory, nation-state endorsed, hegemonic grand-narrative, becomes, in Sedgwick's argument, a creative, affirmative, ultimately restorative search for belonging. This search for belonging does not have to, and indeed mostly does not, lead to anything stable or homogeneous. As Calvin O. Schrag has demonstrated, it is perfectly possible for a hermeneutics based on productive nostalgia to not be logocentric. Indeed, Schrag's definition of a productive nostalgia goes some way towards characterizing the model of reading that I am calling for here:

> Productive nostalgia is a process of meaning-formation that gathers fragments of a remembered past, imaginatively reconstructs them, idealizes their contents, and projects the idealized portrait of the past as a directive for personal and communal actualization.[31]

Both following from and developing on Schrag's argument, I would like to suggest home, rather than *logos*, as a more appropriate descriptor for the object of this hermeneutical exercise. If homemaking is also an act of meaning-making, then the meaning that is being sought is not necessarily the *logos* of absolute Truth, not the Modernist grand-narrative of a single, uncontested, homogeneous Truth, but rather the much more diffuse, fragmented, always-contested, always-changing concept of home. A hermeneutics of nostalgia then is ultimately radical because it does not search for the transcendental *logos* but reflects the much more modest ambition of a space to call one's own. Faced with the immense force of the history of colonialism and its legacies, having to survive in a racist and alienating neo-colonial present, the postcolonial, diasporic subjects I have engaged with in these pages are able to wield this notion of home as a powerfully counter-hegemonic, progressive force that can help to transcend international relations of Empire and capital, and create instead a pan-national space of belonging using the meanings that they write onto objects, places and people. In the face of an overwhelming demand from status quo to be defined in terms of hegemony, whether that be through the nation-state or through capital, exercising the self-indulgence of defining oneself on one's own terms, through one's own narrative of the past and one's relation to it, is a powerfully defiant act.

In *Queer Nostalgia in Cinema and Pop Culture*, Gilad Padva writes movingly of the importance of using nostalgia to rewrite history from a queer perspective. He writes:

> As a journey to the irrecoverable, the written off, the forbidden and the neglected, *queer nostalgia is a creative practice that creates new fields, dimensions, and perspectives of the queer experience*. Fantasized *and* fantastic past are significant parts of every community, as much as official and alternative historical narratives and imperatives. Subaltern sexual communities can be empowered by a glorified past and its mythic playgrounds, role models and halls of fame.[32]

The power that Padva ascribes to nostalgia in its ability to challenge and undermine heteronormativity applies just as much to Empire and its various painful legacies. If queer nostalgia allows spaces within which queer bodies can experience 'a sort of therapeutic process of coming to terms with who we are, what we want to be, and what we *can* be if only we dare to imagine',[33] then a postcolonial nostalgia might just do the same for the various diasporic subjectivities that I have focused on here. Along with Pavda, I argue that the hegemonic derision and disdain for nostalgia, and for nostalgic approaches to the past, is an act of privilege blindness that does great violence by refusing to recognize the fact that 'subaltern communities . . . yearn for communal recollection' because 'for those who are struggling against oppression . . . nostalgia – idealized and fantasized as it is – can be liberating.' When the forces of hegemony have decided that your history is valueless, or worse, non-existent, when your sense of belonging is only safe when it is on terms set by your oppressor, nostalgia 'embraces joyful moments, glamorous eras, spectacular achievements, and sweet times.'[34] In allowing yourself to recover a glorious and fantastical notion of your past, you not only challenge the terms on which certain narratives from certain perspectives of the past are valued over others, but you are also able to challenge the power relations that those same perspectives help construct in the present. As Padva puts it:

> Nostalgia gives us the power to confront bigotry, nationalism, racism, xenophobia, chauvinism, misogyny and homophobia, as it reminds us how beautiful this world could be. If nostalgia is about golden living dreams of visions, then it can truly stimulate our mind's true liberation. Let the sunshine in.[35]

In giving us the opportunity to create a space to belong, in allowing us the tools to make our own home, nostalgia allows us to imagine the revolutionary possibilities that are inherent in the worlding of the home. In short, nostalgia allows one to turn the past into tools that might just transform the future.

For me, like for many other diasporic subjects, nostalgia allows us to dream of a different world, one where our past and present homes do not exist so far apart, one where we do not have to choose between our present and past lives. Nostalgia allows me to imagine a world where home is not just a place where I go on holidays, not full of family members who I can only see once every few years. In the second decade of the twenty-first century, the powers of hegemony are increasingly trying to convince everyone that there is only one way of being a citizen of the nation. Being a citizen of the world apparently means being a citizen of nowhere.[36] In the process, of course, different kinds of citizenship are being put into particular hierarchies. A nostalgic attachment to valueless small objects, a subjectivity that is able to celebrate a past that is at odds with the citizenship that one is supposed to treasure, can, in these circumstances, amount to a rejection of the given value systems. If I can eat my own food, listen to my own music, wear my own clothes in Edinburgh or London or New York or Kolkata or Delhi, then maybe I do not have to choose between citizenship and homelessness. Eating a particular kind of food or listening to a particular kind of music will not bring any change on its own, true, but it does allow me to imagine a world that is structured differently. It allows the luxury to dream of what might one day be possible. It is true that nostalgia does not give any guarantees, but it does at least provide that most valuable and traumatic of things – hope.

NOTES

1. *The Great British Bake Off, Series 6, Episode 10*, BBC1, 7 October 2015
2. Catriona Wightman, "The Great British Bake Off: Was That the Most Emotional Final Ever?", *Digital Spy*, 8 October 2015. Accessed on 16 August 2017, available at: http://www.digitalspy.com/tv/great-british-bake-off/news/a672609/the-great-british-bake-off-was-that-the-most-emotional-final-ever/
3. Rod Liddle, "What the Great British Bake Off really says about Britain", *The Spectator*, 17 October 2015, accessed on 16 August 2017, available at: https://www.spectator.co.uk/2015/10/what-the-great-british-bake-off-really-says-about-britain/
4. Sophie Jamieson, "'I Ain't Sitting near a Muslim': Great British Bake Off's Nadiya Hussain Reveals Racist Incident on Train", *The Telegraph*, 15 December 2016. Accessed on 17 August 2017, available at: http://www.telegraph.co.uk/news/2016/12/15/aint-sitting-near-muslim-great-british-bake-offs-nadiya-hussain/
5. Priya Joshi, "Great British Bake-Off Star Nadiya Hussain's Home Placed under Police Guard after Anti-Muslim Threats", *International Business Times*, 7 January 2016. Accessed on 17 August 2017, available at: http://www.ibtimes.co.uk/great-british-bake-off-star-nadiya-hussains-home-placed-under-police-guard-after-anti-muslim-1536691
6. Johannes Hofer, "*Medical Dissertation on Nostalgia* by Johannes Hofer (1688)" translated by Carolyn Kiser Anspach, *Bulletin of the Institute of the History of Medicine*, 1 January 1934, 381
7. Walter Benjamin, "The Great Art of Making Things Seem Closer", 248
8. Amitav Ghosh, *The Hungry Tide* (New Delhi: HarperCollins, 2004), 3
9. Amitav Ghosh, *The Hungry Tide*, 12
10. Amitav Ghosh, *The Hungry Tide*, 5
11. Michael Ondaatje, *Anil's Ghost* (London: Bloomsbury, 2000), 10
12. Michael Ondaatje, *Anil's Ghost*, 44
13. Michael Ondaatje, *Anil's Ghost*, 54
14. Amitav Ghosh, *The Hungry Tide*, 4
15. Michael Ondaatje, *Anil's Ghost*, 11
16. Amitav Ghosh, *The Hungry Tide*, 250
17. Michael Ondaatje, *Anil's Ghost*, 19
18. Amitav Ghosh, *The Hungry Tide*, 400
19. Michael Ondaatje, *Anil's Ghost*, 29
20. Amitav Ghosh, *The Hungry Tide*, 302
21. Michael Ondaatje, *Anil's Ghost*, 15
22. Michael Ondaatje, *Anil's Ghost*, 68
23. Michael Ondaatje, *Anil's Ghost*, 69
24. Amitav Ghosh, *The Hungry Tide*, 87
25. Amitav Ghosh, *The Hungry Tide*, 400
26. Michael Ondaatje, *Anil's Ghost*, 215
27. Alex Davis, "Coming Home Again: Johannes Hofer, Edmund Spenser, and Premodern Nostalgia", *Parergon*, 33.2, 2016, 20
28. I borrow the phrase from Calvin O. Schrag, *The Resources of Rationality: A Response to the Postmodern Challenge* (Bloomington: Indiana University Press, 1992), 68, though I use it in a rather different fashion than he does.
29. Svetlana Boym, *The Future of Nostalgia* (New York: Basic Books, 2001), xviii
30. Eve Kosofsky Sedgwick, *Touching, Feeling: Affect, Pedagogy, Performativity* (Durham, NC, and London: Duke University Press, 2003), 146
31. Calvin O. Schrag, *The Resources of Rationality*, 74
32. Gilad Padva, *Queer Nostalgia in Cinema and Pop Culture* (Basingstoke: Palgrave Macmillan, 2004), 8
33. Gilad Padva, *Queer Nostalgia in Cinema and Pop Culture*, 11
34. Gilad Padva, *Queer Nostalgia in Cinema and Pop Culture*, 228
35. Gilad Padva, *Queer Nostalgia in Cinema and Pop Culture*, 232

36. Theresa May, Keynote to the Conservative Party Conference, 5 October 2016. Accessed on 17 August 2017, available at: http://www.independent.co.uk/news/uk/politics/theresa-may-speech-tory-conference-2016-in-full-transcript-a7346171.html

Bibliography

Ahluwalia, Kiranjit, and Rahila Gupta, *Provoked: The Story of Kiranjit Ahluwalia*. New Delhi: HarperCollins, 2008.
Ahmad, Irfan, "In Defense of Ho(s)tels: Islamophobia, Domophilia, Liberalism." *Politics, Religion & Ideology* 14:2 (2013): 234–52.
Ahmed, Kamal, "Welcome Back, TSB, as Bank Splits from Lloyds." *The Telegraph*, 7 September 2013.
Ali, Monica, *Brick Lane*. London: Black Swan, 2003.
Andrews, Kehinde, "Colonial Nostalgia Is Back in Fashion, Blinding Us to the Horrors of Empire." *The Guardian*, 24 August 2016.
Athique, Adrian, "Diasporic Audiences and Non-Resident Media: The Case of Indian Films." *Participations: Journal of Audience and Reception Studies* 8.2 (November 2011): 1–23.
Augé, Marc, *Non-Places: Introduction to an Anthropology of Supermodernity*. London and New York: Verso, 1995.
Axel, Brian Keith, *The Nation's Tortured Body: Violence, Representation and the Formation of a Sikh "Diaspora."* Durham, NC, and London: Duke University Press, 2001.
Bachelard, Gaston, *The Poetics of Space*. Boston: Beacon Press, 1994.
Bailey, Sarah Pulliam, "How Nostalgia for White Christian America Drove So Many Americans to Vote for Trump." *Washington Post*, 5 January 2017.
Baird, J.G.A., *Private Letters of Marquess of Dalhousie*. London: William Blackwood and Sons, 1911.
Bance, Peter, *The Duleep Singhs: The Photograph Album of Queen Victoria's Maharajah*. Stroud. Glos: Sutton Publishing, 2004.
Banerjee Divakaruni, Chitra, *The Mistress of Spices*. London: Black Swan, 1997.
Bedi, Rahul, "Shah Rukh Khan Article Spars War of Words Between India and Pakistan." *The Telegraph*, 30 January 2013.
Belsey, Catherine, "Reading Cultural History" in *Reading the Past: Literature and History* edited by Tamsin Spargo, 103–17. London: Palgrave, 2000.
Benjamin, Walter, *Illuminations* edited by Hannah Arendt, London: Pimlico, 1999.
Benjamin, Walter, *Selected Writings 1927–1930* edited by Michael W. Jennings, Howard Eiland and Gary Smith. Cambridge, MA, and London: Harvard University Press, 1999.
Bennett, Susan, *Performing Nostalgia: Shifting Shakespeare and the Contemporary Past*. London: Routledge, 1996.
Bhambra, Gurminder K., "Brexit, Trump, and 'Methodological Whiteness': On the Misrecognition of Race and Class," *British Journal of Sociology*, 68.S1 (2017): 214–32.
Bhatt, Sujata, *The Stinking Rose*. Manchester: Carcanet, 1995.
Bindel, Julie, "I Wanted Him to Stop Hurting Me." *The Guardian*, 4 April 2007.

Binelli, Mark, "Guerilla Goddess," *Rolling Stone*, 29 December 2005.
Bissett, Alan, "The 'New Weegies': The Glasgow Novel in the Twenty-first Century" in *Edinburgh Companion to Contemporary Scottish Literature* edited by Berthold Schoene, 59–67. Edinburgh: Edinburgh University Press, 2007.
Blake, Marc, *Writing the Comedy Movie*. London and New York: Bloomsbury, 2016.
Bond, Anthony, "Welcome to the Slums of Southall." *Mail Online*, 17 October 2011.
Bong Mom, http://www.bongcookbook.com.
Bonnett, Alastair, *Left in the Past: Radicalism and the Politics of Nostalgia*. New York and London: Continuum, 2010.
Boym, Svetlana, *The Future of Nostalgia*. New York: Basic Books, 2001.
Breihan, Tom, "Swet Shop Boys – 'Aaja' Video." *Stereogum*, 2 March 2017.
Brownstein, Ronald, "Trump's Rhetoric of White Nostalgia." *The Atlantic*, 2 June 2016.
Burns, Alice, "The History of the Indian Chain Restaurant Dishoom." *The Culture Club*, 9 February 2017.
Butler, Judith, *Precarious Life: The Powers of Mourning and Violence*. London and New York: Verso, 2004.
Cable, Vince, "Not Martyrs, Masochists." *Daily Mail*, 6 August 2017.
Campbell, Christy, *The Maharajah's Box: An Imperial Story of Conspiracy, Love and a Guru's Prophecy*. London: HarperCollins, 2001.
Cenzatti, Marco, "Heterotopias of Difference" in *Heterotopia and the City: Public Space in a Postcivil Society* edited by Michiel Dehaene and Lieven De Cauter, 77. London and New York: Routledge, 2008
Dames, Nicholas, *Amnesiac Selves: Nostalgia, Forgetting and British Fiction, 1810–1870*. New York and Oxford: Oxford University Press, 2001.
Davis, Alex, "Coming Home Again: Johannes Hofer, Edmund Spenser, and Premodern Nostalgia." *Parergon* 33 (2016): 17–38.
Dehaene, Michiel, and Lieven De Cauter (eds), *Heterotopia and the City: Public Space in a Postcivil Society*. London and New York: Routledge, 2008.
Desai, Jigna, *Beyond Bollywood: The Cultural Politics of South Asian Diasporic Film*. New York and London: Routledge, 2004.
Desai, Jigna, "'Ever Since You've Discovered the Video, I've Had No Peace': Diasporic Spectators Talk Back to Bollywood Masala" in *The Bollywood Reader* edited by Rajinder Dudrah and Jigna Desai, 229–42. Maidenhead and New York: Open University Press, 2008.
Dudrah, Rajinder, *Bollywood: Sociology Goes to the Movies*. New Delhi: Sage, 2006.
Dudrah, Rajinder, *Bollywood Travels: Culture, Diaspora, and Border Crossings in Popular Hindi Cinema*. Oxford and New York: Routledge, 2012.
El-Enany, Nadine, "Brexit Is Not Only an Expression of Nostalgia for Empire, It Is Also the Fruit of Empire." *The LSE Blog*, 11 May 2017, http://blogs.lse.ac.uk/brexit/2017/05/11/brexit-is-not-only-an-expression-of-nostalgia-for-empire-it-is-also-the-fruit-of-empire/.
Fellows, Will, *A Passion to Preserve: Gay Men as Keepers of Culture*. Madison: University of Wisconsin Press, 2004.
Flusser, Vilém, *Writings*. Minneapolis: University of Minnesota Press, 2002.
Flusser, Vilém, *The Freedom of the Migrant: Objections to Nationalism*. Urbana, Chicago and Springfield: University of Illinois Press, 2003.
Foucault, Michel, "Of Other Spaces." *Diacritics* 16 (Spring 1986): 22–27.
Foucault, Michel, *Aesthetics, Method and Epistemology Vol. 2*. New York: New Press, 1998.
Foucault, Michel, *The Order of Things: An Archaeology of the Human Sciences*. London and New York: Routledge, 2002.
Geraghty, Christine, *Now a Major Motion Picture: Film Adaptations of Literature and Drama*. Lanham, MD: Rowman & Littlefield, 2008.
Ghosh, Amitav, *The Hungry Tide*. New Delhi: HarperCollins, 2004.
Ghosh, Palash, "India's War on Valentine's Day." *International Business Times*, 26 January 2012.
Gill, A.A., "Brexit: AA Gill Argues for 'In'." *The Sunday Times*, 12 June 2016.
Glazer, Peter, *Radical Nostalgia: Spanish Civil War Commemoration in America*. Rochester, NY: University of Rochester Press, 2005.

Gopinath, Gayatri, *Impossible Desires: Queer Diasporas and South Asian Popular Cultures*. Durham, NC, and London: Duke University Press, 2005.
The Great British Bake Off, Series 6, Episode 10. BBC1, 7 October 2015.
Gupta, Rahila (ed.), *From Homebreakers to Jailbreakers: Southall Black Sisters*. London: Zed Books, 2003.
Hamilton, Carrie, "Happy Memories." *New Formations* 63 (Winter 2007): 65–81.
Hamilton, Robert, "History of a Remarkable Case of Nostalgia Affecting a Native of Wales, and Occurring in Britain." *Medical Commentaries for the Year 1786* edited by Andrew Duncan, 343–48. Edinburgh and London: C. Elliot & Co., 1787.
Haskins, Chris, "Ireland Is Looking Forward. Britain after the Brexit Vote Is Looking Back." *The Guardian*, 18 October 2016.
Hatherley, Owen, *The Ministry of Nostalgia*. London and New York: Verso, 2016.
Hislop, Leah, "Indian Restaurant Dishoom Voted Britain's Favourite Eatery (Again)." *The Telegraph*, 10 February 2016.
Hofer, Johannes, "*Medical Dissertation on Nostalgia* by Johannes Hofer (1688)." Translated by Carolyn Kiser Anspach, *Bulletin of the Institute of the History of Medicine* (1 January 1934): 376–91.
Huang, C.T., "Heterotopic Ossification," *Spinal Cord Injury Infosheet 12*. March 2009.
Hunt, El, "Swet Shop Boys Have a New Video for 'Aaja (Ft. Ali Sethi)'." *DIY*, 2 March 2017.
Hutnyk, John, *Critique of Exotica: Music, Politics and the Culture Industry*. London: Pluto Press, 2000.
Illbruck, Helmut, *Nostalgia: Origins and Ends of an Unenlightened Disease*. Evanston, IL: Northwestern University Press, 2012.
Iqbal, Nosheen, "BBC Asian Network: 10 Years Old and Still Going Strong." *The Guardian*, 26 October 2012.
Jaffrey, Madhur, *Climbing the Mango Trees: A Memoir of a Childhood in India*. London: Ebury, 2006.
Jamieson, Sophie, "'I Ain't Sitting near a Muslim': Great British Bake Off's Nadiya Hussain Reveals Racist Incident on Train." *The Telegraph*, 15 December 2016. Accessed on 17 August 2017, available at: http://www.telegraph.co.uk/news/2016/12/15/aint-sitting-near-muslim-great-british-bake-offs-nadiya-hussain/
Jaswal, Balli Kaur, *Erotic Stories for Punjabi Widows*. London: HarperCollins, 2017.
Jeffries, Stuart, "The Best Exotic Nostalgia Boom: Why Colonial Style Is Back." *The Guardian*, 19 March 2015.
Joshi, Priya, "Great British Bake-Off Star Nadiya Hussain's Home Placed under Police Guard after Anti-Muslim Threats." *International Business Times*, 7 January 2016. Accessed on 17 August 2017, available at: http://www.ibtimes.co.uk/great-british-bake-off-star-nadiya-hussains-home-placed-under-police-guard-after-anti-muslim-1536691
Katrak, Ketu H., "Food and Belonging: At 'Home' and in 'Alien-Kitchens'" in *Through the Kitchen Window* edited by Arlene Avakian, 263–75. Boston: Beacon Press, 1997.
Katrak, Ketu H., "Changing Traditions: South Asian Americans and Cultural/Communal Politics." *The Massachusetts Review* 43.1 (Spring 2002): 75–88.
Kaye, Ben, "A Bit of Bollywood Romance for the Ali Sethi-Featuring Track." *Consequence of Sound*, 2 March 2017.
Keith, Michael, *After the Cosmopolitan? Multicultural Cities and the Future of Racism*. London and New York: Routledge, 2005.
Khan, Shah Rukh, "Inside My Khanate." *Outlook*, 7 January 2013.
Kun, Josh, *Audiotopia: Music, Race and America*. Berkeley and London: University of California Press, 2005.
Lahiri, Jhumpa, *The Interpreter of Maladies*. Boston and New York: Mariner Books, 1999.
Lahiri, Jhumpa, "Indian Takeout," *Food & Wine*, 1 April 2000.
Lahiri, Jhumpa, *The Namesake*. Boston and New York: Mariner Books, 2004.
Lax, Sigurd F., "Heterotopia from a Biological and Medical Point of View" in *Other Spaces: The Affair of the Heterotopia* edited by Roland Ritter and Bernd Knaller-Vlay, 114–23, Graz, Austria: Haus der Architektur, 1998.
Lefebvre, Henri, *The Production of Space*. Oxford: Blackwell Publishing, 2002.

Lewis, Paul, "Blair Peach: After 31 Years Met Police Say 'Sorry' for Their Role in His Killing." *The Guardian*, 27 April 2010.

Lichtenstein, Rachel, *On Brick Lane*. London: Hamish Hamilton, 2007.

Liddle, Rod, "What the Great British Bake Off Really Says about Britain," *The Spectator*, 17 October 2015.

Lizardi, Ryan, *Mediated Nostalgia: Individual Memory and Contemporary Mass Media*. Lanham, MD: Lexington Books, 2015.

Login, Edith Dalhousie, *Lady Login's Recollections: Court Life and Camp Life, 1820–1904*. London: Smith, Elder, 1916.

Lowenthal, David, "Nostalgia Tells It Like It Wasn't." *The Imagined Past: History, and Nostalgia* edited by Malcolm Chase and Christopher Shaw, 18–32. Manchester: Manchester University Press, 1989.

Lowenthal, David, *The Past Is a Foreign Country Revisited*. Cambridge: Cambridge University Press, 2015.

Ludhra, Aneeka, *Dadima's: Celebrating Grandmother's Wisdom through Indian Cooking*. Sheffield: RMC Media, 2016.

Macgregor, Neil, "Episode 4: Bird Shaped Pestle," *A History of the World in 100 Objects*. BBC Radio 4, 2010.

Mannur, Anita, *Culinary Fictions: Food in South Asian Diasporic Culture*. Philadelphia: Temple University Press, 2010.

Marangoly George, Rosemary, *The Politics of Home: Postcolonial Relocations and Twentieth-Century Fiction*. Berkeley and London: University of California Press, 1999.

May, Emma, "Video: Swet Shop Boys – 'Aaja'." *Spin*, 2 March 2017.

McClarence, Stephen, "Diwali in Leicester: An Indian Adventure on British Soil." *The Telegraph*, 2 November 2015.

Milesi, Laurent, "'Promnesia' (Remembering Forward) in *Midnight's Children*; or Rushdie's Chutney versus Proust's Madeleine" in *Sensual Reading: New Approaches to Reading in Its Relations to the Senses* edited by Michael Syrotinski and Ian Maclachlan, 179–212. Lewisburg, PA: Bucknell University Press; London: Associated University Presses, 2001.

Mishra, Sudesh, "Tazia Fiji!: The Place of Potentiality" in *Transnational South Asians: The Making of a Neo-Diaspora* edited by Susan Koshy and R. Radhakrishnan, 71–94, New Delhi: Oxford University Press, 2008.

Mishra, Vijay, *Bollywood Cinema: Temples of Desire*. New York and London: Routledge, 2002.

Mitchell, Tony, *Dario Fo: People's Court Jester*. London and New York: Bloomsbury, 1986.

Moss, Jonathan, "'We Didn't Realise How Brave We Were at the Time': The 1968 Ford Sewing Machinists' Strike in Public and Personal Memory." *Oral History* 43.1 (Spring 2015): 40–51.

Mukherjee Datta, Sandeepa, *Bong Mom's Cookbook: Stories from a Bengali Mother's Kitchen*. Noida, India: Collins, 2013.

Ondaatje, Michael, *Anil's Ghost*. London: Bloomsbury, 2000.

Ortiz, Brennan, "NYC's Micro Neighborhoods: Little India in Jackson Heights, Queens." *Untapped Cities*, 3 April 2014.

Padva, Gilad. *Queer Nostalgia in Cinema and Pop Culture*. Basingstoke: Palgrave Macmillan, 2004.

Pfleiderer, Beatrix, and Lothar Lutze (eds), *The Hindi Film: Agent and Re-Agent of Cultural Change*. New Delhi: Manohar, 1985.

Puwar, Nirmal, *Space Invaders: Race, Gender and Bodies Out of Place*. Oxford and New York: Berg, 2004.

Rahman, Emdad, "My Friend Quddus Ali: 12 Years On" *Cybersylhet.com*, 14 June 2008.

Rajagopal, Arvind, *Politics after Television: Hindu Nationalism and the Reshaping of the Public in India*. Cambridge: Cambridge University Press, 2001

Raychaudhuri, Anindya, "'Just as Good a Place to Publish': Banksy, Graffiti and the Textualisation of the Wall." *Rupkatha Journal on Interdisciplinary Humanities* 2.1 (2010): 50–58.

Rayner, Jay, "Restaurant Review: Dishoom." *The Guardian*, 15 August 2010.

Robey, Tim, "It's a Wonderful Afterlife, Review," *The Telegraph*, 22 April 2010.

Rodriguez, Gregory, and Dawn Nakagawa, "Looking Backward and Inward: The Politics of Nostalgia and Identity." *Berggruen [Insights]*, Issue 4, 22 July 2016.
Rosaldo, Renato, "Imperialist Nostalgias." *Representations* 26 (Spring 1989): 107–22.
Saadi, Suhayl, *Psychoraag*. Edinburgh: Black and White Publishing, 2004.
Said, Edward, *Reflections on Exile and Other Essays*. Boston: Harvard University Press, 2002.
Said, Edward, *Orientalism*. London: Penguin, 2003.
Samuel, Raphael, *Theatres of Memory: Past and Present in Contemporary Culture*. London and New York: Verso, 2012.
Sarna, Navtej, *The Exile*. New Delhi, Viking: 2008.
Schaffer, Gavin, *The Vision of a Nation: Making Multiculturalism on British Television, 1960–80*. Basingstoke and New York: Palgrave Macmillan, 2014.
Schrag, Calvin O., *The Resources of Rationality: A Response to the Postmodern Challenge*. Bloomington: Indiana University Press, 1992.
Scott, Adam, "Why Brexit and Trump Are to Blame for a Rise in Retro Gadgets – and How Brands Take Advantage." *Wired.com*, 24 May 2017.
Sedgwick, Eve Kosofsky, *Touching, Feeling: Affect, Pedagogy, Performativity*. Durham, NC, and London: Duke University Press, 2003.
Sharma, Sanjay, John Hutnyk and Ashwani Sharma (eds), *Dis-Orienting Rhythms: The Politics of the New Asian Dance Music*. London and New Jersey: Zed Books, 1996.
Shaw, Philip, "Longing for Home: Robert Hamilton, Nostalgia and the Emotional Life of the Eighteenth-Century Soldier." *Journal for Eighteenth-Century Studies* 39.1 (2016): 25–40
Singh, Duleep, *The Maharajah Duleep Singh and the Government: A Narrative*. London: Ballantyne, Hanson & Co., 1884.
Singh, Duleep, *A Reprint of Two Sale Catalogues of Jewels and Other Confiscated Property Belonging to His Highness the Maharajah Duleep Singh*. 1885.
Singh, Gurharpal, and Darshan Singh Tatla, *Sikhs in Britain: The Making of a Community*. London and New York: Zed Books, 2006.
Southall Black Sisters, *Against the Grain*. London: Southall Black Sisters, 1990.
Steinwand, Jonathan, "The Future of Nostalgia in Friedrich Schlegel's Gender Theory: Casting German Aesthetics Beyond Ancient Greece and Modern Europe" in *Narratives of Nostalgia, Gender, and Nationalism* edited by Jean Pickering and Suzanne Kehde, 9–29. New York: New York University Press, 1997.
Stewart, Susan, *On Longing: Narratives of the Miniature, the Gigantic, the Souvenir, the Collection*. Durham, NC, and London: Duke University Press, 1993.
Syal, Rajeev, and Phil Miller, "Margaret Thatcher Gave Full Support over Golden Temple Raid, Letter Shows." *The Guardian*, 15 January 2014.
Therwath, Ingrid, "'Shining Indians': Diaspora and Exemplarity in Bollywood." *South Asia Multidisciplinary Academic Journal* 4 (2010).
Uberoi, Patricia, "The Diaspora Comes Home: Disciplining Desire in DDLJ." *Contributions to Indian Sociology* 32 (November 1998): 305–36.
Ullah, Ansar Ahmed, and Steve Silver, *Commemorating Altab Ali Day 4 May: Against Racism and Fascism*. London: UNISON and Altab Ali Foundation, 2012.
Wainwright, A. Martin, "Queen Victoria and the Maharaja Duleep Singh: Conflicting Identities in an Imperial Context." *Ohio Academy of History Proceedings*, 2013.
Walder, Dennis, *Postcolonial Nostalgias: Writing, Representation, and Memory*. Abingdon, Oxfordshire: Routledge, 2011.
Widgery, David, *Beating Time: Riot 'n' Race 'n' Rock 'n' Roll*. London: Chatto & Windus, 1986.
Wightman, Catriona, "The Great British Bake Off: Was That the Most Emotional Final Ever?" *Digital Spy*, 8 October 2015. Accessed on 16 August 2017, available at: http://www.digitalspy.com/tv/great-british-bake-off/news/a672609/the-great-british-bake-off-was-that-the-most-emotional-final-ever/
Zinkin, Tanya, "Integrating Britain's Immigrants." *The Guardian*, 18 January 1965.

Index

The 4 Skins, 57, 62
9/11, legacies of, 141–142, 146, 147

Advani, Nikhil, 62, 104, 133, 137
Ahluwalia, Kiranjit, 17, 47, 64, 65–69
Ali, Altab, 17, 47, 49–56, 57, 64
Ali, Monica, 50–51, 116
Ali, Quddus, 53, 55–56
Ali, Shaad, 105, 109
Anand, Siddharth, 133, 137, 170
Anil's Ghost. *See* Ondaatje, Michael
Anti Nazi League, 56–57
anti-racism, nostalgias of, 12, 16, 49–52, 54, 57–64, 64, 70, 71, 118, 120, 121, 132, 137, 141, 146, 147, 165, 174, 190
Asian Dub Foundation, 49, 52–56, 58, 64, 153–154, 154, 155, 157, 164, 165, 166, 167, 169, 175
Asian Youth Movements, 49, 57, 61, 64. *See also* Southall Youth Movement
Assassin's Creed: Syndicate, 42–44
Auenbrugger, Joseph Leopold, 7
Augé, Marc, 107–108
Axel, Brian Keith, 23

Bachchan, Amitabh, 105–106, 121, 148–149
Bachchan, Avishek, 138, 148–149
Bachelard, Gaston, 14, 105, 175
Baloch, Qandeel, 120, 125
Bance, Peter, 23

Banerjee Divakaruni, Chitra, 77–78, 91, 109, 111–113
Baracus, Swami, 57–58
Beech, Patrick, 158, 159–160, 160, 161, 172
Belsey, Catherine, 111
Benjamin, Walter, 17, 28, 78–79, 99, 183
Bend it Like Beckham, 62, 87–89, 91, 105, 108. *See also* Chadha, Gurinder
Benn, Tony, 156
Bennett, Susan, 9, 12
Bharatiya Janata Party, 130, 140. *See also* Hindu nationalism
Bhaskar, Sanjeev, xi–xii
Bhatt, Sujata, 86–87, 89
Bhyrowal, Treaty of, 22, 28, 29–30
Bollywood, xi–xii, 17, 21, 55, 57, 62, 89, 102, 104, 105, 107, 109, 115, 118, 119, 122, 123, 129, 130–150, 153, 165, 168, 170
Bonnett, Alistair, 10–11
Boym, Svetlana, 10, 11, 188
Brick Lane. *See* Ali, Monica
Bride and Prejudice, 89. *See also* Chadha, Gurinder
British Broadcasting Corporation, 18; *Apna Hi Ghar Samajhiye*, 157, 159, 166; *Archive Hour: Make Yourself at Home*, 165; *Asian Magazine*, 157, 164–165, 167; Asian Network, 16, 153, 154, 155, 157, 165, 166, 167, 169;

Asian Programmes Advisory Committee, 157, 160–162, 163; Asian Programmes Unit, 157, 162, 163, 172; BBC One, 153, 157, 164, 179, 180; BBC Radio 4, xi, 102, 165; *Desert Island Discs*, xi, xii; General Advisory Council, 159; *Goodness Gracious Me*, 87, 124; *The Great British Bake Off*, 179, 180; Immigrants' Programmes Advisory Committee, 156, 158, 159; Immigrants' Programmes Unit, 155, 156, 157, 159, 163, 165; *A History of the World in 100 Objects*, 80–81; *Mark Steel's in Town*, 102; *Nai Zindagi Naya Jeevan*, 153, 157, 159, 165; *The Noreen Khan Show*, 167–169. See also Bhaskar, Sanjeev; Jaffrey, Madhur
British National Party, 50, 53, 63. See also white supremacy
British Union of Fascists, 50. See also white supremacy
Break ke Baad, 75–76
Brexit, 1–3, 4, 8, 13
Butler, Judith, 28–29

Campbell, Christy, 24, 25, 30, 34
Chadha, Gurinder, 87, 89, 105, 109, 112
Chaggar, Gurdip Singh, 57, 59, 63
Channel 4: *The House That Made Me*, xi–x. See also Bhaskar, Sanjeev
Colonialism and Empire, xii, 22, 24, 25, 29, 30–31, 36, 40, 42, 44, 54–55, 76, 122–123, 123–124, 189; nostalgia against, 11, 29, 40–41, 44, 54, 58, 142, 189; nostalgia for, 2, 3, 8–9
Cullen, William, 7
Curran, Charles, 162

Dalhousie, Marquess of, 25, 32, 33, 34
Dames, Nicholas, 7
Davis, Alex, 5, 8, 15, 19n17, 187–188
Dilwale Dulhaniya Le Jayenge, 129, 132, 135, 136, 138, 139, 142–144, 145, 149
Dishoom, 121–126
Deol, Sonia, 165
Desai, Jigna, 130–131
Dostana, 149–150
Dudrah, Rajinder, 105–106, 131–132, 135, 139, 148

Duleep Singh, Maharajah, 17, 21–44, 65, 183

Elveden Hall, Suffolk, 22, 23, 25, 26, 34, 38, 41
English Defence League, 50, 63. See also white supremacy
Erotic Stories for Punjabi Widows. See Jaswal, Balli Kaur

Fellows, Will, 12
feminism, nostalgias of, 64, 65, 70, 71
Flusser, Vilém, 13, 14
Fo, Dario, 58
food and nostalgia, xii, 5, 8, 16, 17, 62, 67, 69, 75–99, 104, 109–111, 120, 121–124, 125, 135, 142, 180, 181, 183, 186, 190
Foucault, Michel, 17, 103, 105, 107, 111, 114–115

Gandhi, Indira, 36, 149
Gandhi, Mohandas K., 11
Ghosh, Amitav, 183–187
Gill, A.A, 1
Greene, Hugh, 156
Gretton, David, 156–157, 158, 159, 163, 164
Grist, John, 157, 161, 163
Glazer, Peter, 16, 48–49, 71
Gopinath, Gayatri, 167, 168
Gupta, Rahila, 64, 65, 66, 70–71. See also Southall Black Sisters
Gupta, Amit, 75, 104, 109, 112

Hamilton, Robert, 6–8, 15, 16, 187
Hatherley, Owen, 3–4
Heems, 118. See also The Swet Shop Boys
Hindu nationalism, 124–125, 130–131, 139–140, 141, 145, 146
Hofer, Johannes, 5–6, 7–8, 9, 15, 16, 181, 187, 188
The Hundred-Foot Journey, 76–77, 78, 80, 82
The Hungry Tide. See Ghosh, Amitav
Hussain, Nadiya, 181–183
Hutnyk, John, 52, 53
Hynes, Gerry, 162, 163

Ilbruck, Helmut, 15
The Interpreter of Maladies. See Lahiri, Jhumpa
Islam, Nazrul Kazi, 51, 54–55, 56
Islamophobia, 4, 141–142, 145–146, 147, 179–180

Jab Tak Hai Jaan, 140, 141–142, 144–145
Jaffrey, Madhur, 80–81, 94–95
Jadoo, 75, 76, 78, 81, 90–91, 104–105, 109. *See also* Gupta, Amit
Jaswal, Balli Kaur, 104, 105, 117–118
Jhoom Barabar Jhoom, 105–107, 108–109, 109, 131–132, 135, 138, 140, 148. *See also* Ali, Shaad
Jindan Kaur, Maharani, 22, 23, 38
Johnson, Linton Kwesi, 58

Kaif, Katrina, 138, 145, 146
Kajol, 55, 129, 148, 149
Kal Ho Naa Ho, 132, 133, 134, 135, 142, 145, 148. *See also* Advani, Nikhil
Katrak, Ketu, 52, 97
Khan, Shah Rukh, 55, 129, 130, 133, 134, 135, 138, 139, 141, 142, 144, 145–146, 148, 149
Koh-i-Noor, 23, 31, 35, 39, 40, 41, 43
Kuch Kuch Hota Hai, 149–150
Kun, Josh, 168–169

Lahiri, Jhumpa, 79–86, 92–93, 108
Leicester, 75, 103, 104–105, 107, 109, 113, 115
London: Brick Lane, 47, 50, 51, 115, 116, 136; British Museum, 23–24; Buckingham Palace, 42, 136, 138; Houses of Parliament, 42, 136; Metropolitan Police, 47, 51, 53, 57, 138, 141; Southall, xi–xii, 57–64, 71, 89, 101–109, 113, 116, 117–118, 136, 138, 154; Tower Hamlets, 4, 47, 49, 51, 56, 58, 64, 103, 109, 115, 154; Tower of London, 41; Waterloo Station, 105–107, 109, 121, 135, 140; Watney Street, 4, 53, 55, 56, 115, 154
London Dreams, 139–140. *See also* Shah, Vipul
London, Paris, New York, 132, 137
Lawrence, Stephen, 53

Lefebvre, Henri, 102
Leicester, 75, 103, 104–105, 107, 109, 113, 115
Lizzardi, Ryan, 9–10
Lloyds TSB, 101–102
Lowenthal, David, 9
Ludhra, Aneeka, 98–99

M.I.A, 93–94
Mannur, Anita, 10, 86–87
Mansoor, Sarfraz, 165–166
Marangoly George, Rosemary, 14–15, 16
The Mistress of Spices. See Banerjee Divakaruni, Chitra
Mishra, Vijay, 138–139, 142–143
Mishra, Sudesh, 117, 143–144
Misty in Roots, 57, 59, 60
Modi, Narendra, 130, 140, 141. *See also* Bharatiya Janata Party; Hindu nationalism
Mosley, Oswald. *See* British Union of Fascists
Mukherjee Datta, Sandeepa, 95–98
Mundhra, Jag, 66
My Name is Khan, 146–148

Namaste, London, 136, 138. *See also* Shah, Vipul
The Namesake. See Lahiri, Jhumpa
National Front, xi–xii, 47, 50, 57, 62, 63. *See also* white supremacy
Negu Gorriak, 58
neo-liberalism, 17, 76, 130, 139
New York, 77, 81, 103, 108, 119, 132, 133–134, 135, 137, 142, 190; Coney Island, 119; Flushing, 119; Jackson Heights, 75, 103; Lexington Avenue, 103, 108; Manhattan, 77, 108
New York, 133–134, 141

Ondaatje, Michael, 183–187

Padva, Gilad, 16, 189–190
partition, 1947 the, 35, 38, 40, 141
Paris, 25, 31, 37, 75, 138
Patiala House, 62–64, 105, 137–138. *See also* Advani, Nikhil
patriarchy, 66, 67–69, 86, 88, 89, 89–90, 91, 92, 93, 118, 142, 190

Peach, Clement Blair, 17, 47, 56–59, 61, 63, 64
PK, 140, 149
Provoked: A True Story, 66–71. See also Mundhra, Jag
Psychoraag. See Saadi, Suhayl
Punjab, 22, 23, 24, 26, 27, 30, 34, 35, 39, 40, 42, 42–43, 44, 54, 56, 63, 66, 71, 88, 89, 101, 103, 104, 105, 109, 113, 117, 118, 129, 135, 137, 138, 139, 167, 171; Blue Star, Operation, 36, 38; Lahore, 29, 34, 37–39, 40, 140, 141, 172, 173; Patiala, 138
Puwar, Nirmal, 116, 121, 124

Rai Bachchan, Aishwarya, 66, 67, 149
Rajagopal, Arjun, 13
Ramji Londonwaley, 75–76
Ranjit Singh, Maharajah, 22
Raxstar, 154–155, 169
Riz MC, 118, 121, 123. See also The Swet Shop Boys
Rock Against Racism, 56, 60
Rosaldo, Renato, 8–9

Saadi, Suhayl, 170, 171, 171–174, 175
Said, Edward, 24, 37
Salaam, Namaste, 75, 133, 134, 137, 140, 170–171, 172, 174, 175. See also Anand, Siddharth
Samuel, Raphael, 10
Sarna, Navtej, 36–40, 44
Schaffer, Gavin, 155–156, 160, 163, 164, 166–167
Schragg, Calvin O, 188–189
Sedgwick, Eve Kosofsky, 188
Shah, Vipul, 136, 139
Shaheed Minar, Dhaka, 49–50
Sharma, Sanjay, 52, 54

Shaw, Philip, 7, 15
Sidey, Phil, 162
The Singh Twins, 40–42, 42, 43, 44
Southall Black Sisters, 57, 60, 64–68, 71
Southall Youth Movement, 57, 58, 59–60, 64
Steinwand, Jonathan, 12–13
Steel, Mark, 102, 104
Stewart, Susan, 10, 15
The Swet Shop Boys, 118–121, 121, 123, 125

Today's Special, 75, 76–77, 78, 81
Total Siyapaa, 132, 140, 141, 146–147, 149
Tagore, Rabindranath, 11, 49, 50, 51
Thackeray, Bal, 125. See also Hindu nationalism
Thatcher, Margaret, 9, 36
Trump, Donald, 2–3, 4, 8, 13, 120, 125

Uberoi, Patricia, 129, 131, 135

Victoria, Queen, 22, 22–23, 23, 24, 26–27, 30, 31, 34, 39
Vishwa Hindu Parishad, 124. See also Bharatiya Janata Party; Hindu nationalism

Walder, Dennis, 11
Webster, David, 160
white supremacy and racism, 2, 3, 4, 32–33, 47, 51, 53, 56, 62, 113, 116, 118, 120, 132, 137, 141–142, 160
Winterhalter, Franz Xaver, 22, 23, 29, 39, 40

It's a Wonderful Afterlife, 89–90. See also Chadha, Gurinder